D1314039

DATE			

© THE BAKER & TAYLOR CO.

EXECUTIVE'S HANDBOOK OF MODEL BUSINESS CONDUCT CODES

EXECUTIVE'S HANDBOOK OF MODEL BUSINESS CONDUCT CODES

Walter W. Manley II

PRENTICE HALL
Englewood Cliffs, New Jersey 07632

Prentice-Hall International (UK) Limited, *London*
Prentice-Hall of Australia Pty. Limited, *Sydney*
Prentice-Hall Canada, Inc., *Toronto*
Prentice-Hall Hispanoamericana, S.A., *Mexico*
Prentice-Hall of India Private Limited, *New Delhi*
Prentice-Hall of Japan, Inc., *Tokyo*
Simon & Schuster Asia Pte. Ltd., *Singapore*
Editora Prentice-Hall do Brasil, Ltda., *Rio de Janeiro*

© 1991 *by*

PRENTICE-HALL, Inc.

Englewood Cliffs, NJ

10   9   8   7   6   5   4   3   2   1

Library of Congress Cataloging-in-Publication Data

Manley, Walter W.
  Executive's handbook of model business conduct codes / Walter W. Manley II.

    p.   cm.
  Includes index.
  ISBN 0-13-296757-X
  1. Business ethics—United States—Handbooks, manuals, etc.
2. Social responsibility of business—United States—Handbooks,
manuals, etc. 3. Executives—United States—Conduct of life—
Handbooks, manuals, etc.   I. Title.   II. Title: Conduct codes.
HF5387.M336 1991   91-11244
174′.4—dc20   CIP

ISBN 0-13-296757-X

PRENTICE HALL
BUSINESS & PROFESSIONAL DIVISION
A division of Simon & Schuster
Englewood Cliffs, New Jersey 07632

PRINTED IN THE UNITED STATES OF AMERICA

Dedication: To my daughter Marjorie

ACKNOWLEDGMENTS

For over two years I have conducted research in the area of business firms' response to issues in business conduct and their creation and use of codes of conduct. Much of the material in this book has come from the 276 participating firms, among the best managed in this country. Included are publications and codes, together with 1,000 pages of interviews and correspondence with 400 executives, including 85 CEOs and chairmen; 71 executive and senior vice presidents; 77 general counsel; 105 vice presidents; and 65 treasurers, chief auditors, and directors of human resources, employee relations or corporate responsibility. I thank these gentlemen and ladies for their interviews and letters. I have examined over 10,000 pages of business conduct and policy statements and appreciate the permission granted to publish in this book the most useful excerpts of such codes.

I owe many thanks to Kathy McCord, a dear friend and talented journalist; Bob Schucts, David Strong, and Wayne Todd for their support during the writing of this book. Further, I wish to thank Professor William Shrode, Robert Stovall, Nicole Hiers, Kelly Shrode, Kathleen Rice, Paula Bryant, Kay Haberman, Rebecca Einolf, Geir Kjellevold, Patrick Schneider, and Terry Harris for their advice, typing, editing, proofreading, and editorial assistance. I particularly wish to thank Nick Sweers, a learned and accomplished journalist; Joe Riffe, my research assistant for part of 1989; and Barbara Baker and Lois Stille, my wonderful, cheerful typists, for their dedication. Larry Hopcraft, president of Parker-Hannifin's Automotive and Refrigeration Division, offered cogent advice and demonstrated in his encouragement the qualities which have allowed him to be so successful at such a young age.

Tom Power, senior editor in Prentice Hall's Business and Professional Publishing Division, provided sage advice and sincere encouragement.

Cambridge University, Oxford University, and Ridley Hall College have been kind to me, and visiting membership on their faculties served as catalysts for writing the two books, including this one, which I completed in 1990. I particularly wish to thank Cambridge University professors David Thompson, Stephen Watson, Anthony Giddens, J. N. Butterfield, and lecturer Amy Cosh; Ridley Hall College principal Hugo de Waal and Dr. Richard Higginson; and R. J. Smith, chairman of the Oxford Faculty of Law, for their many kindnesses.

Further, I acknowledge the substantial knowledge, insight and encouragement I have received over the last several decades from certain teachers and friends. Harvard professors Rosenblum (now dean of Virginia's Colgate Darden School), Stevenson, Thurston, Korten, Kassarjian, and Trevelyan were excellent teachers and motivators, as were Duke professors Latty, O'Neal, and Pye. Professors Earl Sasser of Harvard and Robinson Everett and Kazimierz Gryzbowski of Duke were not only good friends but probably the best teachers I have ever had. Professor Ken Goodpastor of Harvard has done much to advance the practical application of business ethics. Duke law deans Paul Carrington and Pamela Gann and Fuqua School dean Tom Keller have demonstrated a pursuit of excellence and have, through their ethical leadership, improved the already outstanding Duke School of Law and the Duke Fuqua School. Professors Harold Albert and Robert Akerman encouraged me at a young age to teach; I have attempted to emulate them.

I owe particular thanks to my colleagues who have offered support and encouragement as well: Florida State University professors Ross Heck, Charlie Conn, Mark Martinko, David Kuhn, Glenn Boggs, Bill Gallups, Tom Clark, Dean Ray Solomon, and Grantham Couch, among them.

I owe a special thanks to editors of the seven publishing firms which extended contracts for my two books I wrote in 1989-90. Specifically, I thank Liliane Miller and Lauren Nagy of Greenwood Press, John Mahaney of Wiley, Ann West of Sage, and Karen Hansen and Bob Bovenschulte of Lexington for their support and encouragement.

Finally, I owe my deepest thanks to my students. They have taught me much and have enlivened and enlightened my life.

Walter W. Manley II
Cambridge University
Cambridge, England

FOREWORD

by Bob Stovall

Ethics: "the discipline dealing with what is good and bad or right and wrong, or with moral duty and obligation; the principles of conduct governing an individual or a profession; standards of behavior." So says *Webster's Third International Dictionary.*

But some business observers have a shorter definition for business ethics: an oxymoron. Don't bother looking that one up. It means business and ethics don't mix.

This is patently untrue. Business people have ethics and a truly amazing number of business organizations have their own set of precepts which are set down for employees to see. Most of these business codes of ethics have a common root.

In the Christian-Judeo tradition, the moral law to be observed is found in the Ten Commandments which God gave Moses on Mt. Sinai. It describes acceptable moral behavior for man in the eyes of God. Aristotle and Saint Thomas Aquinas base their moral theses of acceptable human conduct on the "natural law." That law flows from human nature consisting of mind and matter or body and soul. Only when the mind and soul control behavior is a person a truly rational being. According to this philosophy, an act is morally right or wrong as it is compatible with human nature.

One must recognize that great numbers of people do not share these religious or philosophic beliefs; but that there are other instruments which help people decide between right and wrong. One is the voice of conscience or that awareness of the moral good or the feeling to do right or good. Conscience involves personal responsibility for an individual and is a reliable norm of ethical behavior. Another is the ageless doctrine of the Golden Rule: "Do unto others as you would have them do unto you." Following the voice of conscience and the Golden Rule would virtually eliminate corruption in America and elsewhere in the world.

But more needs to be done to aid the moral fabric. Learning right from wrong begins in the home with parents setting a good example and teaching their children honesty, integrity and compassion for others. This requires parents to make sacrifices of time, energy and patience and, out of love, to discipline their children so that they grow up accustomed to living by restraints on personal behavior that society imposes through its laws and customs.

Courses in ethics should be required in high school and colleges. Elementary schools should promote sound moral values, honesty, fairness, compassion, decency, and the respect for people and property through appropriate means. These steps would be a good start on the road back to common decency and trust that are marks of a civilized society.

In addition, it is time that leaders of government, and other social institutions, especially business, be held accountable for the ethical behavior of themselves and their subordinates. This is important in the case of businessmen particularly, not because they are less ethical than leaders in other segments of American society, but because their power, visibility and example have a profound influence on public opinion and their employees' behavior.

Specific corporate statements of ethical conduct mean little when the corporation is found guilty of fraud, checkkiting and laundering of money. The idea that top executives do not know what their subordinates are doing ignores management's responsibility for adequate reporting and control systems that ensure realistic feedback regarding implementation of key policy matters. An environment which facilitates or encourages subordinates to take illegal action is invariably nurtured by attitudes and actions of those at the top. It is they who, above all others, set the moral tone of their organizations.

Leaders in all walks of life must recognize their responsibility to set a good example for those in their organization but also those outside of it. Example is the best form of leadership. Setting an example of honesty and fair play is the greatest service a leader gives to others.

Can business be profitable and ethical? Many doubt it. Among the critics are educators and college students, supervisors and workers and citizens from all walks of life. It is urgent, therefore, for the nation, and especially the business community, to initiate steps to reverse this erosion of moral values. Failure to do so will profoundly change the American way of life because decay in moral values and ethical conduct ultimately leads to loss of confidence in people and their institutions. This sows seeds of distrust and hatred among neighbors, between employer and employees, between voters and their elected officials, and between business and government. In the extreme, it opens the door of government to anarchy!

Consumers who distrust companies don't buy their products. They take their business elsewhere, to another domestic or foreign supplier. It may not be entirely coincidental that the loss of American markets to foreign competition is occurring at a time when moral values in this country are being eroded. We know that the explanation for this loss is not just price, because consumers buy imported goods even where there is a decline in the value of the dollar. Consumers are buying them because of their belief that foreign producers offer quality products and service.

To sum up: a continued decline in moral values creates a political vacuum for demagogues to fill. By offering political alternatives to a system which the public perceives as corrupt, untrustworthy and unresponsive, demagogues may even win substantial political victories. But their price is high. It is the surrender of personal liberty. Similar environments spawned the worst dictators in history who destroyed nations, imprisoned the innocent and brought misery to mankind.

Americans have a stake in restoring moral values in society. That stake is not only individual self-respect but also the survival of our democratic principles and of institutions and the freedom we cherish.

In a remarkable effort of analysis and reportage, the author of this text has created the first seemingly complete guide to the creation and administration of conduct codes in commerce and industry. An early reaction to the scope of this work is surprise that so many business organizations indeed have addressed the subject of codified ethics and promulgate them to employees via formal training and/or corporate communications. This book will be helpful to any management seeking a framework of ethical behavior on which to put its own personal stamp.

It is increasingly accepted that, "good ethics are good for profits." In the realm of morality and ethics, there are laws, standards and mechanisms which can and should be used as norms of moral behavior. Some are written and rooted in religious beliefs while others can be identified through the use of reason. Moral laws lend themselves more to individual interpretation, belief and compliance than do civil laws. Failure to observe moral codes does not result in direct legal or punitive sanctions. The result is that there can be and often are discernible differences in the personal behavior of individuals confronted with similar ethical issues. Nevertheless, standards do exist and it is the obligation of everyone to seek out such standards and live by them.

This book will serve as a carefully-researched guide to the creation, implementation and administration of a code of business conduct to managers and directors who have come to believe that proper business conduct on the part of all employees can enhance profitability.

In a truly prodigious effort the author, Walter W. Manley II, also assembled 70,000 words of excerpts selected from the codes of conduct (10,000 pages reviewed) of 276 of America's best-managed firms. In what promises to be the standard work on the subject, he provides a complete glossary of guides for a firm's creation or modification of a code of business conduct. In essence this is a giant potpourri of "codes of conduct" from which to draw on pragmatically proven methods. Any executive, director, manager or firm owner could use this guide as a reference to the ABCs of creating and using a code effectively.

In terms of the questionnaire which a firm can use to measure the values and attitudes of its employees it is creative and most useful.

The participation of over 400 executives (including 85 CEOs and chairmen, 71 senior or executive vice presidents, 77 corporate counsel, 105 vice presidents; and 65 directors of corporate responsibility, human resources or employee relations, treasurers and chief auditors) is perhaps the most extensive number of high-level executives in leading American firms to be encountered in any manuscript. Their opinions are valuable to any manager.

INTRODUCTION
Why a Firm Needs a Code of Business Conduct

In the September 20, 1976, issue of *Time* magazine, one of the corporate world's giants, International Business Machines, placed an advertisement decrying the public's loss of confidence in American business leadership. The ad stated that just a decade earlier, in 1966, some 55 percent of Americans held a high level of confidence in those who led the nation's businesses. By 1976, the IBM ad pointed out, only 16 percent held that faith. "We believe," IBM proclaimed, "that every company should have a code of conduct...that clearly spells out the legal and ethical obligations of corporate leadership."

More than a decade and a half later, codes of business conduct have been established by an estimated 9,000 of America's 10,000 largest, publicly held firms. But only about five percent of the nearly 3.7 million corporations in the United States have enacted such codes. And public attitudes continue to reflect doubts about the ethical behavior of business. For example, in a 1986 *New York Times* survey, the respondents displayed a lingering suspicion of business and executives in particular. Furthermore, the *Times* reported, 53 percent of those surveyed expressed the belief that "white-collar crime in business was committed 'very often.'"

Business leaders, too, are concerned about the actions and public images of American firms. In a 1987 Touche Ross survey of corporate executives and board members, 94 percent of the respondents agreed with the contention that the nation's business community is significantly troubled by improper conduct.

More of the firms that do not have codes of business conduct might establish such measures if their management understood the advantages and momentum that a code can bring to the business environment. A firm with a code of business conduct often enjoys a competitive advantage with customers over firms that do not have such codes. Studies have shown that firms with codes of business conduct tend to be financially more successful than other firms.

A few definitions are important here. *Values* are specific desires for objects or beliefs perceived as important. *Proper business conduct* is a more general term that refers to concepts of human welfare and the promulgation of principles to enhance human welfare. *Ethics,* meanwhile, are a complex set of rules of conduct associated with a particular class of human actions or associated with a particular group or culture—in this case, businesses, suppliers, consumers, regulators, investors, and many others who influence and affect the daily ebb and flow of business.

A code of business conduct may be only one or two pages in length and deal with values, conduct, and ethical issues in broad, philosophical terms. Or a code of conduct may be a thick document providing detailed directives on how employees, managers, and executives are expected to conduct themselves and make their decisions in a variety of highly regulated environments. Large companies frequently hire consultants to help them formulate codes of business conduct or update portions of their existing codes. Medium-sized or small firms often do not have room in their budgets for such assistance. Fortunately, a company and its leaders can create their own codes and keep their ethical guidelines up to date by drawing upon outstanding examples from codes already promulgated by leading firms. The structure and wording of the examples can be modified as needed to fit the company's unique environment and management's views of what constitutes ethical behavior in business.

Executive's Handbook of Model Business Conduct Codes is intended for anyone who owns, is a partner in, or manages a firm that needs a new or updated code of conduct. The book presents real examples of the ways major corporations address and enforce today's key ethical issues of business conduct. You can use these examples as handy, time-saving, and thought-provoking guides when creating codes suitable for your own unique business situation.

This book also can serve as a useful reference and instructive tool for lawyers who serve as counsel to business; for members of firms' board of directors; for faculty members, scholars, and students of business, philosophy, social science, and law; and for anyone who has an abiding interest in the values and conduct of business.

Executive's Handbook of Model Business Conduct Codes provides procedures for: (1) creating a business code; (2) communicating it to employees and educating them on its importance; (3) interpreting the code; (4) measuring and assuring compliance; and (5) handling violations and imposing sanctions. The book is divided into three sections. The first section examines why it is important for firms to have a code of business conduct and how such a code is created. The second section presents numerous examples drawn from real codes enacted by some of America's most prominent companies. These codes can be reworded and reshaped as needed by firms that want to create their own code of business conduct. The third section of this book examines the steps and procedures necessary to put the code into action and to enforce its provisions. Finally, Appendix A contains a questionnaire that many firms may find useful as a tool for measuring the values and attitudes of employees and managers. The findings from this questionnaire may provide a number of important insights for those who will draft and implement a firm's code of business conduct.

TABLE OF CONTENTS

I

CREATING CODES
OF CONDUCT

Chapter 1

BUSINESS CODES AND CORPORATE IMAGE

Clearly, the past ten years have been rough on the image of American business. Headlines have heralded numerous stories of corruption and crime within key industries and major corporations. Many financial institutions, including banks, savings and loan companies, and brokerage firms, have collapsed, often amid scandal over bad or improper loans, embezzlements, poor management, and allegations of self-serving, unethical, or illegal acts performed by executives, managers, and employees alike. In many industries which supply products to the federal government, the Pentagon, and the space program, numerous whistleblowers have come forward and brought spotlights to bear on cost overruns, falsified safety and maintenance records, and dangerously shoddy products.

The public shock and outcry seemingly have risen in recent years in the wake of such events as the disastrous Exxon Valdez oil spill in Alaska and the major focusing flaw discovered in the Hubble Space Telescope after the long-delayed astronomy satellite finally was put into orbit amid great fanfare and scientific expectations. Television viewers tuning in to the evening news have seen some of Wall Street's once-highest fliers led away in handcuffs for insider trading or illegal junk bond deals and watched some of professional sports' greatest players fall from grace over gambling, drugs, bad investments, or greed born of enormous egos and franchise-endangering salary levels.

From the halls and committee rooms of Capital Hill—which has itself not escaped the spectre of misconduct, scandal, and unethical behavior—to the noontime coffee klatches in the nation's smallest towns, concerns have been raised, and continue to be voiced, about the honesty, integrity, and morality of American business.

So it is not surprising that codes of business conduct recently have become increasingly important strategic and public relations weapons for big businesses. What *is* surprising, however, is that having a formal, written code of business conduct apparently is not yet deemed important by many thousands of medium-sized and smaller firms—even though customers increasingly are seeking out and buying from the companies that promote and practice a highly ethical approach to business.

Codes of business conduct are *not* documents that an executive or manager can whip out in an afternoon. The codes address the very essence and heart of a firm and reflect its soul through the actions and attitudes of its people. The process of creating such an important document can span weeks or even months of research, writing, review, and revisions, especially if all or most of the work is done from scratch.

DRAFTING CODES

Fortunately, there is a simpler way to get the process rolling and completed. Firms drafting their first codes can use the existing codes of successful companies as models for their own efforts.

A Complete Portfolio of Model Business Codes is a product of an intensive, two-year study of how businesses create, implement, and enforce codes of conduct. A few statistics reflect the complexity and magnitude of the project. More than 275 of America's most successful and best-managed firms were surveyed. Some 10,000 pages of business conduct codes were reviewed and gleaned for the examples included in this book. Approximately 400 business leaders were consulted, including 85 chief executive officers and board chairmen, 77 corporate legal counsels, 71 senior vice presidents and executive vice presidents, 105 vice presidents, and 65 others holding prominent positions of corporate responsibility, such as director of human resources, treasurer or chief auditor. During the two-year study, approximately 1,000 pages of interview transcripts and correspondence also were generated, and those efforts, too, are reflected in this book.

FOURTEEN MAJOR BENEFITS OF A CODE OF CONDUCT

This study has identified 14 major benefits that a code of conduct can bring to a firm. These benefits and a number of related advantages are described in the paragraphs that follow:

1. *A code of business conduct provides guidelines to managers and employees that can help them disseminate—and acquaint new employees with—the firm's traditional values and cultural elements.*

According to John Pearson, chairman and chief executive officer of the NWNL Companies: "There is no substitute for the personal dissemination of values and ethics philosophy by the Chief Executive Office[r] and other members of the senior management. However, personal contact with every employee in a large organization is nearly impossible. The next best approach is the formal and official publication of management's philosophy for the widest possible dissemination. This distribution puts the company and its management 'on the record' as to its philosophy. . . ."

In the view of Hershey Foods' chief executive officer, Richard Zimmerman, another important role is filled by the dissemination of values and culture through a code of business conduct. Said Zimmerman: "[O]ften, an individual joins a firm without recognizing the type of environment in which he will place himself and his career. The loud and clear enunciation of a company's code of conduct . . . [allows] that employee to determine whether or not he fits that particular culture."

Codes define the firms' policy in areas of ethical business conduct concern. Most ethical and business conduct issues involve familiar rather than extraordinary matters. Therefore, codes can clearly delineate a company's policy toward—and its response to—most problems. Indeed, in the view of George Roberts, president and chief executive officer of Teledyne, the purpose of a code is to "guide and define."

Of course, every potential example of misconduct cannot be noted in a code of business conduct. Instead, firms often design codes that educate employees about the underlying rationale of code sections. For example, Billy Montague, senior vice president of Branch Banking and Trust Co., contended that well-crafted measures can ensure that the firm will "explain the intent, as well as the letter of the code."

Codes provide guidelines in ambiguous situations where a clearly ethical or proper conduct path is not apparent. In situations where the appropriate actions to take are unclear, codes of business conduct often provide enough direction to effectively manage the dilemmas. They also help (1) reinforce correct conduct and (2) establish parameters to deter improper action. "There is no doubt in my mind that being ethical pays," Kenneth Derr, vice chairman of Chevron has emphasized in *Ethics in American Business*, "because I know in our company, people who sleep well at night work better during the day." Chevron, of course, is a firm that believes in codes of conduct.

In firms without a code of conduct, as former Secretary of Commerce Luther H. Hodges related in *The Business Conscience*, management likely might discover "that everyone in the company had been facing a wide variety of serious . . . [business conduct] dilemmas which they handled case by case without any guidance from one above" and "[w]orse yet, most cases had been resolved in favor of the course that would produce the greatest short-run profit."

Such ambiguous conduct and decisions based solely on maximizing short-term gains can bring disastrous near-term and long-term consequences to a firm. A code of conduct, however, can help provide the guidance a firm's management needs to hold a steady course toward long-term earnings and growth.

Codes can provide overall strategic direction to employees, as well as managers and executives. Employees help plan, implement, and execute business strategies. They make many decisions each day, and sometimes, on behalf of the company, they must choose among several courses of action that have uncertain business-conduct ramifications. When the appropriate course of action is unclear, most employees will rely on the advice of supervisors, fellow employees, or their own personal standards of ethics and business conduct. Firms must fill this potential void with clear guidelines or suffer the consequences of arbitrary and sometimes conflicting standards.

As an example, the highly decentralized firm, Johnson & Johnson, relies on a corporate credo to help provide strategic direction to all who work for the company. According to Johnson & Johnson's chairman, James Burke, "The Credo is our common denominator . . . it guides us in everything we do . . . [and] it represents an attempt to codify what we can all agree upon since we have highly independent managers." The firm's ethical response to the highly publicized Tylenol tamperings a number of years ago illustrates how Johnson & Johnson averted long-term disaster by adhering to the principles in its credo. In the short run, the swift, strategic action of removing Tylenol from the market cost Johnson & Johnson $100 million. But the company quickly recovered and eventually was successful in returning Tylenol to the market, because Johnson & Johnson's overall strategy conformed to public expectations.

Codes provide managers with direction for dealing with outside interest groups. Large firms, particularly those in the public spotlight, usually pay close attention to the influences that outside interests, such as protest groups, consumer activists, or the electronic media and press, can have on the company's activities.

As an illustration, the high-technology Norton Company "welcomes" being in the public limelight, according to information provided by Vice President and General Counsel Wallace Whitney, Jr., because Norton prides itself on being "a highly principled company" in a world where "[t]he behavior of corporations, and particularly multinationals such as ourselves, is continually under searching public scrutiny. . . ."

Other, smaller firms that seldom attract such attention, however, may be unprepared to cope with the sudden appearance of the limelight or public controversy. When outside pressures are brought to bear, a strong ethical base, embodied in a code of business conduct, can help managers deal with the pressures and lessen the consequences. Unfortunately, many firms compulsively dwell on—and waste valuable company resources on sparring with—the uncontrollable outside interest groups. Instead, these firms should concentrate their energies on what they can control: proper business conduct.

Codes assist managers in controlling business relationships and communicating the firm's expectations to suppliers, customers, and agents. "[C]odes [of conduct] disseminated to vendors and available for public bodies show the policy of the company where it concerns actions of parties outside the company," Marshall McDonald, chief executive office of FPL, noted.

Each day, a company creates business relationships that can be cooperative, collegial, or adversarial. The health of the relationships with suppliers, customers, and other parties determines the firm's success. Codes of conduct that introduce fairness principles into these dealings can provide valuable guidance for building and maintaining healthy business relationships.

Moreover, well-drafted ethical provisions can provide a deterrent to questionable or improper requests from customers, suppliers, or others. Codes also can outline procedures for handling and reporting such requests and terminating a business relationship, when necessary.

"We have found on many occasions that suppliers as well as customers attempt to achieve preferential treatment by practices which, while not technically illegal, nevertheless do not follow good business practices," said Cliff Whitehill, General Mills' senior vice president and general counsel. "Being able to cite the General Mills code quickly ends such attempted acts or influence."

Codes outline managers', employees', and the firm's rights and duties. "Written codes of ethics serve to document the company's values and responsibilities," Hewlett Packard's chief executive officer, John Young, asserted, because "[by] making the implicit more explicit, such codes help guide people's actions and thus strengthen the firm's culture. . . ."

One of the most useful goals of a code of conduct is to accurately define and clearly delineate the rights and duties of managers and employees. By having such a code, the firm can ensure that managers and employees are respected and knowledgeable members of a team.

"The value of the [code] appears [to be in part] a management guide to corporate policy, particularly in areas of divisional turf and required procedures," according to Arthur Hilgart, executive director of corporate planning and development for Upjohn.

Codes enable firms to respond to complex government regulation and intense scrutiny. "Codes," Tenneco CEO James Ketelson has said, "enhance firms' responses to complex government regulations and intense scrutiny." Zealous government agencies have increased their investigations into the propriety of firms' business practices. The threat and imposition of more government regulations have shocked many firms into augmenting internal policing and self-regulation. Codes of conduct are excellent control mechanisms, and they comprise a central element of self-regulation. They also can be highly effective in assuring proper business conduct.

Codes provide stable guideposts compared to inconsistent and subjective individual or management standards of conduct or ethics. Without a code of conduct to draw upon, managers and employees who face ethical dilemmas rely on their immediate organizational framework for direction, primarily supervisors, managers, and colleagues. Codes supersede individual guidance and direct all employees toward the firm's overall goals and standards.

2. *Codes improve the firm's public and consumer image and its business reputation.*

During the twentieth century, business firms have emerged as central elements in American life, and society's expectations of them have changed immensely from firms' historic purpose: the creation of goods and services at a profit. Today, society also expect firms to consider its well-being and to assign a high priority to societal concerns, such as preserving a clean environment. When a firm actually lives up to its stated standards, its code of conduct can be a marvelous public relations tool. Bad ethics, on the other hand, repel consumers; they naturally associate management or employee misconduct or shoddiness with the firm's product or service. So in an era when society is examining more closely the conduct of business and its managers and employees, a firm should be willing to use any legitimate tool, such as a code of conduct, to minimize unethical conduct and build public trust.

"[W]e succeed or fail according to the trust consumers have in us," William Smithburg, chairman and CEO of Quaker Oats, has stated in *Ethics in American Business*. "Their trust in our brands is simply the basis of our prosperity . . . our brands, trademarks, and goodwill are more important than our plants and equipment, which can always be replaced. Unethical behavior would undermine the trust that has been placed in our company and our brands, at an incalculable cost."

3. *Codes offer protection in preempting or defending lawsuits.*

According to Detroit Edison CEO Walter McCarthy, "In this time of increasing media coverage of the acts of people in positions of high responsibility, it is essential to tell employees what management expects them *not* to do as well as *what* to do." If firms do not act to prevent unethical or improper conduct by employees, managers, and executives, then society, government, courts, and juries may hold the business responsible for the misdeeds of their personnel. Companies that enact codes of conduct can point to them as evidence of good faith and attempts to comply with statutes and government regulations. Moreover, if an employee's conduct violates the ethical standards expressed in the firm's code of conduct, the firm can reduce its liability in any reducing lawsuit. As the president of one Fortune 500 company has put it bluntly: "The code has saved our skins on a number of occasions."

4. *Codes improve firms' financial performances.*

Several studies have demonstrated the link between (1) firms that make proper business conduct and ethics a priority and (2) enhanced financial performance. Codes also are credited with providing a new source of competitive advantage, plus enhanced productivity, and fewer information gaps between buyers and sellers or third parties.

5. *Codes enhance morale, employees' self-image, pride, loyalty, and the recruiting of outstanding employees.*

A code establishes a standard of conduct that is expected of each employee, regardless of status or tenure. When codes apply equally to everyone, employees generally respect the standards because they sense that no one receives preferential treatment. "People feel better working for a firm with a code which enforces high standards of ethics," contends Ed Kilburn, ITT vice president and general counsel.

6. *Codes of conduct help satisfy management's responsibility to create a workplace climate of integrity and excellence.*

Codes of conduct encourage the development of an open working environment where people can share ideas and improve their service to clients. Other important byproducts are opportunities to improve communication, entrepreneurship, and synergy, and demonstrate leadership through competence and behavior based on values.

7. *Codes of business conduct help preempt the growth of new regulations, and they are important requisites for effective leadership.*

When firms abide by standards higher than those required by law, they help reduce outside pressures to impose more regulations. Within the firm, high standards of conduct and honesty among the company's leaders dramatically affect the conduct and honesty of those who look to their leadership for direction.

8. *Codes act as catalysts for constructive change, and they provide a counterbalance to address the concerns of society at large.*

Businesses are voices of power and authority in American society, and they help lead change. Developing a code of conduct thus can increase a firm's awareness of society's needs. As Peter McColough, former Xerox Corp. CEO, has commented: "No matter how well we run . . . a company, if the society in which we live goes to pieces economically or socially, we aren't going to prosper very much . . . [Consequently] I think that it really is an advantage to business to play a role generally in society. We simply have an obligation to make our society better."

9. *Codes enable firms to clearly enunciate their interests and goals and thereby assist in the goals' realization.*

A code of business conduct becomes an effective and positive control mechanism when it expresses the firm's interests and goals and spells out acceptable behavior for the managers and employees who will pursue them. For example, the Coors Vision statement "defines what we are as a business . . . [and] leads the charge for growth and profitability and clarifies for everyone what we dream of being," according to Adolph Coors CEO Jeffrey Coors. At the same time, the Coors Vision "helps us be aligned in our strategic thinking."

10. *Codes help satisfy the needs of highly principled stockholders who pride themselves on making ethical investments.*

Most investors want businesses to act in the common good. With the growing emphasis on ethical investing, firms that neglect the ethical views and concerns of those who buy their securities often can suffer reduced demand for their products and stock.

11. *Codes encourage frequent, open, and honest communications within the firm.*

Codes of conduct are principles, sometimes very detailed, that typically encourage respect for the views, rights, and diversity of employees and managers. Proper code compliance requires a continuing discourse concerning correct behavior, so codes can help create open and sometimes novel channels of communication. Improved communication at all levels of a firm increases efficiency and understanding.

12. *Codes help integrate or transfer cultures of (1) merged or acquired firms and (2) far-flung or entrepreneurial operations of one firm.*

Codes of business conduct help smooth an often-difficult transition period when firms merge or join through acquisition. Employees and managers of the organization being acquired can quickly learn the operating principles and precepts of their new parent firm by reading its code of conduct.

13. *Codes help prevent managers from requiring subordinates to perform improper acts,* *and the codes also help stop subordinates from trying to get managers to perform* *improper acts.*

    A code of conduct can give managers and employees a way to refuse a directive or request to perform an unethical or illegal act. They can use provisions in the code as guidelines for reporting the superior's or subordinate's request to the proper authority, and they can seek resolution or sanctions as called for in the code.

14. *Codes promote market efficiency, especially in areas where the marketplace and laws are* *weak or inefficient.*

    With codes of conduct or ethics established, markets can be more efficient in rewarding the best and most ethical producers of goods and services, while punishing the inefficient producers who cut ethical corners to survive. Also, the law, a traditional regulator of business activities, is unable to restrain business behavior in many areas because of high enforcement costs and potential conflicts with rights such as those guaranteed by the First Amendment. Codes of conduct, ethical values, and the dynamics of the marketplace then become the major regulators.

    Firms are reflections of the conduct of their people, so each person who works for a firm has a continuing obligation to ensure that the business acts properly in all dealings with customers, suppliers, employees, shareholders, and the public. The responsibility for keeping pace with the firm's legal and ethical obligations thus lies in the people, not in a set of rules and philosophical statements. Nonetheless, a code of conduct is an important element in enhancing and building a firm's public image, its growth, and its long-term profitability.

    The next chapter of this book prevents guidelines for preparing a code of business conduct.

Chapter 2

GUIDELINES FOR CREATING CODES OF CONDUCT

The process of creating a code of business conduct begins with three key decisions: (1) who will approve the code in its final form; (2) how the code will be drafted; and (3) what will be the source of the ethical values that the code will reflect. Once these decisions are settled, the code-creating process then can become a matter of choosing an appropriate structure and approach and following a set of general guidelines that draw upon the experiences and advice of others who have produced successful codes. This chapter is designed to guide you through the steps of creating a code of business conduct.

WHO APPROVES THE CODE

Generally, the chief executive officer (CEO) or board chairman has the final say in promulgating a firm's code of business conduct. However, when a code is in its draft and review stages, it often must meet with approval from managers, employees, corporate legal counsel, and sometimes, outside consultants, before it is delivered to the CEO or chairman for its final okay.

HOW CODES ARE DRAFTED

For many business leaders and entrepreneurs, codes of conduct define the very essence of the business. Consequently, the effort and enthusiasm a firm puts into creating its code reflects its willingness to examine its internal and external environments and mission. In the process of creating a code of business conduct, a firm's executives literally can rediscover the company's key success factors.

There are many different ways to create successful codes of business conduct. One approach or a combination of several approaches may be right for your firm.

The process used at Security Pacific Bank provides one illustration. Executive Vice President Irving Margol has described the bank's code-creation effort as a "top-down bottom-up" approach. More than 75 top-level executives of the bank volunteered to help formulate the code's first draft, with the assistance of an outside consultant. The bank's CEO identified the key objectives, then the senior-level executives offered the consultant some examples of difficult business-conduct decisions they had faced. Later, the senior-level executives were divided into two discussion groups. The tasks of the two groups were: (1) to identify the entities to whom the bank owed certain ethical obligations; and (2) how the bank handled conflicts with those entities. The consultant used all of these inputs to compile the first draft of the credo. Then the first draft was reviewed and revised into its final form by the bank's legal counsel and selected senior managers.

At some firms, a specific individual or a small group is assigned the task of creating and implementing a complete code of business conduct. At other firms, every employee—from custodians and secretaries to executives—may be asked to participate in the process. In all cases, however, top-level management's commitment to the codes is a critical element for successful implementation.

The Roles of CEOs and Chairmen in Creating Codes. CEOs and chairmen frequently initiate and oversee the creation of codes of conduct, because initiating a code or enlarging an existing one can strengthen their control of the business conduct of the firm and its employees. A study by the Ethics Resource Center found that in 41 percent of the surveyed firms, the CEOs had initiated the codes. For example, Teledyne's president and CEO, George Roberts, promulgated his firm's codes, according to Dan Reed, Teledyne's ethics officer. And because the codes were put in place by the firm's leader, "not many incidents of ethics problems" have been encountered, Reed said.

In instances where a CEO or chairman has access to a parent firm's code of conduct, he may use it to form a new code for his own firm. Thomas Rami, director of public policy development for Southwestern Bell, recalled that while AT&T's code provided the pattern for Southwestern Bell's code, it was Southwestern Bell's chairman who led the drive to mold the finished form of that firm's code.

The Role of Boards of Directors in Code Development. Boards of directors sometimes provide pivotal leadership in code development. A firm's board usually initiates such action through an audit committee or similar group. Once it receives the audit committee's recommendations, the board can implement a code of business conduct or revise an existing code. For example, according to Roger Ericson, general consul for Temple-Inland, that firm's audit committee "initiated a review of existing conflicts of interest policies at its initial meeting and subsequently has been responsible for developing the company's Standards of Business Conduct Policy and monitoring its compliance."

The Role of Corporate Legal Departments. The desire to develop codes of conduct sometimes stems from concerns over legal liability, a worry that has expanded rapidly in the last two decades. As Donald Smith, general counsel and senior vice president at GEICO, points out: "Our legal department drafted the code, because preventing fraudulent activities, especially in the claims process, was the firm's primary concern; the firm's top executives felt lawyers were best equipped in this regard." Meanwhile, at First American, according to Senior Vice President Ronald

Roberts: "There is no doubt that Jack Stringham, the firm's General Counsel, was the catalyst for the code's creation, because conflicts of interest are major concerns of any financial institution, and Jack acted on that concern; however, our code is not simply a 'thou shalt not' document. It is a disclosure-based code."

Finance and Human Resources Departments. At many firms, departments such as finance and human resources draft at least parts of the codes. Upjohn's finance department, for example, created a portion of that firm's business code of conduct, according to Arthur Hilgart, executive director of corporate planning and development. The finance department at General Motors also played an important role in developing the automotive giant's code, according to GM's legal counsel, Roger Herrington.

Sections of codes dealing with employee rights and conduct frequently are developed by human-resources directors. And human-resources departments sometimes are tasked to develop at least the rough draft of entire codes of conduct. Boatmen's Bancshares, for instance, directed its human-resources group to produce that firm's code, according to John Wells, the senior vice president of human resources. Then the finished draft was "reviewed by legal counsel and approved by the Chief Executive Officer," Wells added.

Communications Departments. Some firms rely on their communications departments to generate the first draft or assist in creating the final draft of a code of business conduct. Amdahl and 3M are two examples of firms that used this approach.

Corporate Task Forces. To get the code-creation process underway, firms often organize special task forces made up of managers and, occasionally, employees of various ranks and functions. William Verplank, vice president of corporate human resources at Combustion Engineering, recounted how his firm used that approach: "[A] task force of mid-level managers selected to represent all segments of the Company . . . w[as] charged with reducing results of focus group discussions that centered on the Company's culture and value system to a representative set of values. Through several meetings of this task force, the company's Statement of Guiding Principles was developed."

A similar tack was used successfully by Bank of America, according to that firm's legal counsel, John Huffstutler. "A task force of distinguished managers from audit, personnel, legal divisions, and the business units of Bank of America comprised a task force under the CEO's supervision which drafted our most recent code in the 1980's—this approach gave us a better, more versatile code," Huffstutler noted.

Employees. In numerous firms, employees play at least one and sometimes two key roles in the development of a code of business conduct. In the first role, employees serve as a sounding board for the initial drafts of the code. In the second, less-common role, employees participate in the entire formulation of the code. In either role, employees can readily identify the potential pressure points where violations of proper conduct might occur. Employee participation enhances the likelihood that the firm's workers will accept and adhere to the code's provisions.

Also, the focus on ethics can heighten their sense of values in the workplace, and overall morale tends to improve, some firms report.

A number of firms have experienced good results by letting their employees, rather than managers or the CEO or chairman, create the codes of conduct. One example is Washington Mutual, where employees served in "colleague groups that developed the values," according to Kim Alexander, a management training specialist. The firm's rationale, she said, was that by letting employees create the values in the code, there would be greater cooperation and not just passive acceptance once the code was enacted.

Consultants. Firms typically hire consultants to (1) help them come up with ideas for their codes of business conduct, and (2) write the initial drafts of the codes. In a few cases, consultants may be hired to perform the entire process, from concepts to promulgation. Most firms, however, are reluctant to delegate the most important work to outsiders. For example, Security Pacific delegated the responsibility of choosing the values to its senior managers, then retained an outside consultant to write the first draft of the code of conduct. In this way, the consultant assisted, but did not dominate the process. Bowater, meanwhile, took an opposite approach with the same result. Its executives drafted the code, but sought recommended wording from outside advisers.

SOURCES OF CODE VALUES

Once it has been decided who will create or update the code and who will provide the final approval, the next step is to identify the ethical values that should be incorporated into the codes. Some of the existing documents that can be used as research include old versions of a firm's code of conduct, policy memoranda or statements of procedures, and current laws or regulations that affect the firm. The values of the firm's founder, chairman, board members, executives, managers, and employees also should be considered.

As an important time-saving and effort-saving measure, many companies examine codes of conduct developed by other firms and adapt and rewrite some of those measures to better fit their own business environment. To help streamline this important step, the next section of this book presents numerous examples drawn from real codes. These examples show how leading firms have addressed key ethical issues in today's competitive environments. The codes can be employed as models during the process of drafting a new code, and they can be expanded, shortened, or reshaped as needed.

Using Existing Codes. The precedent for using others' codes as a starting point is well-established. Some of the best-known names in American business have turned to the respected credos of other firms for models. Champion International executives, for example, studied many companies' approaches to the subject of corporate responsibility, but they were most impressed with the essence of Johnson & Johnson's corporate credo. That credo became the starting point for Champion's own credo: "The Champion Way." Both ARKLA and Pacific Gas & Electric (PG&E)

used other utilities' codes as guides when they created their own codes. PG&E also incorporated elements of California's state conflict of interest policy into its code.

Existing Laws and Regulations as Sources for Code Values. When constructing a corporate code of conduct, it is often necessary to consult certain legal standards, laws, and regulations. Firms frequently use existing statutory or case law as sources of values for their codes of conduct. As an example, Centel's code is based in part on statutory regulations that set the firm's operating parameters, according to Senior Vice President Karl Berolzheimer.

The laws that firms incorporate as values or guides in their codes of conduct typically center on five areas: (1) corporate fiduciary duties; (2) the corporate duty of care; (3) agency duties; (4) securities laws; and (5) special industry regulations.

Fiduciary duties are the laws a firm must adhere to in order to protect the interest of its shareholders and customers.

The corporate duty of care involves the board of directors' legal duty to exercise prudence in managing the firm's activities.

The agency duty is also known as the duty of loyalty and obedience. This requires employees or other agents of the firm to act in the best interests of the firm and its customers.

Meanwhile, most firms employ the observance of federal and state securities laws in sections of their codes of conduct. And special industry rules and practices sometimes provide the starting point for major parts of a firm's code of conduct.

Many sources of material and inspiration are possible and available to those charged with drafting a code. But certain other issues also must be addressed during the drafting process. These issues are discussed in the paragraphs that follow.

Structure. The persons drafting the code have to choose from an array of possible structures. The structures of existing codes provide a good starting point. Or, structure may depend on the sources of the values, as well as the objectives of the code. For example, a code that relies heavily on existing law as its source may also adopt the structure of the law.

Types of Authority Expressed in the Codes. Codes typically are anchored by some type of authority principles. These principles usually are metaphysical or legal-political in form. The metaphysical principle most commonly cited in codes is that "virtue is its own reward" and finds expression in language such as: "The company principles of honesty and integrity require that employees and the firm conduct business in a lawful and ethical manner." A commonly employed legal-political principle which adds substance to a code is the social contract—the notion that business should conduct its affairs on a level playing field, because civilized, advanced society dictates it. This view often is reflected in code statements such as: "The firm will maintain its good citizenship by adhering to the laws and to ethical behavior."

Constituency Relationships. Through a code of conduct, the firm can identify persons, groups, and agencies toward which it acknowledges a degree of responsibility. Here, firms often address employees' rights and duties and the firm's obligation toward them. Other constituency relationships addressed by the codes may include customers or consumers, suppliers, federal, state and local governments, competitors, local communities, shareholders, and employees' families.

Defining and Drafting Codes by Objectives. A wide array if objectives can be achieved through a code of conduct. But three types of objective-oriented codes are common: (1) the employee guidance code; (2) the public relations code; and (3) the corporate identity code.

The *employee guidance code* points to potential problem areas that employees may encounter in work-related activity. The code then states the firm's policy on these issues and indicates how such situations should be handled or where counsel should be sought. The principle disadvantage of employee guidance codes is that they tend to be narrowly focused within the firm and do not address the larger needs of society.

A *public relations code* can be little more than a broad, externally directed document used to pacify certain outside groups, such as the media, government, and consumer and public-interest groups. These codes usually lack clear operational substance and instead respond to broad public issues in a general way.

A *corporate identity code*, meanwhile, is built from a blending of the employee guidance and public relations codes and constitutes the best approach for many firms. In a corporate identity code, a firm can emphasize the role it seeks to play in society, its responsibilities to its various constituencies, and the standards by which it will conduct its operations.

Joining Purpose, Values, and Objectives to Operations. To be credible, a code's statement of purpose should be operationally relevant. The firm can link the code's statement of purpose, values, or objectives to the firm's operations in several ways, for example, by connecting the code statements to the firm's internal planning process. Many corporations now include a wide range of societal objectives in their strategic planning goals.

Legal and Nonlegal Issues. Many codes emphasize compliance with federal and state statutes, and regulations such as the Clayton Act, the Sherman Act, the Foreign Corrupt Practices Act, the Securities Exchange Act, and the Equal Opportunity Act. Yet, while laws establish minimum standards of acceptable behavior in certain areas, ethical behavior in business requires that employees, managers, and executives act responsibly at all times toward the well-being of society, shareholders, customers, suppliers, and their fellow workers, as well as their firm. As William Smithburg, chairman and CEO of Quaker Oats, has observed in the publication *Ethics in American Business*, "ethical behavior involves more than just conforming to laws. . . . To me, ethical corporate behavior requires moving beyond strict honesty to being honorable in everything you do and setting the best example possible so that you earn respect for your products, the way you do business, and the way you behave in the community."

Negative vs. Positive Codes. The first tendency, a natural one, is for a firm to devise a negative code that details every inappropriate or undesirable act. Yet, codes with a negative tenor and a great many restrictions imposed from the top of the organization inspire little support or respect. Also, a manager or employee can face a severe conflict of interest when he must decide if a provision prohibited in a negative code of conduct really applies to the conduct he wishes to pursue. And the effectiveness of a negative provision will depend on the attitudes of the regulators who enforce it and on the respect those who are regulated are willing to direct to the provision. These can vary significantly, depending on the parties' perceptions of the prohibitions' importance and the advantages or risks involved in not adhering to them. Since a negative code is no better than a manager's or employee's conscience, the preferable approach is an affirmative credo that incorporates a code of honor.

GUIDELINES FOR PRODUCING THE CODE

Once the method for drafting the code has been determined and the persons have been selected who will draft the code, provide its ethical values, and review and approve it, then the work can begin on actually producing the measures. The 18 guidelines that follow are drawn from the experiences of some of the nation's leading firms. These guidelines can be used by your firm to save time and effort and keep a code-creation project on the desired path.

1. *The firm's chief executive officer (CEO) must be a leader in the code's development.*

According to Phil Morrison, director of auditing for Firestone: "One of the critical success factors of our code was the adamancy of our CEO, Richard Riley, and president, John Nevin, that we have a top-drawer code—and no buts about it." As the head of operations, a firm's CEO can ensure that the code does not include unrealistic standards. The code-creation role of the CEO at Harris Corporation was very direct, said O.W. Hudson, Director of Business Conduct and Corporate Secretary. "The CEO . . . not only fervently endorsed the code, he . . . assumed a functional role by serving with five senior executives on the Management Ethics Committee to help administer the code—now that is a strong signal to the company's employees."

2. *The CEO or those under his immediate direction should identify the firm's key objectives, which can serve as ground rules in the creation of the code.*

For example, the CEO of Security Pacific Bank identified the following objectives: (1) the code shall describe both current ethical practices as well as ideals for the future; (2) it shall apply to all sectors of the firm; (3) it shall be sufficiently generic to address varied issues while being operationally oriented; (4) the firm's management shall participate in all facets of the code's development; and (5) the entire staff shall continue its involvement in the implementation of the code.

3. *Although input from large groups is helpful, the code should be drafted by a small operating group of three to six people, including someone from the legal staff.*

A small group can, with more facility, develop and analyze numerous ideas. At the same time, the group's small size is conducive to taking decisive action. One representative should be drawn from each major facet of the firm's operations (e.g., marketing, finance, human resources, management information systems, accounting, or legal).

4. *The code should contain: (1) a preamble or opening section that asserts the need for the code; (2) expectations of high standards of conduct; (3) an explanation of how to interpret the code; and (4), the firm's position on code enforcement, decision making, and sanctions.*

5. *The code should be more than merely a treatise on existing statutes. It should clearly distinguish between ethical and legal requirements.*

Addressing ethical issues, of course, requires a person to look beyond the mere satisfaction of the minimum standards established by law in certain areas. For instance, as Aetna Counsel Tom Calvocoressi asserted during the process of revising that firm's code: "One of the code's objectives is to clearly put all employees on notice that we want them to conduct themselves in an ethical manner—mere compliance with the law is only the starting point—for instance, the code makes it clear Aetna will not transact business with vendors who sexually harass our employees—no law requires that company response." Another firm, Norton, also sought to move beyond mere compliance when it declared that it was aiming "for a standard of conduct well above what the law demands—not just to keep us above reproach, but to nourish our self-respect and sharpen our sense of purpose."

6. *The code shall require employees to comply with all relevant laws and professional standards.*

Firms employing professionals (e.g., accountants, lawyers, doctors) often incorporate the profession's code of conduct by reference or summary into the code of conduct. The main goals here are (1) to eliminate inconsistencies between an individual's responsibilities to his profession and to the firm and (2) to raise his awareness of his professional duties.

7. *The code should emphasize key values of the organization.*

Codes of conduct should include the organizations' core values and mission, in order to provide employees with a sense of the firm's purpose and objectives. For example, Thomas Smith, Dow Chemical Director of Public Affairs, described the scope of "Dow's code as crystallizing our common core values and facilitating a discussion of them."

8. *The body of a comprehensive code contains approximately 25 to 35 topical sections, covering areas such as compliance with the law, dealing with customers and suppliers, conflict of interest, and employee rights.*

In each such section, the objectives, principles, and guidelines for decisions and conduct should be thoroughly presented, followed by the relevant regulations the firm intends to enforce. The code can present interpretations of the enforceable directives at the end of each section. However, the firm should be less concerned with the length of the code and more concerned with its relevance, utility, and credibility.

9. *The code sections should be comprehensive and concise, not voluminous.*

An excessively detailed code is difficult to administer because employees may not have the time or inclination to read and comprehend every section. Furthermore, a lengthy, detailed code increases the likelihood that employees will try to take advantage of loopholes. If the code does not specifically describe the questionable activity, the employee may incorrectly assume the conduct in question is permissible. Clearly understood guidelines, on the other hand, usually compel employees to ask questions of supervisors and expose ethically difficult situations for discussion and resolution.

10. *A code should incorporate operating principles, so that employees, by virtue of complying with the code of conduct, can assist the firm in properly executing its daily operations and activities.*

11. *A code should include specific examples, illustrations of the code in action, and factual situations.*

If possible, some of the history of the firm and some examples of unethical behavior should be woven into the code to bring to life the importance of the code principles and directives to the firm's employee's. Further, the code should identify a resource person or section to be consulted by employees who need interpretation of code provisions or assistance in settling business conduct dilemmas.

12. *A code should fully describe the most commonly encountered conflicts of interest.*

This is important, because (1) it answers many questions before they have to be asked; and (2) a firm competing closely with another company for a major contract might be evaluated on the basis of the internal ethical conduct of its employees.

13. *A code should include a declaration that the firm expects the employee to exercise upright behavior in all business dealings.*

The requirement that transactions be conducted on an arms-length basis establishes a level of objectivity in the business interaction.

14. *Through code provisions, the firm should exercise reasonable care and prudence by responding to all likely questions posed by employees.*

The code should also detail how an employee can resolve problems and list appropriate action steps. The code should admonish all employees to exercise prudent behavior in the daily conduct of their affairs. A code standard of reasonable conduct is appropriate. For instance, if the employee takes action in response to a business conduct dilemma that he reasonably believes others in a similar situation would take, then he usually adequately protects his own interests and those of the firm.

15. *A number of guidelines addressing employees' conduct should be incorporated into the code.*

Employees should be mindful of their actions at all times and seek to conduct themselves in accordance with the firm's code of conduct. While doing so, employees should consider the following questions:

a. Will the employee's action in question comply with the intent and purpose of company policies and practices? Of primary importance to the firm is the employee's ability to comply with the firm's code of conduct. The employee should examine every action taken on behalf of the firm in this manner. An employee's properly evaluating his actions in relation to the firm's code assists the firm in achieving its objectives.

b. Before carrying out any questionable activity, the employee should pose the query: Can the employee defend the action in question in front of supervisors, other employees, and the general public? Greg Koczanski of Citicorp, who wrote that firm's brochure, "Ethical Choices," believes "the code should encourage employees facing ethical or business conduct dilemmas to discuss the matter with others—the employee should ask: 'If I read about my action in *The New York Times*, would I be proud?'" Employees facing activities with questionable ethical implications should seek guidance from a supervisor to resolve the situation. Encouraging employees to take such steps, via a code of conduct, can protect the firm from significant, perhaps irreparable, damage.

c. Will the action in question compromise the employee's position if it becomes known to his supervisor, co-employees, friends, or subordinates? Actions that would compromise an employee are probably in violation of the firm's code of conduct. The above question encourages the individual to consider many different perspectives.

d. Is the action in question honest in every respect? Employees should forthrightly represent themselves in all actions and activities to protect themselves and the firm from charges of impropriety.

e. Could the action in question appear to be inappropriate even if it is, in fact, ethical? Employees should be careful to take actions that demonstrate the highest moral and ethical character. Furthermore, employees should be cognizant of the firm's reputation and public image. An employee focusing his attention on his job and actions will not act in a manner that would appear inappropriate, even if the activity is ethical.

f. Can the employee be comfortable in undertaking the action in question, or does it violate his personal code of conduct? While on the job, employees should comply with the firm's code of conduct. Moreover, if the firm's code was developed using the guidelines above, the employee's personal code of conduct may already be incorporated in the firm's code of conduct. If an employee feels uncomfortable taking an action, he should discuss the activity with his supervisor and explore the ethical and public-relations implications of the proposed action. In raising and spurring discussions of such questions, employees serve the long-term interests of the firm.

16. *The CEO must carefully and candidly review the first draft of the proposed code of conduct.*

As leader of the firm, the CEO's input is vital, and his additional participation at this stage will increase the legitimacy of the firm's code in the eyes of employees and managers.

17. *The draft code should be circulated within the firm for comment.*

Additional observations at this stage increase the likelihood that employees and management will accept the finished code, because more viewpoints are being considered, and thereby respected.

18. *The final draft of the code should consist of the modified draft that reflects the incorporation of employee comments.*

Once employees determine that their comments have been considered and incorporated in the firm's code, the likelihood of the employees' obeying the code will improve because they, too, will have invested time in the code's development. The code becomes the creation, even by derivation, of every group in the firm.

CONCLUSION

In the opinion of the late novelist Ernest Hemingway, what was "good" was what he felt good after, and what was "bad" was what he felt bad after. If every employee used such judgment without any guidelines from his employer, chaos of the most arbitrary kind would ensue. To avoid this, a firm should create a comprehensive code of conduct with an emphasis on ethical behavior. If it fails to do so, the business firm abdicates responsibility for making judgments on the critical issues of the day.

The next section of this book presents numerous model codes drawn from codes of conduct enacted by some of America's most prominent and respected firms.

SECTION II

MODEL CODES OF BUSINESS CONDUCT

Chapter 3

BUSINESS CONDUCT

The daily conduct of business raises many personal ethical issues very similar to those introduced by any other human activity. As a result, many firms' codes often begin with a general statement of ethics and mission, presented in the form of a personal letter from the chief executive officer or chairman to all managers, employees, and others associated with the business. Other firms rely on a summary introduction designed to stress the ethical standards, fairness, and importance of complying with the codes.

In the examples that follow, some of America's most prominent business leaders introduce their firms' codes of business conduct.

INTRODUCTORY LETTER FROM THE CHAIRMAN OR CEO

Firestone

To my fellow employees,

Today, Firestone conducts its business in a complex, competitive environment governed by numerous laws and regulations. Observance of the highest standard of business conduct is a firm Company commitment and is essential if the Company is to meet its obligations to the public, its stockholders, customers and employees.

Firestone's business reputation is the reputation of all its employees, and it is important that each employee carry on his or her responsibilities in a manner consistent with the Company's commitment.

The rules and principles we observe to assure that the Company's business is conducted in a lawful and ethical manner are published in a variety of policies, manuals, and other Company publications. This booklet outlines those policies in general terms, making the rules and principles clear for everyone associated with the Company.

A number of the subjects discussed in this booklet may, at times, involve complex situations, and the Company policies with respect to such subjects are necessarily more detailed than the general principles included here. If you at any time have any questions at to whether or not some action on your part might be in conflict with Firestone's standards of business conduct, you should discuss the matter with your supervisor. Your supervisor will be prepared to discuss with you the specifics of the applicable Company policies and, if necessary, to refer you to others in the Company for further guidance.

If you at any time believe that you have been asked by a supervisor or management to engage in a course of action that is not consistent with Firestone's standards of business conduct, you should bring that matter to the attention of your supervisor. If your questions are not satisfactorily resolved, you should request a meeting with your supervisor and his or her immediate superior. The purpose of this course of action is to eliminate the possibility of any employee erroneously concluding that he or she has been directed to engage in activity inconsistent with Firestone's standards of business conduct. If you continue to believe that the action requested of you would contravene the Company's policies and standards of business conduct, you should contact the Law Department.

Compliance with the Company's business standards is vital to the integrity and well being of Firestone and our employees. I suggest that you periodically review the contents of this booklet, and if you are a supervisor, discuss it with each new employee and review it annually with your staff.

John J. Nevin

IBM

Our company has an outstanding reputation for ethical behavior and fair dealing, one that you and your fellow IBMers have earned over the years.

That record is a source of pride for everyone in IBM. Because it enables us to build our business on the basis of trust and confidence, it is also a most valuable asset.

In many cases, decisions about what is ethical or fair are, and always will be, clear-cut. There will also be times when the changes in or industry, our company, and our ways of doing business can make it more difficult for you to be certain of the right course of conduct. This version of our *Business Conduct Guidelines* has been updated to provide advice and counsel on some of the new questions and circumstances you may encounter.

But guidelines, however comprehensive, cannot anticipate every situation or all of the changes that are still ahead of us. That is why I want to emphasize, as we always have, a principle that is not subject to change:

we expect every IBM employee to live up to the highest standards of conduct, in every business relationship—with each other, with the company, with our customers, business partners, and competitors.

Doing the right thing begins with the basic honesty and integrity of individual IBMers—you and your colleagues. More than ever, it also depends on your good judgment and sensitivity to the way others see us and how they may interpret our actions.

In the future, as in the past, IBM's fine reputation is largely in your hands. I am confident you will keep what you have already done so much to earn.

John F. Akers

Proctor & Gamble

The principle foundation on which Proctor & Gamble has been built is the character of the people in the organization. From its people, the Company itself has developed a strong tradition of character. Honesty, integrity, fairness and a respect and concern for others have been characteristics of P&G people and Company activities ever since its founding in 1837. The Company's continued success depends heavily on each of us doing his or her share to maintain and enhance our tradition of character.

While Proctor & Gamble is oriented to progress and growth, is vital that employees understand that the Company is concerned not only with results but with how results are obtained. We do care. And we will never tolerate efforts or activities to achieve results through illegal or unfair dealings anywhere in the world.

What follows in this booklet does not cover every possible subject or potential situation. It does discuss broad areas of policy and principles which should guide us in our daily work worldwide. Detailed guidelines covering many of our activities have long existed and those which pertain to your job are available to you through your department manager's office. While the more important ones are summarized in these pages, you should carefully review, and be thoroughly familiar with, all those which cover your own responsibilities.

Ethical conduct in Proctor & Gamble has historically been developed and communicated by the manner in which we make and execute our daily decisions. However, as we continue to grow worldwide with a constant flow of new people into the Company, it seems more appropriate than ever that we remind ourselves, and especially new employees, of what these standards and guidelines are. This is why I urge you to read this booklet carefully.

John G. Smale
Chairman and Chief Executive

INTRODUCTIONS TO CODES

Walt Disney

Today, the name Walt Disney is known throughout the United States, and virtually every other company around the world as a symbol of "The Finest in Family Entertainment." This is a legacy that has developed through more than 50 years of bold pioneering achievements . . . a harmonious blend of creative genius and plain hard work.

Walt Disney believed that the right kind of entertainment would appeal to all people . . . young and old alike . . . in every walk of life. Walt believed that our audience would accept, above anything else, quality and good taste in entertainment.

Time and time again throughout his career, he virtually bet his entire organization on this belief . . . often in the face of skepticism and predicted failure by others. His philosophy rejected gimmicks and the fast buck, embracing instead a different and vastly more difficult philosophy . . . to produce a quality family entertainment product. This philosophy has brought to the name "Disney" a hard-earned public trust unparalleled anywhere else in the entertainment business.

This public trust, above all else, is the basis for the remarkable success of the Disney organization . . . a foundation built on a half-century of great traditions which we are dedicated to preserve as our organization continues its dynamic growth. We are determined that our size will never adversely affect our product but, if anything, will help us improve it. And we remain dedicated to the same basic principles of family entertainment which have always guided the Disney organization.

Our traditions have kept us up with the future . . . but our future demands that we keep our traditions. Our challenge . . . to which "The Disney Management Style" is dedicated . . . is to continue to produce for future generations . . . "The Finest in Family Entertainment."

Bowater

The success of Bowater Incorporated depends on the goodwill of our customers, suppliers, shareholders and employees. As the minimum standard, we must conduct our business in compliance with the law; but mere compliance with the law does not protect our single most important asset, which is our reputation for integrity and ethical conduct. In building and protecting this reputation, each of us is totally interdependent on the others. For as our individual business conduct determines the reputation of the organization, so does the reputation of the company we represent reflect on our personal reputations.

This statement of Policy relates to Bowater Incorporated's companies. It is a guide to assist employees in making judgments in their business conduct. If you have any questions about the meaning of this policy or specific situations which may arise, you should seek the advice of your supervisor who will assist in resolving your questions. Where necessary, you should obtain help or interpretation from the Legal Department.

New employees are asked to read and sign a letter from the Chairman, President and Chief Executive Officer of Bowater Incorporated recognizing their full awareness of, and intention to adhere to, this Policy. Each signed letter will be kept in the employee's personnel file.

Annually, the Secretary of Bowater Incorporated will distribute a Certification Letter . . . to key management personnel. This letter will serve to reconfirm that management personnel, and their respective departments, understand and are continually abiding by this Statement of Policy. This letter will require signature, and will be kept on file by the Corporate Legal Department.

Mellon Bank

Please read this Code of Conduct carefully and retain it for future reference. As an associate, you are expected to be familiar with it. From time to time, you may be asked to certify in writing that you have followed the Code, so be sure you understand it.

For more than one hundred years, this Corporation and its predecessors have endeavored "to be a premier financial services organization in every respect." One measure of the success achieved is the high respect accorded Mellon worldwide. This reputation is one of our most important assets.

Another measure of our success is our financial performance. One important goal has been and remains increasing our corporate earnings. The reason for this is that earnings are the locomotive that makes it possible for us to do what we want and need to do for our constituencies.

Only by conducting our business in a accordance with highest ethical, legal and moral standards can all our goals be achieved. And since corporate behavior is the sum total of individual behavior by associates, this code is articulated so associates may know the individual ethical, legal and moral standards required by Mellon.

Mellon has many important constituencies including five core constituencies: associates, communities, creditors, customers and shareholders. Toward all we wish to apply only the highest ethical, legal and moral standards and each of us as individuals must so conduct ourselves.

There is an old expression that people are judged by the company they keep. For this reason, among others, Mellon does *not* wish to do any business of any kind with recognized criminal elements. In addition, business may *not* be transacted on behalf of Mellon with any person who would use the benefits of such transaction to further an unlawful purpose.

This code should help associates recognize their ethical, legal and moral responsibilities. It formalizes the principles, obligations, and high standards of behavior Mellon expects. It does not attempt to detail all responsibilities, but rather sets general guidelines of professional conduct to be followed by all associates.

W.W. Grainger

The nature and scope of the Company's nationwide operations place a significant trust in individual employees. The Company rewards each employee's contribution to the Company by providing challenging employment, competitive compensation and benefits, pleasant working facilities, and attractive retirement plans.

The importance of ethical conduct to the success of the Company is further emphasized in our statement of Company Operating Principles. These principles commit the Company: **To operate with the highest moral and legal standards, and to employ persons who are dependable and loyal and who have high standards and integrity.**

Employees over the years have understood and met the high ethical standards demanded by the Company. With continued growth and the addition of new employees, however, it is appropriate to be more specific concerning how the Company's ethical standards apply to certain business situations. For this reason, the Company has prepared the following *Business Conduct Guidelines.*

All employees are expected to study the *Business Conduct Guidelines,* and to pledge personal commitment and compliance. A response card is provided for you to acknowledge your receipt of the publication. In addition, all supervisory employees have a special obligation to maintain exemplary business conduct as a model for their subordinates.

I am confident that Grainger people will appreciate this expression of the ethical standards that are vital to the continued success of the Company and its employees. All of us are on a team. We must be able to depend on our teammates to support these standards for the mutual benefit of all of us.

Chapter 4

BUSINESS DEALINGS AND RELATIONSHIPS

Often, in the business arena, there is significant pressure, explicit or implicit, on executives and employees to practice deception for their firms' or their own profit. This deception may be aimed at customers, suppliers, labor unions, government officials, superiors, their fellow employees, or competing companies.

Management styles in some earlier decades emphasized the ruthless pursuit of pursuit. But the successful manager in the 1990s must emphasize profitability only within the confines of obedience to the laws and standards of ethics. By so doing, the manager will act to preserve and validate the integrity of his firm and the economic system. Toward this end, a firm should establish and publicize its standards on business dealings and relationships through a code of conduct. A healthy working environment that emphasizes production, truthfulness, and trust—and not deception, bluffing, and puffery—can revitalize a flagging firm.

The following excerpts from major firms' codes reflect renewed emphasis on forthright business dealings, truthfulness, integrity, and avoiding deception.

PRESERVING THE FIRM'S REPUTATION

Citicorp

Citicorp's reputation for integrity has been built by the men and women who work here now, and who have worked here in the past. A good reputation is a fragile thing which must be earned on a continuing basis by conducting all of our affairs in a fair and honest way, complying not only with the letter, but also with the spirit of the law.

Cummins

For Cummins, ethics rests on a fundamental belief in people's dignity and decency. Our most basic ethical standard is to show respect for those whose lives we affect and to treat them as we would expect them to treat us if our positions were reversed. This kind of respect implies that we must: A. Obey the law. B. Be honest—present the facts fairly and accurately. C. Be fair—give everyone appropriate consideration. D. Be concerned—care about how Cummins' actions affect others and try to make those effects as beneficial as possible. E. Be courageous—treat others with respect even when it means losing business. It seldom does. Over the long haul, people trust and respect this kind of behavior and wish more of our institutions embodied it.

The reason for such behavior is that, in the long run, nothing else works. If economics and societies do not operate in this way, the whole machinery begins to collapse. No corporation can long survive in situations where employees, creditors, and communities don't trust each other. Since a corporation lives by society's consent, it must plan on earning and keeping that consent for the duration. Successes we have today—in securing sales, completing negotiations, obtaining credit, enlisting that others have learned to expect that Cummins will deal with them fairly. What we do today will maintain or undermine that legacy.

Our aim is that Cummins—its individual members, each of its distributors, and their people—all be known worldwide as trustworthy in all respects. "In all respects" is important. We can't operate by one set of standards internally and by another set externally. We cannot say one thing and do another. Our ethical standards should not tolerate split behavior.

Upjohn

The Company's reputation is one of our most valuable assets. The Company's operations must be characterized by integrity, and the products and services we sell must be of the highest quality.

Proctor & Gamble

Integrity without results will not support a successful business. But, results without integrity not only betray our heritage but carry with them the seeds of their own destruction. Our consumers and our suppliers who suffer from any lapses from our principles will never forget it. While we can always bounce back to get better results tomorrow, there is no way to fully restore your good name once you lose it. As Proctor & Gamble managers, it is our responsibility to maintain this heritage and high standards it represents. Making this system work requires personal responsibility and individual integrity from each of us in the Company. We must constantly remind ourselves that even though there will always be pressure for results, we can't allow this pressure to make us forget who we are. We must teach all our people—with actions and deeds—that our corporate integrity is not something locked in a vault in Cincinnati at the General Offices. It's the composite of the individual integrity of each of us.

There is no way that any one person can guarantee that all employees will maintain our good name. What each of us can do is see that the people who work for us are helped to understand this message clearly and often. When we make a decision on principle, we should make sure that our people understand that's precisely what we're doing. They must learn this at our knees, from our deeds. and not from articles in the Company magazine or from speeches. As one of our senior executives once put it, "The outstanding characteristic of Proctor & Gamble is that it has character."

INTEGRITY

Tandy

Integrity is something to be proud of, something most possess and yet it must always be protected and defended. Integrity is the moral fiber of ourselves individually and our society. Unfortunately, there are those in our society that "shortchange" their fellow man by setting their standards for integrity too low. For those of you that do maintain high standards, I congratulate you and encourage you to maintain that example.

While we rarely describe it that way, we all have as one of our jobs the security and well being of our corporate assets. Prevention of shoplifting, protection of office equipment from removal, prompt bank deposits, stopping the mysterious disappearance of tools and materials, and the security of our merchandise in distribution are major opportunities for us to insure integrity. Much of our paperwork is also a major opportunity to preserve and report our assets. The bottom line is: integrity should always be with us. A number of years ago when my father passed away, as an impressionable young man, I recall one thing very distinctly that the minister said at his funeral: "When he spoke, you had the feeling he was telling you the closest thing to the absolute truth that he knew." Honesty and integrity are virtues that we all should practice everyday in all our endeavors. Society is depending on you and me.

HONESTY AND FAIRNESS

Proctor & Gamble

A third principle central to the character of P&G is a total commitment to honesty in all our business dealings . . . inside the Company and out. Our decision-making process has been described as a "democracy of ideas." This helps insure we can choose the best decision from among *all* the possible alternatives that the organization can generate . . . not just the ideas of one person or a few people. For this democracy of ideas to exist, we must deal honorably and openly with others. We simply cannot tolerate bending the facts or withholding information in order to make a sale. We can't operate with other P&G departments on the basis that "what they don't know won't hurt them."

Similarly, in our dealings outside the Company, we strive to be honest and fair. We must try to do the right things with our suppliers. We are a major purchaser of goods and services, and depend upon our suppliers to successfully conduct our business. We may well be tough bargainers, and we never spend money needlessly. However, we should be prepared to pay a fair price for value received, and then expect first quality. And, in all our dealings we never tolerate kickbacks, bribes, or conflict of interest to make our business dealings easier or clear away apparent obstacles. As these practices are increasingly subjected to public scrutiny, we can be very proud of Proctor & Gamble's record. It is, perhaps, the best in all industry.

IBM

Everyone you do business with is entitled to fair and even-handed treatment. That should be true no matter what your relationship with an outside organization may be—whether you are buying, selling or representing IBM in any other capacity.

Control Data

Control Data expects you to be fair with everyone you deal with on behalf of the Company. Sometimes, however, it may be hard to define what is fair.

In some situations, the law will determine what is fair. Control Data will abide by all applicable laws wherever it does business. Be aware, however, that many of our policies ask more of us than is required by the law. Another way to look at this area of fairness is to imagine yourself in the other person's place. How would you expect to be treated?

Parker-Hannifin

Parker expects from each of its employees honesty and openness in dealings with others. Employees, for example, must be willing to accept responsibility for their mistakes. We must each be willing to tell our supervisors the bad as well as the good news—such as the reasons for potential product problems and unexcused absences or tardiness. Supervisors have a corresponding responsibility for honesty in their treatment of subordinates. Performance reviews should include an open discussion of subordinates' strengths and areas for improvement. Performance problems or interpersonal conflicts should be dealt with and discussed when they first appear and should not be left unresolved.

Employees are expected to raise ethical concerns and report any actual or suspected ethical misconduct to their supervisors and to the Office of General Counsel or the Corporate Security Director. Honesty also requires that employees refuse to participate either actively or passively in any cover-up of such misconduct. Each employee is expected to cooperate fully in any investigations of ethical matters by Parker and its counsel. "Looking the other way" on potential ethical violations is in direct contradiction to Parker's commitment to honesty and integrity and will not be tolerated.

All Parker employees are expected to treat their fellow employees with fairness and respect. All employees must be given an equal opportunity to succeed regardless of their race, color, sex, religion, age, national origin, or personal idiosyncrasies. Harassment or unequal treatment of fellow employees based on such arbitrary standards has no place at Parker. The diversity of Parker's workforce is one of its great strengths, and each employee's uniqueness should be treated with tolerance and respect. Parker's supervisors are expected to foster an environment that encourages each employee to develop his or her capabilities to the fullest without interference from discriminatory unequal or harassing treatment.

UNDESIRABLE BUSINESS

First Commerce

Employees are encouraged to actively solicit profitable business, but dealings with persons of questionable reputation should be avoided since such transactions often result in losses, adverse publicity or other embarrassment. When questions of this nature arise, a decision to accept or reject the business should be made only after consultation with an executive officer of the Company.

COMPETITION AND COMPETITORS

Atlantic Financial

In its many business activities, Atlantic Financial engages in vigorous, but fair and ethical competition.

Digital Equipment

We never criticize the competition publicly. We sell by presenting the positive features of our own products. We want to be respectful of all competition, and collect and analyze all public information about competitors. When we hire people from competitors, we should never ask them for confidential, competitive information, nor should we use confidential literature they may have taken with them.

First Bank System

In offering financial services, FBS engages in vigorous, fair, and open competition. Conducted from an ethical base, this competition is healthy and helps to inform and serve customers.

As a representative of FBS, you are expected to observe the highest standards of ethical conduct with FBS competitors. It is against FBS policy to disseminate rumors or make disparaging, negative statements about our competitors. You may not inform FBS competitors about any FBS plans that are not general, public knowledge.

First Virginia

Competition with other financial institutions should always be conducted in a positive rather than a negative manner. Better service and a friendly personal interest in the customer are far more effective and permanent than criticism of competitors. Derogatory statements which could be interpreted as damaging to the business or reputation of a competitor should not be made.

Holiday

We will be leaders, not followers in our industry and we will accurately monitor our key competitor's direction and long-term strategy in order to stay ahead.

We will compete in the marketplace as a law-abiding company with the highest standards of integrity and ethical conduct. We expect our competitors to do the same. In all cases, our integrity, reputation and ethical standards will come before any competitive pressures.

IBM

If you work in a marketing or service activity, IBM asks you to compete not just vigorously and effectively but fairly as well.

It has long been IBM's policy to sell products and services on their merits, not by disparaging competitors, their products or their services. False or misleading statements and innuendos are improper. Don't make comparisons that unfairly cast the competitor in a bad light. Such conduct only invites disrespect from customers and complaints from competitors.

Johnson Controls

Johnson Controls believes that leadership in our businesses comes from providing products and services of a quality and value that are superior to those of our competitors. Our intent is to compete fairly and vigorously.

Planning or acting together with any competitor to fix prices or to agree about the nature, extent or means of competition in any market is against company policy and in violation of antitrust laws.

Premark

Competition based on quality, service, and price is the heart of the free enterprise system. The Company, which enthusiastically accepts this challenge, competes on a positive basis, not by derogating its competitors, their products, services, programs, or management.

Quaker Oats

As a competitor in the marketplace, we continually seek economic knowledge about our competition. However, we will not engage in illegal or improper acts to acquire a competitor's trade secrets, customer lists, information about company facilities, technical developments or operations. In addition, we will not hire competitors' employees to obtain confidential information or urge competitive personnel or customers to disclose confidential information.

GIFTS, FAVORS, AND BUSINESS ENTERTAINMENT

Eaton

The purpose of business entertainment and gifts is to create goodwill and sound working relationships. Their purpose is not to gain special advantage with customers. You have crossed the line into unethical behavior when your actions unduly influence recipients, make them feel obligated to pay Eaton back or violate their own standards of conduct. It is your duty to exercise good judgment and to *act with moderation* in offering entertainment or gratuities.

Practices in offering and accepting business gratuities vary among the markets we serve. With most commercial and industrial customers, reasonable entertainment and gratuities are customary. However, such activities are strictly forbidden when dealing with the U.S. government. The promise, offer or delivery to an officer or employee of the U.S. government of a gift, favor, or other gratuity (i.e., *anything* of value) would not only violate Eaton policy; it could also be a criminal offense.

It's also important to observe a customer's regulations regarding gratuities. Never offer to anyone something he or she is prohibited from receiving. It is clear that you must take special care when working with U.S. government employees. And you should investigate whether there are regulations imposed upon other customers you serve—state, local and foreign government employees *and* representatives from the commercial sector. Awareness will help you avoid inappropriate and possibly illegal situations.

Obviously, relatives or close friends employed by government agencies may be entertained socially; but care should be taken so that the entertainment is personal and is perceived as personal, and in no way can be viewed as related to Eaton business.

Avon

Employees shall select and deal with those who are doing, or seeking to do, business with the Company in a completely impartial manner, without any considerations other than the best interests of the Company. This means that no employee shall seek or accept from any such person or firm any gift, entertainment, or favor of a type that goes beyond common courtesies consistent with ethical business practices. Any appearance of possible impropriety must be avoided.

RELATIONSHIPS AND CONDUCT WITH GOVERNMENT AND PUBLIC OFFICIALS

Mead

Government—federal, state, and local—has a substantial impact on the goals, strategies, and operations of Mead. It is the company's policy to develop and maintain good relationships and effective communication with all levels of government. However, contacts with government officials must never be conducted in a way that would be in violation of applicable laws or regulations or could cast doubts on the company's integrity.

Working relationships with legislators and government administrative employees for the purpose of legitimately influencing the formulation of law or regulations will be conducted according to the highest ethical standards and in a framework of mutual respect and arm's length dealing. Employees responsible for formulating or presenting Mead's positions on public issues are expected to take into account any special concerns of the company and to balance them with the public interest. Mead will conform to all lobbying or representation requirements and rules.

No corporate contributions will be made, directly or indirectly, to political candidates, their political committees, or to political parties, either federal, state, or local. However, the corporation does bear the administrative costs of employee political participation programs and encourages individual participation in the political process. Mead also may make its position known on public issues, and corporate support related to ballot issues is quite acceptable.

Employees may properly serve in consulting or advisory positions to governmental bodies where their expertise will contribute to government effectiveness. In such circumstances, or in the case of an employee who chooses to enter government service (either elective or appointed), an arm's length relationship between Mead and the employee or former employee will be maintained. In addition, all parties should be alert to possible conflicts of interest.

Any payment, gift, loan, donation or reimbursement to a government employee (including elected officials) of money, property, services or anything of value, whether made directly or indirectly, and which might be construed as a payoff, bribe or other improper influence is expressly forbidden. Certain expenditures which are permitted to facilitate the conduct of business include such things as: meals or refreshments during the course of a meeting or activity which has a business purpose; transportation or accommodations, but only in unusual circumstances (e.g., remote or inaccessible locations) for a specific trip with the approval of the government employee; honoraria and travel expense reimbursement if a government employee is speaking, as an individual, to an identifiable group to whom his expertise and message are relevant.

United Technologies

The laws and regulations governing contracting with the government impose requirements not traditionally associated with purely commercial business transactions. For example, it is a criminal violation—a felony—knowingly to make a false claim or false statement to the government. Violations of these and other statutes can subject us to damaging litigation, reduction of negotiated contract prices, suspension of UTC's eligibility to receive government contracts, and debarment from doing business with the government. Violations also may subject the corporation and its individual employees to civil lawsuits or criminal prosecution, with possible resultant fines, debarment or suspension, and prison sentences.

Adolph Coors

Hospitality toward public officials shall be of such a scale and nature as to avoid compromising the integrity or impugning the reputation of the public official or the Company. All such acts should be performed in the expectation that they will become a matter of public knowledge.

LOBBYING

Chevron

Lobbying is a necessary and constructive part of the political process. Essentially, lobbying involves attempts to influence the decisions of public officials through advocacy, either by direct communication or by encouraging employees, shareholders and others to express their own views.

The laws and regulations that govern lobbying and the tax deductibility of lobbying expenses vary greatly. Employees who represent the company in legislative or regulatory matters are responsible for understanding and complying with all such laws and regulations. Employees planning to participate in any activity that involves contact with public officials on behalf of the company should first determine the extent, if any, of the registration and reporting requirements that apply to them or to the company. In the U.S., you should contact the Government Affairs staff on these matters.

PURCHASES OF GOODS AND SERVICES

Boston Edison

The Company spends millions of dollars annually to purchase goods and services. All Company employees involved in the procurement function should be above reproach and impartial when making procurement-related decisions. These functions include but are not limited to: establishing need; developing specifications; requisitioning, purchasing, receiving, and inspecting goods; and paying vendors. To remain fair and impartial in making decisions, employees involved in these processes should: [1] Follow established policies and procedures for all steps of the purchasing process. [2] Avoid "backdoor selling" when doing business with vendors. Backdoor selling occurs when vendors circumvent established procedures to work directly with requisitioners and to influence procurement decisions. [3] Be impartial in making decisions that affect the purchasing of goods and services, and avoid being influenced by pressure from inside or outside the Company. [4] As already discussed in detail, neither seek nor accept gratuities, favors, or other payments from vendors or customers. [5] Not use Company funds to make personal purchases.

Union Carbide

Purchasing personnel will adhere to the highest standards of business integrity and ethics and will respect and comply with all applicable laws, regulations and customs.

In addition to complying with the Corporate Policies regarding business integrity and ethics, Union Carbide endorses the Standards of Purchasing Practice of the National Association of Purchasing Management and International Federation of Purchasing. Furthermore: [1] Transactions and communications with vendor representatives must be sincere, factual and straightforward. The confidence of the vendor must be respected. [2] Purchasing personnel must keep themselves free from any type of personal obligation to any vendor. Personal gifts, loans or compensation will not be accepted from vendors. Imprinted sales promotional or advertising items or other items of small value are the exception. [3] Prudent judgment will be exercised when considering acceptance of entertainment. Acceptance of entertainment invitations must be approved by the individual's management. [4] Purchasing personnel shall be familiar and comply with antitrust laws, such as the Sherman Act, the Clayton Act, the Federal Trade Commission Act and the Robinson-Patman Act. [5] Any question of interpretation of this policy should be referred to the Field materials Administrator.

Gannett

Gannett is committed to the concept of free, fair and open competition for suppliers, customers and competitors. To achieve that, the people of Gannett will:

[1] Avoid actions that restrict freedom of competitive opportunities. We will not disparage our competitors or their products or services. [2] Maintain an arms-length relationship in all dealings, including those with suppliers or others dealing with the Company. This includes any credits or return of money for services such as from collection agencies. [3] Keep senior management informed on any matters that might be considered sensitive to preserving the Company's reputation, even when less candor might seem to protect the Company or its management from criticism.

Consolidated Freightways

... the Company believes that fair competition is fundamental to continuation of the American free enterprise system. Accordingly, we support those laws which prohibit unfair practices and abuses of economic power.

We have a legal right to choose our suppliers and customers, and to refuse to buy from or sell to anyone. But this right must be exercised independently by us, without consultation outside the Company, with competitors or others.

An agreement between competitors not to sell or buy from certain individuals or firms is illegal. Never suggest that a competitor, supplier or customer should not sell to or buy from anyone.

Our Company purchases solely on the basis of price, quality, terms and service. Never imply that a supplier must purchase from us in order to sell to us. Never imply to a customer that the purchase of our services or products will result in sales to us.

Firestone

Employees must also conduct all dealings with customers and potential customers fairly and in conformity with the spirit and intent of the above principles. This means that any kickback, under-the-table payment, illegal or unethical rebate, or other similar improper favor to customers and their employees or representatives is strictly prohibited. Prohibited conduct includes providing expensive gifts or lavish or otherwise inappropriate entertainment to customers, potential customers or their employees and representatives, for the purpose of influencing them to do business with the Company.

The boundary line between ethical and unethical competition, or legal and illegal conduct, is not always well defined. This is particularly true in international activities, where differing local laws, customs and practices come into play. The following standards, therefore, are provided to serve as general guidelines only to appropriate conduct in dealing with customers: 1. All employees should make every effort to know and fully comply with all state and federal laws governing relations with customers as well as competitors. 2. All employees engaged in government contracts, or contracts and other dealings with quasi-governmental entities, must also be aware of the specific rules and regulations covering those relations. 3. Employees may not provide any gift to customers, their employees or representatives, except an item of nominal value, which fits the normal and customary pattern of the Company's sales efforts for a particular market. 4. Entertainment for any customer must fit regular business practices. The place and type of entertainment and the money spent must be reasonable and appropriate.

CONTRACT BIDDING, NEGOTIATION, AND PRICING

Motorola

In the negotiation and pricing of most negotiated U.S. Government contracts, subcontracts, and modifications exceeding $100,000 in value, cost and pricing data must be submitted to the Government before agreement on price. Motorola must also certify that this cost or pricing data is current, accurate and complete. Moreover, it is Motorola policy to disclose to the Government all data which a reasonable buyer or seller would believe might significantly affect price. Company guidelines and specific training are provided to employees involved in such negotiations, submissions, and certifications. Each Motorola employee bears individual responsibility to deal with the Government fairly, and to comply with disclosure requirements when pricing and negotiating contracts, subcontracts, and modifications.

BRIBES, KICKBACKS, AND IMPROPER PAYMENTS

H&R Block

All of the business affairs of the Company and all of its representatives acting on behalf of the Company with all other parties, including suppliers, customers and competitors, shall be conducted on an ethical, legal and arm's-length basis, and shall be based on commercial merit and not on considerations personal to the representative acting on behalf of the Company or the person with whom he or she deals. No payment or gift shall be made by a Company representative (whether in the form of a commission, loan, kickback, rebate, bonus, salary, profit participation arrangement, financial inducement or otherwise) for the purpose of securing preferential consideration for the Company, not shall a Company representative accept any payment or gift of such nature as a personal inducement to enter into any transaction on behalf of the Company. Nothing in this policy is intended to prevent payments with Company funds of legitimate charges made for services rendered to the Company or items purchased by the Company, nor to modify the Company's existing policies with respect to ordinary and necessary business expenditure for travel and entertainment on behalf of customers or suppliers to the Company, so long as all such expenditures are documented and supported by proper records and receipts.

Chapter 5

INTERNATIONAL BUSINESS RELATIONSHIPS AND PRACTICES

The "World Competitiveness Report," a business survey of 32 nations issued in July, 1989, by the World Economic Forum, ranked the United States third in international economic competitiveness behind Japan and Switzerland. The authors of the report defined competitiveness as "the ability to take advantage of opportunities in the international marketplace." In addition, the report ranked the United States "sixth, behind Finland and Sweden in 'innovative forward orientation.'"

"Perhaps for the first time since the United States became a modern industrial economy, the most important influence shaping the trend of business conditions in the years ahead will be our external trade . . . a shift of historic proportions," the economist Paul McCracken has noted.

Yet, for a variety of reasons, primarily lack of knowledge and formidable bureaucratic obstacles, few American firms export: A mere 250 U.S. companies account for about 85 percent of the nation's exports. The General Accounting Office has estimated that another 11,000 domestic firms could export their goods and services, and if they did, they would generate at least $4 billion in sales and create 125,000 jobs. Moreover, by the end of 1992, the European community was expected to become the world's largest trading bloc—320 million people annually producing $2.4 trillion worth of goods and services—by eliminating all barriers to free trade among its members. Leading economists contend that the United States, with more than 247 million people and $3.9 trillion in annual economic output, must expand its international trade to transform the European challenge into an opportunity.

Succeeding in the international sector requires a firm's determined commitment to developing a strategy based on the interrelationship of three factors: the market, the product, and the business person. While mastery of the first two elements assists in determining a starting point for export operations, the last is more important in actually maintaining export activities. And it is essential that the firm establish a code of conduct that encompasses ethical behavior in international business relationships and practices.

Another method of increasing foreign business is through countertrade, which some observers believe is a market equal to at least 30 percent of the more than $2 trillion in international sales. Countertrade is an umbrella term encompassing a wide range of barterlike activities in international trade. In such transactions, a buyer may require payment in goods rather than cash. Counterpurchase is a prevalent form of countertrade in which the contract is specifically stated in a selected currency. The seller delivers the desired products to the purchaser, and the seller agrees to purchase products from the original buyer equal to more than a portion or all of the original price.

In addition, successful international advertising conducted in one country can be a critical sales factor in others, as well. The firm's next step is assuring, after examining its product advertising in a major market, that the "buying proposal," the content of the advertisement, actually transfers to the international market's consumers.

The Foreign Corrupt Practices Act of 1977 (FCPA) is one of the United States' most controversial laws. The FCPA deems it unlawful for any U.S. business firm or "any individual who is a citizen, national, or resident of the United States" to use an instrument of interstate commerce (such as the telephone or the mail) in furtherance of a payment or offer to pay money or "anything of value" directly or indirectly to any foreign official with discretionary authority, any candidate for foreign political office, or any foreign political party, if the purpose of the payment or offer is made "corruptly" to induce the recipient's act or refraining from an act in such a manner as to assist the firm in obtaining or retaining business for or with or directing business to any person.

In 1988, the Congress enacted an omnibus trade bill, of which Part I is titled "Foreign Corrupt Practices Act Amendments." These amendments modify the FCPA in several important aspects, including foreign-trade practices, penalties, and injunctive relief, and accounting and control standards.

Of course, a firm dealing in the international market should incorporate clear and complete recapitulations of the FCPA, and in addition, conflict-of-interest policies in its code of conduct that require the disclosure of such prohibited activities. Moreover, the code should address any federal sanctions, boycotts, or policies regarding specific foreign markets and discuss the Export Administration Act, which controls the import of U.S. technology by an adversary nation.

There is no easy formula for success in international business. But to create and keep customers, firms must be innovative and entrepreneurial and, most of all, develop a global strategy with appropriate business-code guidelines. The following examples show how several major firms have combined ethics and the need for compliance with complex regulations.

INTERNATIONAL RELATIONSHIPS AND INVESTMENT AND SUPPORT FOR FREE ENTERPRISE AND PLURALISM

Mead

Because Mead does business in other countries, care must be taken that managers and employees who handle the international business of the company recognize the different rules and regulations, customs, manners, and values that exist abroad. Mead's guidelines for proper business behavior apply not only to Mead employees but also to independent agents in their dealings on Mead's behalf.

The guidelines covering payments and gifts, competition, purchasing, and conflict of interest apply to dealings in the international arena in generally the same manner as described in preceding sections of these guidelines.

Mead is an Ohio corporation. While Ohio law does not have a substantial impact on Mead's activities outside the United States, such activities are subject to applicable U.S. laws and regulations. This means Mead's international managers must accept responsibility for compliance with such laws and regulations, even though locally owned competitors need not do so.

Ordinarily U.S. laws and regulations affect operations in other countries only where they may affect American trade or commerce, or impact on American consumers or investors. Examples of such laws are: antitrust, boycott legislation, foreign corrupt practices, and taxes.

The laws of many other jurisdictions may impact any Mead operation. These laws include not only those of the United States and of the country in which the operation is conducted, but those of other countries in which the operation does business. Supranational law, e.g., European Economic Community, must also be observed.

Local laws may be expected to contain differing requirements relating to, among other things: use of language, labeling and packaging, safety and health, taxes, custom duties, dealer and agency relationships, employee rights, inventors' rights, and dumping.

Mead attempts to furnish legal and business guidance to its international managers, both here and abroad, and urges them to seek advice when in doubt. Mead also looks to its managers to keep Mead advised of changes and new developments in local laws and practices affecting their operations.

PepsiCo

PepsiCo firmly believes that, in fostering economic growth, international commerce strengthens both understanding and peace. Our goal is to achieve commercial success by offering quality and value to our customers, to continue to provide products that are safe, wholesome, economically efficient, and environmentally sound, and to provide a fair return to our investors while adhering to the highest standards of integrity.

Our objective is to continue to be a good corporate citizen in every country in which we do business, and to maintain open and constructive communication with local community and business leaders in order to bring to fruition mutually acceptable objectives. As a company based in the United States, we recognize our responsibility to the interests of our country. In addition, we recognize and pay particular attention to each host country's priorities respecting economic and social development, including industrial and regional growth, environmental quality, the availability of employment opportunities and the transfer and advancement of technology and innovation.

PepsiCo will continue to state its position on issues of national and international importance which may have an impact on it or its operations throughout the world.

As a company with operations in most nations of the world, PepsiCo obeys all laws and regulations and, to the maximum extent feasible, respects the lawful customs of host countries. In managing our financial commercial operations, we take into account the established objectives and related rules and regulations of host countries regarding balance of payments and credit policies.

We believe that a fundamental principle of international investment is mutuality. Thus, we pursue investment with financial interest indigenous to host countries where these are mutually beneficial. We welcome and encourage ownership of PepsiCo stock and PepsiCo's other publicly traded securities by citizens of every country. We give preference to raw materials and products of the host country where they are fully competitive in price, quality, availability and other respects.

PPG

PPG is a product of the private enterprise system operating for profit is a free market economy. Many aspects of the Company's culture reflect that experience. We respect the power of the free enterprise system operating to generate a high standard of living for its people. Recent history and experience have shown that free, fair competition in a market-based economy can bring similar advantages to other parts of the world as well. And we are prepared to share the benefit of our experience with all those who seek it.

At the same time, we recognize that the world consists of a wide array of races, religions, languages, cultures, political systems and economic resources. We accept these differences as legitimate and desirable; we recognize that each country must determine its own way. As a global corporation with operations in many different countries, PPG seeks nothing more from its host governments than the opportunity to compete fairly and on the basis of merit wherever the markets for its products exist.

PPG recognizes that the pluralism of the world we operate in can be a strength, bringing the insight and experience of many different cultures to bear on common problems and opportunities. The Company has no desire to impose a uniform code of behavior on its people worldwide simply for the sake of uniformity; we wish to benefit from the variety of human experience, not to suppress it.

Accordingly, where conduct resulting from adherence to Company policies is inconsistent with local law, custom and prevailing practice, provision has been made to allow for *compatible* area or country codes which more definitively anticipate local operating conditions, laws, customs, and cultural differences. Such codes, dealing with geographic areas outside the United States, must have *prior* approval of PPG's Management Committee before they can be practiced, published or incorporated into the Company's overall code.

You should contact either your own supervisor or PPG's Law Department to clarify questions concerning Code Interpretation or to report any difficulties presented by observing PPG's Worldwide Code of Ethics in your country.

FOREIGN TRANSACTIONS, PAYMENTS AND THE FOREIGN CORRUPT PRACTICES ACT

Transco

(Foreign Transactions and Payments.) Having due regard for the responsibilities relating to international operations, it is the Company's policy that all employees and agents comply with the ethical standards and applicable legal requirements of the Foreign Corrupt Practices Act and of each foreign country in which its business is conducted.

The Foreign Corrupt Practices Act makes it a criminal offense for a United States company or agent acting on its behalf to pay anything of value to any foreign government official to influence any official action in securing, retaining, or directing business. This prohibition applies to bribes, kickbacks or like payments made directly to such foreign officials or indirectly through seemingly legitimate payments, such as commissions or consulting fees paid to overseas agents or representatives. Because of the broad reach of this statute and its harsh criminal penalties for a violation, each employee should consult with the General Counsel before concluding any transaction which even appears to involve a foreign payment.

The Foreign Corrupt Practices Act of 1977, which is part of the federal securities laws, has significantly expanded the authority of the federal government to deal with improper business practices and, perhaps more significantly, to determine just what constitutes such improper practices. While American's commitment to the highest standards of corporate conduct is reflected throughout its internal policies and procedures, in view of the broad reach of the Act it is important that American's management employees have a basic understanding of this law and of the program which American has adopted to assure compliance with it.

The Act deals primarily with three areas: (1) record keeping, (2) internal controls, and (3) prohibited foreign activity. In summary, the provisions of the Act in each of these areas are as follows:

Record Keeping Provisions. Companies subject to the Act are required to make and keep books, records and accounts which, in reasonable detail, accurately and fairly reflect the transactions and disposition of the assets of the company. The purpose of this requirement is basically to prevent the occurrence of the following types of abuses.

1. Records that fail to record improper transactions.

2. Records that are falsified to conceal improper transactions which are otherwise correctly recorded.

3. Records that accurately record the existence of a transaction but which fail to reveal the illegal or improper purpose of the transaction.

Internal Controls Provision. This position of the Act requires companies to devise and maintain a system of internal accounting controls sufficient to provide reasonable assurances that the following objectives are achieved:

1. Transactions are executed in accordance with management's general and specific authorization.

2. Transactions are recorded in a way which will permit the preparation of proper financial statements and will maintain accountability for assets.

3. Access to assets is permitted only in accordance with management's general and specific authorizations.

4. Audits are conducted at reasonable intervals and appropriate action is taken with respect to any deficiencies in accountability for assets.

Prohibited Foreign Activity. This portion of the Act makes it a criminal offense for any U.S. business to offer a bribe, directly or indirectly, to a foreign official, foreign political party, party official or candidate for foreign political office for the purpose of obtaining, retaining or directing business to the company or any other person. This highly publicized provision carries with it fines of up to $1 million for a violation.

Becton Dickinson

In 1977, after several highly publicized disclosures of American companies making questionable foreign payments, Congress enacted the Foreign Corrupt Practices Act. The Act makes it a crime for any Unites States citizen or company, or anyone acting on their behalf, to give anything of value to a foreign official, a foreign political party, or a candidate for foreign political office for the purpose of obtaining, retaining, or directing business. The Act also requires the setting up of internal accounting controls.

A violation of the Act by an individual could result in a $10,000 fine and a five year prison term. Companies can be fined $1 million under the Act.

All payments which are intended to influence the recipients to misuse their official position or to use than their best judgment in the taking or influencing of discretionary official action are prohibited. Certain payments, however, which are made merely to expedite the movement of a matter toward an eventual act or decision without any intent to influence the outcome, or are made in connection with matters which do not involve any discretionary action, may not be unlawful.

No payment to a foreign official, political party or candidate for foreign office should be made without determining whether such payment is prohibited by the Company policy or the Foreign Corrupt Practices Act. Any questions as to whether a payment would be prohibited should be referred to the Law Department.

Jostens

The Company will scrupulously adhere to the letter and spirit of the Foreign Corrupt Practices Act, which prohibits giving money or items of value to a foreign official to influence decisions made by a foreign government. The Act further prohibits giving money or items of value to any person or firm when there is reason to believe that it will be passed on to a government official for this purpose. All matters that may involve these laws must be coordinated and carefully reviewed by the Legal Department.

APPOINTMENT OF FOREIGN SALES REPRESENTATIVES, DISTRIBUTORS, AND CONSULTANTS

FMC

Commission or fee arrangements shall be made only with firms or persons serving as bona fide commercial sales representatives, distributors or consultants (hereinafter referred to as "representatives"). Such arrangements may not be entered into with any firm in which a government official or employee is known to own an interest. All commission and fee arrangements with regular foreign sales representatives shall be covered by a written contract. The contract should contain, in addition to other normal terms and conditions, a clear description of the representative's services to be rendered, a commitment by the representative to abide by applicable law, and a statement that FMC may be required to disclose the existence and terms and conditions of the contract to authorized governmental agencies. (The Company's model international Sales Representative and Distributorship agreements are recommended for this purpose.) Representatives in single transactions whose arrangements are not covered by a regular representative's contract shall also be advised that such a disclosure may be required. Any commission or fee to be paid a representative for assistance in securing orders and for after-sales service must be reasonable as to amount and consistent with normal practice for the industry, for the line of products involved and for the services to be rendered. Percentage commissions should normally be scaled downward as sales volume increases. Payments to a representative should not be made in cash. Payments to a representative should also be made to its business office in the country where it is located unless the Law Department has approved otherwise.

FINANCIAL RECORDKEEPING PROVISIONS OF THE FOREIGN CORRUPT PRACTICES ACT

Ashland

"Internal Accounting Controls" section . . . describes the internal accounting controls which have been established to govern management of the company's assets. Ashland has adopted these controls in accordance with generally accepted accounting principles, the guidelines of the Financial Accounting Standards Board, internal needs, and the requirements of various other applicable laws and regulations. Because of its far-reaching provisions, one of these laws, the Foreign Corrupt Practices Act, deserves further explanation.

The Foreign Corrupt Practices Act (FCPA) became law in 1977. All American citizens and companies, whether publicly traded or privately held, are subject to one or more provisions of the act.

The FCPA has two basic parts: 1) the anti-bribery provisions and 2) accounting and recordkeeping requirements. The anti-bribery section prohibits payment of a bribe to a foreign official or foreign political party, party official or candidate for political office. The FCPA defines a bribe as anything of value given or offered to a foreign official for the purpose of influencing an act or decision to obtain, retain or direct business. "Anything of value" can include things other than cash. This part of the FCPA applies to all American citizens and business enterprises.

Despite its name's reference to foreign practices, the FCPA's accounting and recordkeeping provisions apply to domestic as well as foreign operations of publicly traded American companies. These requirements act as a control system to complement the anti-bribery section and are primarily intended to prevent or detect unreported slush funds or illegal payments.

While the accounting provisions basically are a restatement of generally accepted accounting principles, it's important to understand that strict accuracy in documentation and reporting is required. These provisions can be interpreted to include relatively small sums from petty cash funds.

HCA

HCA has established and maintains a high standard of accuracy and completeness in its financial records. Those records serve as the basis for managing the Corporations' business, for measuring and fulfilling the Corporations' obligations to patients, shareholders, employees, suppliers and others, and for compliance with tax and financial reporting requirements.

Proper accounting of assets and liabilities is now mandated by law. The Foreign Corrupt Practices Act requires American companies, including HCA, to maintain reasonably complete and accurate books and records and to devise "sufficient" systems of internal accounting controls. Failure to comply with these provisions could result in fines for the Corporations and fines or imprisonment for individuals.

It is the policy of HCA on its own behalf and in connection with the operations of its Controlled Affiliates to comply with the recording and reporting requirements of applicable law and established financial standards and generally accepted accounting principles. In particular, the practices of the Corporations shall comply with the following requirements: a) All items of income and expense and all assets and liabilities are entered on the financial records of the Corporations and are accurately and adequately described as appropriate for legitimate business purposes and as required by law, and in accordance with generally accepted accounting principles. b) Reports submitted to governmental authorities are accurately made. Specifically, the Corporations make available to authorized governmental agencies information as necessary for such agencies to make appropriate determinations with respect to matters under their jurisdictions. c) Transactions are executed in accordance with management's general or specific authorization and access to assets is permitted only in accordance with such authorization.

EXPORTS, IMPORTS, BOYCOTTS, AND RESTRICTIVE TRADE PRACTICE

Morton Thiokol

All employees shall strictly comply with (1) the anti-boycott provisions of the Export Administration Act of 1969, as amended, and the rules and regulations with respect thereto and (2) anti-boycott laws and regulations pursuant to the Internal Revenue Code. To insure such compliance, Group and Division Counsel and the Tax Department shall keep appropriate personnel advised as to the specific application of these rules to proposed transactions of their business unit.

In general, these laws require the company to avoid any conduct or agreement which has the effect of furthering or supporting a restrictive trade practice or boycott fostered or imposed by a foreign country against a country friendly to the United States or against any United States person, firm or corporation. Various nations and communities of nations have enacted laws that prohibit or restrict the export of certain goods and technology. In most cases, restricted goods or technology may be exported to certain listed countries, if at all, only after required permits or licenses have been obtained. It is vital that each exporting entity be thoroughly familiar with these laws because they may apply by reason of Company affiliations. For example, if an employee of a Company subsidiary in England approves an export sale from the English subsidiary of a product to a country that is on a U.S. government restricted list without obtaining U.S. government approval, the Company could be guilty of violating United States law.

Control Data

Many types of commercial data, products, software and associated technical data may not be exported without prior written approval from the U.S. government. Control Data is responsible for ensuring that items delivered overseas are not diverted to restricted countries.

Many different types of transactions can be considered an export: [1] Shipping data or software to a Control Data facility in another country is considered an export. [2] Unpublished design data normally cannot be released overseas without specific U.S. government approval. [3] Performing a technical service in a foreign nation is considered an export and may require a license. [4] Conversations of a technical nature with a citizen of another country may be considered an export, even when the foreign citizen is in the United States. You must have written U.S. government approval to release certain technical data even in casual conversations. [5] Presentation of unpublished research to an audience that includes foreign citizens may be restricted if the U.S. government has sponsored the work. [6] When foreign visitors tour Control Data facilities, what they see can be considered an export, and therefore may require advance approval.

If you have any doubt about a pending situation, check with Control Data's Export Administration function or a Control Data attorney.

AT&T

United States Export Control Laws govern all exports of commodities and technical data from the United States, including items that are hand-carried as samples or demonstration units in luggage. AT&T's policy is to comply fully with the Export Control Laws.

Failure to comply with these laws could result in the loss or restriction of AT&T's export privileges, which in turn could damage or even destroy a significant portion of the Company's business. Violations of these laws can also result in fines and imprisonment for individual employees. Employees are responsible for understanding whether, and how, the Export Control Laws apply to their job activities and for conforming to these laws.

The International Law Division's Export Control and Compliance Organization is responsible for AT&T's export licensing program. It also serves as the focal point for AT&T's export control and compliance program, and a clearinghouse for information on export control matters. Any questions concerning export control should be directed to that organization.

... AT&T's policy is to comply strictly with U.S. laws pertaining to prohibited foreign economic boycotts.

These laws prohibit a wide variety of activities connected with such boycotts, including: refusing to do business with boycotted countries, their nationals, or blacklisted companies; furnishing information about the Company's or any person's past, present, or prospective relationships with boycotted countries or blacklisted companies; furnishing information about any person's race, religion, sex or national origin or membership or support of charitable organizations supporting a boycotted country; discriminating against individuals or companies on the basis of race, religion, sex or national origin; and paying, honoring or confirming letters of credit containing boycott provisions. The law also requires that boycotting requests be reported to the U.S. Government.

Violation of these laws can result in fines for the Company and fines and/or imprisonment for employees. Each employee is expected to follow Company practices in boycott matters. Any questions concerning the boycott laws should be referred to the International Law Division.

PPG

In their efforts to expedite the transfer of new technology into their countries, some developing nations have been less than vigorous in their enforcement of laws protecting the holders of foreign patents. In other instances, national policies may restrict the secure flow of proprietary information. This issue is of particular concern to PPG because our business depends to a great extent on the security of proprietary technical and business information.

Accordingly, in its dealings with host governments as well as with international agencies, PPG will work to create an atmosphere in which technology ownership is recognized and where appropriate compensation for its transfer is accepted practice. At the same time, PPG respects the legitimate security and economic needs of its host countries and will endeavor to conduct its operations in a manner consistent with those needs.

Quaker

When traveling on Company business, employees must adhere to each country's laws regarding declaration and importation of money, negotiable instruments and goods. Any goods for which an import license has not been obtained should not be carried into a country by an employee. Any questions regarding specific rules for each country should be referred to the Corporate Law Department.

Becton Dickinson

From time to time various countries attempt to boycott trade with other countries and restrict and impose sanctions upon companies who trade with the target country or its citizens. Most of these boycotts have been directed against Israel by Arab countries, although on occasion other countries are the targets of restrictive practices.

It is the policy of Becton Dickinson to refuse to cooperate with restrictive trade practices or boycotts even if this refusal results in loss of business opportunities to our Company.

Furthermore, severe penalties can be imposed under the Tax Reform Act of 1976 and the Export Administration Act of 1979 for compliance with restrictive practices and boycotts not sanctioned by the United States government. The Export Administration Regulations prohibit Becton Dickinson and its subsidiaries, foreign and domestic, from cooperating with restrictive trade practices or boycotts imposed by other countries, except under certain very limited exceptions, and requires reporting of boycott requests. The Tax Reform Act requires a company doing business with countries demanding participation or cooperation with an international boycott to file a report with the U.S. Treasury Department. Under this Act, companies that comply with boycott demands are deprived of important U.S. tax benefits.

UAL

The Company will not take any action, directly or indirectly, which will have the effect of furthering or supporting international restrictive trade practices, including boycotts not sanctioned by the United States government. The Company may, however, comply with some restrictions on imports into or exports from a foreign country. All employees should seek advice from the General Counsel's office through normal channels whenever they receive a request for present or future Company action involving any international restrictive trade practice.

Chapter 6

RESPONSIBILITIES OF
MANAGEMENT

Management, it can be argued, is a delicate balancing act, and managers are the tightrope walkers. Their task is to make it across the highwire to the common good while juggling a variety of needs and forces that could pull them off in other, possibly disastrous, directions.

Just a few of the needs and forces that management must juggle include: near-term and long-term economic responsibilities to shareholders, suppliers, and lenders, as well as to the firm; conflicts between duties owed to society and the firm and managers' own values or moral beliefs; a higher sense of social responsibility on the part of consumers, investors, and employees; increased federal and state regulations of business operations and environmental impact; and the necessity to build and improve management itself.

The model codes that begin below address a diversity of key management issues, including: (1) style of management; (2) strategic and tactical planning, operation and control; (3) management development; (4) management's responsibilities toward company personnel; (5) the use of outside professional services; (6) management's responsibilities to owners and shareholders; (7) the requirement that key managers not travel together and endanger the firm's operations if a disaster occurs; (8) managing amid decentralization.

MANAGEMENT STYLE

Holiday

Management has significant responsibilities—to their colleagues, to their fellow employees, to the company's stockholders, franchisees and other investors, and to the communities in which we operate. We will lead by example, beginning with personal conduct, on and off the job, which exemplifies discipline and integrity. We will adhere to the letter and spirit of the company's beliefs and business principles, and all management decisions and actions affecting the company will be unencumbered by conflict with any personal interests. These will be considered the minimum standards of ethical performance.

We will set management examples by: (1) dealing honestly, openly and effectively with all employees; (2) developing employees with potential for positions of greater responsibility and reward, and dealing promptly and effectively with unsatisfactory performance; (3) rewarding the best results, and recognizing outstanding efforts; (4) insisting by personal competence, effort, and example, that all work is performed at the highest level of quality, on time and within budget; (5) planning for the future by anticipating and managing change and rigorously reviewing performance against plans; (6) communicating regularly and openly with employee groups; (and 7) realizing that most success is based on team performance and recognizing team members as contributors to the success of any undertaking.

We consider the values of teamwork, mutual respect and support, open discussion of issues and a supportive rather than adversary management environment as fundamental to the success of the enterprise. This is particularly true in a business environment of rapid change.

San Diego Gas and Electric

In our Utility operations, we will pursue a management style that will: (1) Encourage innovation and be responsive to the changing business environment. (2) Encourage open expression of new ideas and divergent opinions, while leaving the responsibility for final decisions with the accountable person. (3) Delegate the responsibility and authority for decisions to the lowest practical level of accountability; employees will be evaluated and rewarded based on both short-term results and achievement of long-term goals and strategies. (4) Result in the maximum utilization of Company resources.

AmeriFirst

The management of AmeriFirst understands that loyalty must be earned both by employer and employees. The concept of loyalty implies a positive and mutually supportive attitude one to the other. For its part, the Bank demonstrates loyalty by treating every staff member honestly and generously. In return, the Bank expects the members of the staff to be loyal to the Bank and their fellow workers. Loyalty is the catalyst that helps make an organization an entity.

STRATEGIC AND TACTICAL PLANNING, OPERATION, AND CONTROL

Union Carbide

The Corporation and its businesses will maintain strategic plans which, along with annual operating objectives and budgets derived from those plans, will be reviewed periodically and approved by responsible managements. Control systems at Corporate and business levels will seek to ensure that all resource commitments to businesses and functional departments are consistent with approved strategic plans and operating budgets.

Panhandle Eastern Corporation

Panhandle Eastern Corporation will develop and maintain a long-range strategic plan which is designed to guide and offer measures of performance for the business activities of the Corporation and its subsidiaries and affiliates. The Corporate Strategic Plan is the umbrella under which the various companies and departments may develop such specific plans as may be required to carry out the Corporation's objectives and strategies. The Chief Executive Officer of Panhandle Eastern Corporation will appoint periodically a senior management group to oversee the development of the Corporation's strategic plans. The Corporate Vice President–Planning is responsible for all coordination for the planning system.

The top management group of the Panhandle Eastern Companies will be afforded the opportunity to input and critique the strategic plans prior to completion of their development. The Corporation's Strategic Plan will be reviewed by the Board of Directors and the Chairman will seek any appropriate Board actions. The Corporate Planning Department will support the senior management group in the development of the strategic plans, will call upon the various Panhandle Eastern Companies for forecasts and other information, and will be responsible for assuring compatibility of all data and information used in the strategic planning activity. Upon request of any of the operating units, the Corporate Planning Department will monitor key elements of the external environment as well as various internal activities and recommend the need to review the strategic plan when significant changes in circumstances have occurred.

Corning

We will maintain a system of strategic planning, management information, and controls which is detailed enough to allow management at all levels to exercise their responsibilities, but which is not unnecessarily burdensome.

MANAGEMENT DEVELOPMENT

Squibb

Far more than plant, property and equipment, our human resources are our most valuable assets. We are committed to developing the skills of our people at all levels of the organization. Management development, career planning and succession planning are at the core of our operating philosophy.

RESPONSIBILITIES TOWARD COMPANY PERSONNEL

PPG

The relationship between PPG and its personnel at every level is one based on mutual respect, reciprocal trust and shared objectives. Furthering the recognition of these ties, strengthening our common bonds and enhancing their impact on the Company's day-to-day activities is the ongoing responsibility of every PPG manager. Even though local circumstances vary from one PPG location to another, certain principles and expectations concerning the relationship of PPG to its associates transcend local conditions. Those principles define the implicit understanding which exists between PPG and every individual employed by the Company.

USING OUTSIDE PROFESSIONAL SERVICES

American Airlines

American Airlines maintains professional staffs in such specialized areas as Audits and Security, Credit and Collections, Data Processing, Legal, Management Training, Medical, Properties and Facilities, Corporate Communications, Purchasing and Taxes and Insurance. The experience and expertise of these specialized service divisions are available to all executives in the course of their duties. It is American's policy not to employ outside professional services except where it is not practical to rely upon our own resources.

The proper procedure for an executive seeking approval of outside professional services is to consult first with the Company department head who specializs in the area of the required services. If it is agreed that outside help is desirable, the request should be submitted in accordance with AA Regulation 10-13. When all approvals have been obtained, the Legal Department should be consulted to determine the appropriate form of retention agreement between American and the organization to be retained.

MANAGEMENT RESPONSIBILITY TO OWNERS AND SHAREHOLDERS

Holiday

We hold that the prime objective of management is to increase stockholder value. In planning for the future, we will formulate and execute our plans toward that objective. Our financial performance is the basic measurement of how well we are accomplishing our objective. We believe that increased profit permits new investment, new career opportunities, and additional resources for our communities, all to the ultimate benefit of our stockholders. We will focus our activities in the hotel/casino businesses in which we have exceptional expertise. Specifically, we will concentrate on the management, franchising and development part of the hotel business, thereby generating profits based primarily on our management expertise.

We measure our financial performance by attention to earnings, return on equity, return on investment and cash flow as we believe these are the best measures of the economic vitality of our businesses and our management performance. We expect long-term growth in earnings and cash flow to be generated from operations through unit growth, new product development, and productivity and profitability improvements, in addition to general levels of inflation. Unit growth in hotels can be achieved in a planned and orderly manner. Unit growth in casino gaming must, by its nature, be somewhat opportunistic and limited to the jurisdictions which allow gaming. New development will be financed to the greatest extent practical with prudent levels of risk by using capital from external sources in order to maximize Holiday Corporation's return on equity.

We will strive to constantly improve our productivity and to achieve greater results with fewer resources. We will establish specific productivity goals and measurements throughout the company to continually improve operating margins. We will assure that there is an active, well-informed and independent board of directors. We are committed to attracting and retaining a board of outstanding quality which lays a foundation of professional management throughout the company. We seek directors with a proven record of accomplishments in diverse fields. Our board will be an active, independent and thought-provoking force in our efforts to realize our opportunities and meet the needs of our various constituencies. We will maintain open, effective communication with our stockholders, our employees, the investment community and the public so they can properly evaluate our performance and future prospects.

Lafarge

Lafarge Corporation's ability to develop and sustain our business depends on the support of our investors. This means the Company must always strive to provide a competitive return on their investments. Each operating unit is therefore expected to contribute to our overall financial performance. Our success will not be measured by growth in terms of sheer size but rather by long term earnings per share improvement and greater financial strength and flexibility.

Marion

We have a responsibility to our shareholders to build the business on their behalf. This requires prudent investment in the development of people, products, and facilities necessary to sustain long-term growth in profits and return on shareholder investment.

Warner-Lambert

We are committed to providing a fair and attractive economic return to our shareholders, and we are prepared to take prudent risks to achieve sustainable long-term corporate growth.

San Diego Gas and Electric

We are responsible ultimately to the owners of the Company. We believe that by fulfilling our obligations to our many constituencies we will best serve the needs of our shareholders: preservation of their capital and an attractive return on their investment. Thus, we will: (1) Operate the Corporation to maximize the long-term shareholder value. (2) Inform shareholders about current Company activities and future plans.

First Alabama Bancshares

To the shareholders, the Company strives to: provide a fair return on their investment by conducting business in a sound and profitable manner. To all of these entities, the Company has a responsibility to formulate, implement and enforce a code of conduct to insure that these important responsibilities to the Company's constituencies are met.

MANAGEMENT TRAVEL

Upjohn

Travel in the Same Conveyance. The Chairman and President will not travel together, and the Corporate Senior Vice Presidents will not travel together. No more than five corporate officers or executive directors will travel with the officer to whom they report, and not more than three Divisional directors or managers will travel with the executive director to whom they report. A majority of employees in a particular area or all members of a research or project team may not travel together. This policy applies to travel in Company, commercial, or privately owned aircraft, automobiles, trains, busses and steamships.

DECENTRALIZATION, PARTICIPATION, AND COORDINATION

Deere

Decentralization has been a basic philosophy of the Company throughout its long history. Accordingly, broad authority has traditionally been delegated to managers close to the point of action. Corporate and divisional objectives, policies and procedures are intended to set a coordinating framework within which decentralized operating decisions are made and carried out. Decentralization imposes special requirements on us to communicate well and to be sensitive to the contribution each unit and each employee can best make to success of the enterprise. Experience has taught us that, properly used, it stimulates superior performance and fosters many important values including better decisions, more innovation, and greater personal involvement and growth. We have a high appreciation for the experience and ingenuity of all employees. We seek to involve them in the management process and get the fullest benefit of their ideas and judgment.

Medtronic

The company has split its operations into a number of business units each with its own mission and objectives. Within this system each business will be accorded the right to manage its own affairs and to make its own operating decisions in line with the long-range plans and annual operating plans as approved by the Corporate Center. Currently these business units are Pacing, Blood Systems, Neurological, AMI, Ventures, and Worldwide Distribution, which includes U.S. Cardiovascular Sales and Marketing and International Sales and Marketing. To achieve the advantages of a common customer, we have elected to sell our products, wherever practical, through a shared distribution system. In the U.S., our Pacing and Blood Systems products are sold through the U.S. Cardiovascular Sales Force while Neurological and AMI products are sold through their own distribution system. In international markets, most Medtronic products are sold through the International Sales organization.

Where businesses use our shared distribution system, the product business unit is responsible for: 1) setting the strategic direction of the business, 2) product planning and development, and 3) manufacturing and technical support. Worldwide Distribution is responsible for: 1) identifying market needs, 2) implementing marketing programs, and 3) managing distribution. The business units, including the Worldwide Distribution organization, will share the responsibility for the financial return of each business as defined by our financial systems. To maximize the leverage of our worldwide operations, we will conduct research, product development, and manufacturing activities in various international locations. In order to achieve advantages of scale, it is in the interest of all of our business units to share certain staff services. Those corporate employees not in the Corporate Center are in Corporate Shared Services. They provide services to the business units and to the Corporate Center. All expenses of Corporate Shared Services are allocated to the users who decide which services they desire to purchase.

Chapter 7

RIGHTS AND RESPONSIBILITIES OF EMPLOYERS AND EMPLOYEES

A well-crafted code of business conduct addresses many different issues related to the rights and responsibilities of employers and employees. On the one hand, a code may reflect the firm's strong commitment to hiring, training, and keeping good employees. On the other hand, the code's contents also may reflect the statutory and judicial erosion of employer rights and the growing signs of increased employer liability in the 1990s.

Perhaps the most important reason for firms to react positively to employees' new expectations is that concepts such as privacy and due process are esteemed values in our society at large. Incorporating relevant guidelines into the code of conduct helps balance the firm's prerogatives to manage, on one hand, and the employees' rights, on the other, to enjoy such values in the workplace.

Recent successful lawsuits against firms in the areas of wrongful discharge and invasion of privacy demonstrate a shift of balance away from the established doctrines of the omnipotent employer. And in an era of social and economic upheaval, disagreement between employer and employee is inevitable. Management therefore must understand the current status of various employment doctrines and promulgate effective procedures.

In its code of business conduct, meanwhile, a firm should carefully avoid or eliminate words such as "permanent," "career path," "job security," "partnership track," and "long-term growth." These terms also should be eliminated from the firm's advertisements and job-applicant interviews. The firm can use qualifiers such as "usually" and "in most cases" in its personnel manuals. The business also can consider using other precautions, including a form to be signed by new employees declaring that the firm can terminate employment at any time, with or without good cause. It should be noted, however, that courts have varied in their interpretation of such disclaimers.

The following excerpts show how some leading firms have responded in their codes to a variety of issues, including: the commitment to employees; rights of employees; political activities and contributions; union relations; employee privacy; employment conditions, contracts, and termination; time recording, labor charges and work schedules; employee contacts with the media; and protection and use of the firm's equipment, supplies, and funds.

COMMITMENT TO EMPLOYEES

Dana

The commitment and ability of Dana people are the most important elements in making Dana globally competitive. Because they play this crucial role, Dana people are the most important asset in determining Dana's success. We must make every effort to assure that Dana people have the tools, skills, and motivation they need to meet their responsibilities as we face our competitive challenge.

The Dana Style includes a number of specific practices which increase the competitiveness of Dana people as our most important asset.

Promotion from Within: Job openings with Dana beyond the entry level are filled by career Dana people, utilizing the world-wide Dana Management Resource programs. Dana people are encouraged to move across product, discipline and organizational lines (where not conflicting with operational efficiency) to fill positions; and supervisors are encouraged to discuss job opportunities with their people. On-the-job training in Dana's different disciplines (sales, engineering, finance, manufacturing, etc.) is important preparation for promotion from within. Dana people are encouraged to take the initiative in preparing themselves to seek promotional opportunities within Dana.

Education: Continuous education and training makes all Dana people more competitive. The full range of available educational resources should be used: Dana University regular and advanced degree courses, seminars and training sessions at the Center of Technology, regional education programs around the world, in-plant training (such as Excellence in Manufacturing, and statistical process control techniques), and non-Dana training resources (including seminars, university courses, state educational programs, and technical programs). The goal of any Dana educational activity should be improved on-the-job performance.

Recognition: As Dana's most important asset, Dana people should be involved in setting their job goals and judging their job performance. In addition, all Dana people should have their job performance reviewed at least once a year by their supervisor. Wages and benefits are determined by each business unit, in line with individual performance, competitive, and local conditions. All Dana people should be evaluated based on their ability and their competitive performance.

Ryder

For our employees we will strive . . . to provide a working climate of mutual trust, respect and support . . . to provide meaningful jobs that stimulate development of knowledge and skills . . . to establish clear job objectives and fair performance standards . . . to provide timely feedback on contributions to the business . . . to provide opportunities to develop potential for growth and advancement . . . to provide equal opportunity in hiring and promotion based on ability, performance and experience . . . to compensate in a manner that recognizes our pay for performance philosophy . . . to set an example which inspires integrity, honesty, and sincerity . . . to acknowledge the need for a balanced life including business, personal, family and community activities.

San Diego Gas and Electric

Employees are the Company's most important resource. In our day-to-day relations with them, we will: [1] Treat employees fairly and with respect. [2] Recognize and reward significant achievements and contributions by employees. [3] Communicate regularly and candidly with employees and encourage an environment of open and two-way communication. [4] Provide regular formal performance appraisals and ongoing informal performance feedback. [5] Emphasize the selection and development of high-quality supervision at all levels. [6] Provide appropriate training and opportunities for self-development. [7] Maintain safe working conditions and strive to provide suitable facilities for employees consistent with the requirements of their jobs. [8] Provide a work atmosphere free of racial, religious, age or sexual discrimination or harassment. [9] Ensure that all operating organizations treat their employees fairly and with respect. [10] Encourage the use of compensation programs appropriate to the specific industry or entity. [11] Encourage thorough and open communications to and from the operating organizations and their employees.

Warner-Lambert

We are committed to attracting and retaining capable people, providing them with challenging work in an open and participatory environment, marked by equal opportunity for personal growth. Performance will be evaluated on the basis of fair and objective standards. Creativity and innovation will be encouraged. Employees will be treated with dignity and respect. They will be actively encouraged to make suggestions for improving the effectiveness of the enterprise and the quality of work life.

RIGHTS OF EMPLOYEES

Marion

Those who produce should share in the results. Each Marion associate has the right to: Be treated as an individual; be rewarded for performance; know what is expected on the job and where we stand in relation to that expectation; get problems resolved and be heard; a safe and healthy workplace; share in the growth of the company through personal and career growth; [and] we earn these through our high productivity and commitment to quality in all that we do.

Deere

We must provide conditions of employment and management practices that will earn and support superior performance by our employees. This is the only way we can be more successful than our competitors. Each individual's contribution must be respected and appropriately rewarded. All employees must be given every reasonable opportunity to grow and advance to the full extent of their abilities. Neither religious preference, race, sex, nor age should enter into appraisals of individuals for employment, salary review, or promotion. Outside the workplace, each employee must feel free to participate in community life according to his or her own desires and beliefs without fear of retribution or coercion by the company. We must respect individual privacy by retaining only that employee information which is important for legal or business purposes, and by keeping all such information strictly confidential.

Combustion Engineering

Human resources are one of the most important assets of the Company. The Company considers all of its employees to be essential assets. As such, all employees are expected to comply with relevant laws, obligations, and Company policies applicable to decisions and conduct in the workplace. Compliance includes the taking of actions that are consistent with laws forbidding discrimination (and this includes prohibitions against sexual harassment) and actions consistent with the Company's Equal Employment Opportunities efforts.

Harris

We will provide our employees with equitable compensation, good working conditions and an environment for growth that includes an opportunity for personal development limited only by the individual's ability and desire to advance. Our goal is to provide continuity of employment for productive, dedicated and loyal employees.

Dow

Employees are the source of Dow's success. We treat them with respect, promote teamwork, and encourage personal freedom and growth. Excellence in performance is sought and rewarded.

Lowe's

1) We, as management, must realize, accept and promote the Company's policy in regard to Employee Relations. We have a legal and moral obligation to adhere to the employment policies and practices of non-discrimination as it relates to sex, race, color, religion, national origin, age or handicap. 2) All employees are

expected to conduct themselves in such a manner as to maintain a working environment free from discrimination of any kind, including sexual or racial harassment. 3) All of us, most particularly management, must respect and preserve the individual rights and dignity of every Lowe's employee.

POLITICAL ACTIVITIES AND CONTRIBUTIONS

Wells Fargo

Although the Company encourages your active interest in the political and governmental process, you may not: [1] Represent the Company in political matters without the approval of the manager of the Public and Governmental Affairs Department; or [2] use the Company's name or address in mailed material, fund collection, or any political advertisement or literature. If you want to run for an elective political office or accept an appointment to a federal, state or local government office, discuss your plans with your designated officer to assure the demands of the office and time away from Wells Fargo will not interfere with your job performance. You should also discuss your plans with the manager of the Public and Governmental Affairs Department, who will review with you applicable laws and restrictions on Company contributions, transactions, and lobbying. You must obtain approval from your designated officer before agreeing to serve on finance or investment committees of political campaigns or political subdivisions. If approval is granted, carefully indicate to the committee that your opinions are personal and not those of Wells Fargo.

It is illegal for a person representing Wells Fargo to make a cash or other gift (including donated services) from the Company's resources to any public officeholder or candidate for federal office. Wells Fargo & Company contributions are legal on the state and local levels, and can be made after clearance with the Public and Governmental Affairs Department. Wells Fargo may host gatherings attended by political figures at which banking and governmental issues are discussed. These should be cleared ahead of time through the Public and Governmental Affairs Department.

Aetna

Individual participation in the political process is essential to the preservation and improvement of our society. Employees should, however, separate personal political views and activities from those of Aetna to avoid possible misunderstanding and legal difficulties. Expenses must not be incurred on Aetna's behalf in connection with personal political activity. A decision by an employee to contribute personal funds for political purposes is strictly his or her own. The Company will in no way pressure employees to make personal contributions. Nor will it pay any additional compensation to any employee who contributes funds. The Company may solicit employees to participate in a political action committee, but any such participation is strictly on a voluntary basis. Senior management will not inquire about any such contribution nor will the employee's supervisor.

Avon

Political contributions by the Company are prohibited. By political contributions are meant direct or indirect payments in support of political candidates, officeholders or political parties. In addition to cash payments, these include the loan of corporate personnel during paid working hours, the purchase of tickets to fund-raising events, or the payment for advertisements, printing or other campaign expenses.

U.S. employees may, of course, make personal contributions to their Political Action Committee for the support of candidates for public office in the United States.

Mobil Oil

Mobil encourages its employees to participate, as individuals and on their own time, in such political undertakings as they may desire. A decision by an employee as to whether he or she will contribute any personal time, money, or other resources to a political campaign or political activity is a voluntary one.

Should an employee decide to make a contribution of time or money, reimbursement or compensation from Mobil or its affiliates is specifically forbidden.

Cooper

Employees shall not use Company funds or assets for contributions of any kind to any political party or committee or to any candidate for, or holder of, any office in the U.S. government, whether local, state or national, without meeting the following criteria: 1) The contribution is not in contravention of any existing law; 2) The proposal must be submitted to the Senior Vice President, Administration, for Corporate approval before the contribution is made; 3) the contribution must be recorded in the appropriate records of the Company; and 4) the contribution may not exceed $1,000 in value. In countries other than the United States, the policy shall be determined in accordance with local law and practice as well as U.S. law; but under no circumstances shall contributions be made that have not met the above criteria.

Chevron

The Chevron Political Action Committee has been established under federal law to receive contributions from interested employees and retired employee stockholders for candidates for federal office and candidates for state office in certain states. All donations are completely voluntary and are confidential except to the extent that the law requires them to be disclosed on Political Action Committee reports. They are limited to $1,000 per person annually. Administrative expenses are borne by the company, and a detailed accounting of all contributions is sent to each contributor annually.

Coors

Coors Industries may make political, civic or charitable contributions in states or countries when permitted by law, but only as authorized by Adolph Coors Company's Board of Directors.

Centel

Employees may be solicited to contribute to the Centel Corporation Good Government Fund, a Federal political action committee, or to a trade association or state political action committee authorized by Centel to solicit its employees.

Gannett

Personal contributions to political parties or candidates are a matter of individual choice. Such contributions may not be represented as being on behalf of the Company. Gannett funds cannot be used for political contributions.

Bethlehem

Bethlehem has established written policies with respect to political contributions and reference should be made to them for a more detailed explanation. Bethlehem's policy is to comply strictly with all applicable and valid laws and regulations relating to the making of corporate political contributions. No political contributions for any candidate for Federal office shall be made for or on behalf of Bethlehem by any Bethlehem employee. Even in those jurisdictions where corporate contributions are legal, no employee is authorized to make any political contribution, including the purchase of tickets to raise political funds and the furnishing of any goods or services, for or on behalf of Bethlehem, unless it has been cleared in accordance with established corporate procedures and has been reviewed and approved by the General Counsel. Monetary contributions so approved shall be made only by corporate check payable to the candidate or political committee in question.

Bethlehem believes that it is inadvisable to become involved in the internal political affairs of a foreign country. Accordingly, neither Bethlehem nor any employee may make a foreign political contribution for or on behalf of Bethlehem. Bethlehem encourages its employees at all levels to exercise their rights of citizenship by voting, by making personal political contributions if they wish to do so with their own funds, and by being otherwise politically active, in support of candidates or parties of the employee's own personal selection. It should be clearly understood that such political activity by Bethlehem employees must be engaged in strictly in their individual and private capacities as responsible citizens and not on behalf of Bethlehem. No Bethlehem employee may receive any direct or indirect reimbursement or offsetting refund of any nature whatsoever with respect to political contributions made by them in any form.

UNION RELATIONS

Public Service Indiana

The Company fully recognizes the rights granted to its union employees by law and the terms of the existing labor agreement and does not interfere in any way with its union employees in their exercise of those rights. Company managers and supervisors exercise the same high ethical and professional standards followed in other areas of its business in administering the labor agreement and dealing with its union employees' certified representative.

EMPLOYEE PRIVACY

St. Paul Companies

The Company recognizes the paramount importance of preserving the dignity and privacy of each individual. Of course, in today's complex society, certain information must be collected and maintained for current employees as well as applicants for employment. For prospective employees, this can include necessary but **work-relevant** personal information on background and habits. For current employees, this includes information necessary for administering Company benefit programs.

AT&T

Over the years, privacy of communications has been basic to AT&T's business, not only because it is required by law, but because the public has placed its trust in the integrity of AT&T's people and its service. AT&T customers expect, for example, that their conversations will be kept private. In recent years, with the ever-increasing volume of data transmission over the network, that trust has taken on a special significance. Today it is the responsibility of every AT&T employee to protect not only the privacy of conversations on the network, but also the flow of information in data form that in the wrong hands could have serious economic or legal consequences for the parties involved. The basic rules for privacy have not changed. Violating any one of them could tarnish a reputation AT&T has earned over many years. The basic rules are [1] Don't tamper with or intrude upon any transmission, whether by voice , non-voice or data. [2] Don't listen to or repeat anyone else's conversation or communication, or permit them to be monitored or recorded except as required in the proper management of the business. [3] Don't allow an unauthorized person to have access to any communication transmitted over AT&T facilities. This includes divulging information about who was speaking or what was spoken about, except as authorized by the customer or required in the proper management of business. [4] Don't install or permit installation of any device that will enable someone to listen to, observe, or realize that a communication has occurred, except as authorized by an official service or installation order issued in accordance with Company practices. [5] Don't use information from any communication, or even the fact that a communication has occurred, for your personal benefit or for the benefit of others. [6] Don't disclose information about customer billing arrangements, or the location of equipment, circuits, trunks, and cables to any unauthorized person.

Contact the AT&T Corporate Security Organization if you believe that the privacy if any communication has been compromised, or if you receive a subpoena, court order, or any other type of request for information from anyone (including law enforcement and other government agencies) concerning any AT&T service.

NWNL

In the collection, custody and distribution of personal information concerning both individuals to whom the Company provides insurance coverage and other services and the Company's employees and Field force, the Company will give due consideration to an individual's right to privacy and will take reasonable precautions to avoid any unwarranted invasion of that right.

BellSouth

Privacy of communications is basic to the BellSouth companies' business, both legally and because the American public trusts the integrity of our employees. Today, that trust applies not only to protecting the privacy of conversations on the network, but also to the flow of information in data form.

The rules for privacy are: 1) No transmission is to be tampered with or intruded upon by wiretap or any other method, including the employee's personal telephone or service. 2) No conversation, transmission of data, or other non-voice communication should be intentionally listened to or monitored by wiretap or any other method, and its existence or contents should not be divulged, except as required in the proper management of business and as permitted by law. 3) Communications arrangements with customers, and information about billing records, equipment, or circuits, are not to be disclosed to any unauthorized person. 4) No information on the location or purpose of telephone company equipment shall be disclosed to any unauthorized person. 5) Employees must not discuss information gained through their jobs regarding military installations, communications arrangements, etc., with friends, family or relatives. 6) The above secrecy requirements apply to all modes of communication offered by the company.

If a law enforcement organization, or any other government authority, asks for private information, the request should be referred immediately to the Security Department or other appropriate organization. Employees guilty of violating these procedures may be subject to disciplinary action which could include dismissal.

EMPLOYMENT CONDITIONS, CONTRACTS, AND TERMINATION

Bankers Trust

None of the policies contained or referred to in this Code constitutes or grants a legal right of any nature to any employee of the Corporation, nor do they confer any right or privilege upon any employee or any particular group of employees. Employment with the Corporation in all cases is at will. Each employee has the right to resign from the Corporation at any time. Conversely, the Corporation has the right to terminate the employment of any employee at any time in its sole discretion.

U.S. Savings Association of Texas

(a) The Association shall not enter into any employment contract the terms of which could lead to material financial loss or damage to the Association; as may occur when an employment contract provides for an excessive term or termination costs. (b) The Association shall not enter into any employment contract the terms of which could lead to material financial loss or damage to the Association; as may occur when an employment contract provides for an excessive term or termination costs. (c) No employment contract shall contain any terms which would preclude termination of employment by the Board of Directors; provided, however, termination other than for cause need not prejudice the officer's or employee's right to compensation or other benefits under the contract. No employment contract shall provide any officer or employee any right to receive compensation or other benefits for any period after termination for cause. "Termination for Cause" shall include termination because of personal dishonesty, incompetence, willful misconduct, breach of fiduciary duty, intentional failure to perform stated duties, willful violation of any law, rule, regulation, or final cease-and-desist order, or material breach of any provisions of the employment contract. (d) All employment contracts of persons assuming the title of Senior Vice President or higher of the Association shall be approved by the Association's Board of Directors.

Champion

Assure all employees that no one will lose employment because of work redesign. Reductions in force which result directly from implementation of employee work redesign projects will be handled through attrition, voluntary severance programs, or reassignment. Explain to all employees that in all other situations where jobs must be eliminated, the company will make a good-faith effort to do what is right for the business and what is fair for the employees.

When reorganizations, capital improvements, a change in market conditions, or other circumstances cause a temporary or permanent decrease in jobs, the company will try to handle those reductions by attrition, voluntary severance programs, or reassignment. However, there may be conditions under which layoffs or terminations cannot be avoided.

Establish an atmosphere in which promising new ideas are encouraged and can be tested. It is a responsibility of leadership to encourage risk and experimentation that may produce benefits to the company even though some promising initiatives will fail.

AllTel

Inability of an employee to meet job requirements will disqualify that employee from being maintained on that job. For example, an employee employed in a job which requires driving is expected to retain a valid license. While the company tries to accommodate requests for temporary emergency changes in job duties, no guarantees of any accommodation can be made. Each situation must be evaluated by management on its own merits.

Summit

All documents, lists, directories, other writings and all other information obtained or created during employment ends. In addition, the staff member shall not make any copies of or share that information with any person outside of the Corporation.These rules shall apply to all information generated during employment which deals in any way with the business of the Corporation, whether or not the relationship between the staff member and the situation, customer or transaction involved predated employment with the Corporation.

EMPLOYMENT AT WILL

Chevron

Our employees are our most important assets. Their integrity, abilities and commitment to their jobs are the basis of our success. Our concern for them came long before the numerous laws and regulations regarding employee rights that now exist in many countries. While the company hopes to provide stable employment, it does not guarantee employment for any particular period of time for any employee, nor is any company employee authorized to make such a guarantee. Generally, either an employee or the company is free to terminate the employment relationship at any time unless there is a written contract to the contrary.

The company will take steps to end a person's employment only after it has determined that such an action is proper. If a collective bargaining agreement or written contract is applicable, it will control.

The many benefit plans for employees reflect our concern for our employees. The care with which these plans have been administered by the company is now supplemented, with respect to U.S. plans, by extensive federal regulation chiefly under the Employee Retirement Income Security Act (ERISA) of 1974. Other important U.S. laws affecting employees include the Fair Labor Standards Act and various state laws regulating rates, hours, and working conditions. Beyond our obligation to comply with these laws are several subjects meriting special attention.

Meridian

Employees ending employment with Meridian voluntarily should complete a resignation form or letter, directed to their supervisor, at least two weeks prior to their last day of employment. Last working day is defined as the last day an employee is physically on the job excluding sick, personal or vacation time. Human resources will then schedule and conduct an exit interview. At that time, the employee must account for and return all Company property, i.e., teller stamps, manuals, ID badge, keys, etc. Employees resigning voluntarily and wanting to maintain account relationships with the Company will be advised at the exit interview regarding the appropriate procedures.

Becton Dickinson

The Company recognizes and understands the desire for job security at every level of employment. No business has the power, however, to guarantee a lifetime job to anyone. Businesses have declined and failed as well as prospered. Becton Dickinson, of course, is a long-lived firm. It has grown and prospered over the years, despite recession, depression, war, and an ever-changing society. The Company believes the best way to assure continued success and job security is through the good work that reflects itself in the superior products and services we offer our customers. Job security, then, is not something the Company provides to you so much as it is something you create through your own skills and dedication.

EMPLOYEE CONDUCT

US West

Dishonest or illegal activities on company premises or while on company business will not be condoned and can result in disciplinary action, including dismissal and criminal prosecution. The following illustrates activities that are against company policy, and which will not be tolerated on company premises, in company vehicles or while engaged on company business: 1) Consumption and storage of alcoholic beverages, except where legally licensed and authorized by an officer of the company. 2) The use of controlled substances, prescribed and non-prescribed drugs or alcohol by an employee is of concern to US West when it interferes with job performance, conduct, attendance, safety or when in violation of the law. The unlawful manufacture, distribution, dispensation, possession, transfer, sales, purchase or use of a controlled substance by employees while on company premises or while on company business is prohibited. 3) Conducting company business, which includes driving vehicles or operating company equipment, while on company business. Even employees with permits or licenses may not carry weapons on company property or while on company business.

The company reserves the right to inspect any property that may be used by employees for the storage of their personal effects. This includes desks, lockers and vehicles owned by the company. It is a violation of company policy to store any contraband, illegal drugs, toxic materials or weapons on company property.

EMPLOYEE RESPONSIBILITIES

EG&G

All full-time employees will be expected to report any part-time employment or consulting activity to their supervisor and to receive his/her approval that such activity will create no conflict of time or business interest. You are EG&G in the eyes of others. As a result of your employment with EG&G, all people who recognize this employment will look to you as a reflection of the company. This will be true during working hours as well as non-working hours. We wish to be proud of you and we expect you to be proud of the company. Consequently, we expect you to give a good impression of the company and of your colleagues at work, to be loyal and faithful to the objectives of the company and the duties of your job, and to behave in a manner which does credit to yourself and the company. How you discuss the company and business activities formally or informally will be accepted by other people as characterizing EG&G. Be mindful of this. If you are unable to act in this manner, discuss your concerns with your supervisor. You should be able to at all times to feel proud that you are an EG&G employee.

Federal Express

All employees are Federal Express representatives. This is true whether the employee is on or off duty. But, this is particularly important to remember when the employee is wearing a Federal Express uniform or badge. All employees are encouraged to observe the highest standards of professional conduct at all times.

Washington Mutual

The Human value recognizes that we deal with many people in many relationships—customers, fellow staff, vendors, neighbors, shareholders, investment bankers, analysts, people who solicit our charity. Every one of these contacts—and every one of these relationships—should be caring, courteous, dignified and always pleasant. The importance of courtesy and dignity is obvious. But it's by being truly caring and always pleasant that we set ourselves apart. Caring means that we put ourselves in shoes of others. We make their problems, their dreams, their concerns, our own. And we act accordingly—giving our all to solve customer and shareholder problems and concerns, providing a positive work environment for our employees, and supporting and volunteering for programs that help people in our communities. Pleasantness is always desirable—but is it always possible? Can anyone be pleasant when dealing with an obstinate defaulting borrower? Yes. We all have unpleasant tasks. But just because a task is unpleasant doesn't mean that you have to do it unpleasantly.

Chairman Lou Pepper tells a story about a customer who wrote a letter about an employee who said no to a request she had made. Her complaint was not that the employee said no, but that he had done so "with readiness and pleasure." "It was, in my judgment, an error on our part—not in what was done, but in how it was done," Lou said. "The employee should have put himself in the customer's shoes. He should have shown he regretted having to say no, thereby making the refusal as pleasant as possible for the customer." The Ethical value is based on the fundamental principle that everything we do meets the highest ethical standards. It means complying with both the letter and the spirit of the laws and regulations under which we operate. But it also means more.

It means always selling customers the product that best meets their needs—even if we have to send them somewhere to get it. We also fully explain all aspects of our products and any penalties they may carry as well as the benefits, and we never sell a customer something he doesn't understand. We live up to the trust our customers place in us. For our crew, it means we provide fair and equitable treatment and conduct our business with respect.

Delta

In addition to the basic requirements of loyalty to the Company and compliance with the law, all of us must adhere to and comply with the overriding moral and ethical standards of our society in the conduct of business. The Company's interest can never be served by corner-cutting in the interests of a seemingly quick profit or temporary advantage.

Boatmen's Bancshares

An employee's personal behavior concerns the corporation as it reflects on the Boatmen's organization. Employees should conduct their personal affairs in such a way as to avoid discredit or embarrassment either to themselves or Boatmen's. Personal behavior and mode of dress should always be governed by common sense and good taste. Financial transactions should be for reasonable, ordinary purposes. Speculative ventures outside of one's financial capacity should be avoided. Employees must never use their position with Boatmen's to influence public officials, customers, suppliers or others for personal gain or benefit.

First Alabama

It is essential to the protection of the Company's values and the meeting of the Company's responsibilities that every individual employee has a strong commitment to meeting ethical standards in the performance of his duties. It is important that each employee be: loyal and dedicated to the achievement of the Company's goals; honest and trustworthy in personal and business matters; competent, reliable and cooperative in the completion of his or her duties; knowledgeable of the standards set by this Code of Conduct, and committed to following these standards.

Kansas City Power & Light

An employee who wishes to endorse a commercial product or service must clearly specify that they are not representing the Company, may not use the Company letterhead stationery or indicate that they are employed by the Company.

BB&T

Employees shall not make any commitment of their time or energy toward any activity inside or outside the Corporation, which may, in the opinion of the management, detract from the employees' or the Corporation's efficient operation and image.

NCNB

NCNB Corporation is committed to the highest standards of ethical and professional conduct. This commitment has both personal and corporate implications. Because the Corporation is judged by the collective performance of its employees, each of us has a responsibility to act in a manner that merits public trust and confidence. Specific guidelines, regulations and procedures are contained in manuals related to your corporate duties. Basic principles of personal conduct can be stated simply: [1] You must not take any action, either personally or on behalf of the Corporation, that will violate any law or regulation affecting our business. [2] You must perform your assigned duties to the best of your ability and in the best interest of the Corporation, its stockholders, and its customers. [3] You must avoid all circumstances that could produce conflicts or the appearance of conflicts between your personal interests and those of the Corporation. [4] You must respect the confidentiality of information obtained in the course of business, whether related to the financial affairs of customers or to the investment value of any business enterprise, including your own. [5] You must exercise absolute candor in providing facts and information requested of you by organization superiors or other authorized officials in providing such information, however, you should avoid voicing opinions that cannot be completely substantiated. [6] You must not misuse corporate resources or your corporate position in pursuit of personal interests or in violation of any law or regulation.

Boise Cascade

Employees have the responsibility to maintain the highest ethical standards in the daily conduct of their work, to avoid work-related conflicts of interest, to properly utilize the company's resources, and to perform their work to the best of their abilities. Whenever an ethical situation arises about which they have doubt as to the proper course of conduct, employees should seek advice. Whenever they observe other employees engaged in conduct which may violate these standards, they should remind them of their responsibilities. Serious or repeated violations should be reported to a supervisor.

Meritor

The management of the personal finances of a member of a financial institution requires prudence consistent with employment in such an organization. Employees should avoid becoming involved in situations which might influence judgments made or advice given on behalf of Meritor or which are clearly speculative. Employees and their immediate families may invest in securities as they choose, provided that the investments are not, or do not appear to represent a conflict of interest or use of confidential information. Investments should be avoided, however, if their magnitude in relation to an employee's net worth would appear to influence their judgment on behalf of Meritor. Investments should also be avoided in closely held companies with which an employee has business dealings on behalf of Meritor. Certain stock exchanges prohibit their members from opening a margin account for an employee of a financial institution without advance permission from the institution. Consequently, employees should obtain permission from the Director of Human Resources prior to establishing a margin account.

Carteret Savings

It is extremely important that each director, officer and employee maintain a sound personal financial condition. Failure to do so can only create a distraction and may lead to a compromise of the Code of Ethics. Personal finances, if handled improperly, can undermine your impartiality, credibility, and judgment.

AIG

It is extremely important that each employee maintain a sound personal financial condition. Failure to do so can only create a distraction which will surely prevent him or her from carrying out his or her responsibilities to AIG in an efficient manner.

CONFLICTS OF INTEREST

Puget Sound

Employees are expected to be sensitive to the interests of the Company and render their best impartial judgment in all matters affecting the Company. Even the most well-meaning person may be swayed—or appear to others to be swayed—if the personal economic interests of the individual or of the individual's immediate family are altered by business transactions made by that individual on behalf of the Company. To maintain independence of action and judgment, it is necessary to avoid such potential compromise or appearance of compromise. [Guidelines] 1) Employees who render services, with or without compensation, to any person or group who sells or is attempting to sell to the Company, and employees who have a significant financial interest in any organization that sells to or is attempting to sell to the Company, must clear such conflicts of interest in writing with the Treasurer. 2) Requests or acceptance of money or services for an employee's personal use from any customer, vendor, or person attempting to do business with the Company in return for favorable Company action will be considered a bribe and is illegal. 3) Acceptance of gifts, samples, entertainment, travel or services by the employee or the employee's family that create an obligation of favorable Company action is unacceptable. 4) The Company will never offer or give money, gifts or unpaid services intended for the personal use of an individual or an employee or agent of another corporation, organization, or government in return for favorable business decisions. 5) Use of the name of the Company and/or the purchasing power of the Company to obtain discounts or rebates on purchases made for personal use, other than offers made to all employees, is inappropriate.

Avon

No Avon employee should place himself, or allow himself to be placed, in a situation in which his personal interests might conflict with the interest of the Company. The Company recognizes and respects the individual's right to invest or participate in activities outside of one's Avon employment provided that these in no way conflict with the Company's interest or welfare, and do not interfere with the individual's responsibilities to Avon or the effectiveness of one's job performance.

Ashland

A conflict of interest exists when there is a conflict between an individual's obligation to the company and personal self-interest. Other potential conflicts arise in situations where a competitive, regulatory or adversary relationship should exist. Generally speaking, employees and closely related family members should not engage in activities that compete with any of the company's lines of business, provide service or assistance to a competitor, or interfere with the performance of job duties. In addition, you should not use company assets for your personal gain. In other words, the work you do for the company belongs to the company. You may not exploit inventions, patents or copyrights belonging to the company.

This policy is based on the legal principle that requires directors, officers, majority stockholders and employees who handle company money or property, or who transact company business, to serve the company with undivided loyalty. These individuals are strictly prohibited from taking what in all fairness belongs to the company. If a business opportunity should belong to Ashland, taking it for personal gain is similar to taking a corporate asset.

Sears, Roebuck

Investment and dealings prohibited to Sears employees must also be avoided by the members of the employee's family who act on the information or advice of the employee. Such family members include an employee's spouse, an employee's children and their spouses, an employee's brothers and sisters and their spouses, and an employee's parents and parents-in-law.

Lincoln National

The Company is aware that in the course of a director, officer or employee's tenure with the Company strong personal relationships will be established. Such a relationship with a director, officer or employee who has left the Company could, however, adversely affect or influence the judgment of an incumbent director, officer or employee in any transactions of the Company directly with the departed director, officer or employee or his or her new employer. The Company therefore expects its directors, officers and employees to exercise a high degree of prudence in this area.

IBM

Your private life is very much your own. Still, a conflict of interest may arise if you engage in any activities or advance any personal interests at the expense of IBM's interests. It's up to you to avoid situations in which your loyalty may become divided. Each individual's situation is different, and in evaluating your own, you will have to consider many factors. . . .

NEGOTIATION FOR FUTURE EMPLOYMENT

Polaroid

1) If you are representing the Company in its dealings with any outside person, you should not negotiate for your future employment by such person. If you desire to negotiate for employment by any such person, you may ask to be relieved of the

specific assignment which interferes with such negotiation. 2) You should not undertake to act on behalf of the Company in any matter that, to your knowledge, directly or indirectly affects any outside person with whom you are negotiating for your future employment.

EMPLOYMENT OF RELATIVES BY THE COMPANY, CUSTOMERS, SUPPLIERS OR COMPETITORS

Citicorp

Citicorp permits the employment of relatives. Relatives, as used here, include husband, wife, child, parent, brother, sister, brother-in-law, sister-in-law, mother-in-law and father-in-law. The following guidelines reduce the possibility or perception of favoritism and avoid placing related staff in embarrassing positions: [1] Related staff may not be assigned to positions where one relative may have the opportunity to check, process, review, approve, audit, or otherwise affect the work of another relative. [2] Related staff may not be assigned to positions where one relative might influence the salary progress or promotion of another. The Chief Auditor or designee must be advised of existing situations where relatives of staff are employed.

Dominion Bankshares

The Corporation recognizes that the employment of relatives may create potential conflicts of interest. Consequently, the Corporation has adopted a policy which restricts such employment practices. For more detailed information, the specific policy statement should be consulted, which is available from the Human Resources Group.

Burlington Northern

The Company does not prohibit spouses, parents and children and other persons related by blood or marriage from working for the Company simultaneously. However, all such employees must be hired by disinterested personnel strictly on the basis of merit and without regard to family relationships. Reporting relationships between family members are to be avoided to the maximum extent possible, to eliminate even the appearance of possible favoritism based on family ties.

Tambrands

The Company encourages the hiring of relatives of employees in the hourly and salaried non-exempt classifications, because such employees will tend to have greater loyalty and commitment to the Company. However, this practice does not extend into the management group, because family relationships within management may affect or appear to affect judgments about promotions and job assignments. Thus Tambrands Inc. will not hire any relative of a member of management in any position throughout the Company.

U.S. Bancorp

Relatives of U.S. Bancorp employees may be hired and retained as employees of U.S. Bancorp and its subsidiaries with the following exception: No relative shall be employed within the same branch, department, region, division, group, subsidiary or in any line of authority within U.S. Bancorp when such assignment would place one in a position of exercising supervisory, appointment or grievance adjustment authority over the other.

Wells Fargo

Members of the same family may be employed, but: One family member may not directly supervise another; Two family members may not control a double custody arrangement; One family member may not process, review, or audit the work of another, whether in the same or different accounting units; Manager and designated officer approvals are required for family members to work in the same accounting unit; and Family members of senior vice presidents and above may only be employed with the written consent of the manager of Employee and Retiree Relations. For purposes of Standards, "family" is defined as: Spouse, children, parents, brothers, sisters and dependents, whether or not living in the same household; All other relatives who live in the same househhold; Any individual or organization which represents or acts as agents or fiduciary for those listed above; Other individuals or organizations through which those listed above may receive a personal benefit; and Persons who live together in non-marital, non-related arrangements.

Zenith

Members of the same family (related by blood or marriage) may be employed by Zenith. As a general rule, salaried employees who are related should not be placed in or remain in assignments where one is in a position to influence the other's remuneration, expense accounts, work environment or progress within the company. In no case may a salaried employee work under the direct or indirect supervision of a relative. To assure that employee/company conflicts of interest are avoided, upon hiring or reassignment, salaried employees with such relationships are required to inform the local Salaried Personnel/Industrial Relations Manager that the relationship exists. Management and Human Resources will determine if any conflict exists and, if so, what course of action should be taken.

Mobil

The fact an employee's spouse, member of the employee's family or close relative occupies a position of responsibility with a customer, supplier or competitor does not require present action provided the employee: (a) Calls the supervisor's attention to this connection before making any recommendations that might affect dealings between Mobil and the company in question. (b) If decisions are normally made that might affect such dealings, discusses all the circumstances with the supervisor so the supervisor, rather than the employee, may make the decision.

Cigna

1. The acceptance of gifts or favors, or outside business or financial involvement by a member of an employee's immediate family (spouse, children or parents) may, under some circumstances, impute a possible conflict of interest to the employee. Each employee discloses any such circumstances to his or her immediate supervisor if the employee reasonably believes that a conflict or apparent conflict exists. 2. Managers do not employ or place, or in any way influence or attempt to influence the employment or placement of relatives.

St. Paul

It is the policy of the Company not to hire relatives of officers and directors on a regular, full-time basis. Relatives of other employees may be employed, but not in same department or reporting to a relative. No person may participate in decisions regarding compensation, promotion or termination of a relative. For the purposes of this policy a relative is any one of the following: spouse, father, mother, son, daughter, brother, sister, nephew, niece, uncle, aunt, first cousin and any such "in-law."

COMPENSATION AND BENEFITS

Rohm & Haas

All payments to employees as wages, salaries, bonuses, etc. must be justified based on services rendered the company and recorded as compensation on the company's books and tax reports. No employee may be asked to refund a portion of his compensation or to spend it in an illegal or unethical manner.

Baxter

All employees shall be compensated in the country in which they reside and in the currency of that country unless appropriate steps are taken to ensure that all applicable tax and foreign exchange laws are complied with and the exception is specifically approved in advance by the General Counsel.

ARMCO

To provide not only fair pay, but the best compensation for service rendered that is possible under existing economic commercial and other competitive conditions. To develop an organization of such spirit, loyalty and efficiency that it can and will secure results which will make it possible for individuals to receive better compensation than would be possible for providing similar service in other fields of effort.

IBM

We seek motivated, intelligent, educated people who understand and embrace our values, work hard, have fun working, are flexible and often creative. Compensation is based on results, and promotion on results and ability.

Wells Fargo

Wells Fargo maintains levels of pay for employees which compare favorably with those of competing employers. In implementing its compensation programs, Wells Fargo seeks to provide incentives and rewards for individual performance while maintaining overall fairness.

OUTSIDE EMPLOYMENT AND INTERESTS

Cooper Industries

It is the policy of Cooper Industries to employ only persons who do *not* engage in outside jobs or other business activities involving a firm which is competing with, selling to or buying from the Company. Further, persons engaged in outside jobs or business activities may be hired or retained only when such activities do not interfere in any way with the job being performed for Cooper. Cooper's policy is to pay fair and competitive compensation for full-time work. The normal demands of full-time employment are not compatible with "moonlighting," and supplemental or secondary employment is discouraged. Under no circumstances may employees have outside interests that are in any way detrimental to the best interest of the Company.

Midlantic

No Officer shall engage in any outside employment (including becoming a general partner or director or trustee) with a business enterprise organized for profit without first obtaining the approval of Midlantic's Corporate Office. Such approval will not be given if such employment will: (a) in any manner interfere with the proper and effective performance by the Officer of his official duties; (b) create or appear to create a conflict of interest; or (c) reflect adversely upon Midlantic or its Subsidiaries. This paragraph deals only with outside employment with business enterprises and does not affect Midlantic's practice of permitting Officers to be associated with governmental, municipal, educational, charitable, religious, or other civic organizations.

Detroit Edison

In general, employees have the right to be employed outside the Company and to have financial or managerial interests in outside companies. However, these outside interests must not conflict with Company interests or with the employees' duties and responsibilities to the Company. Employees are not permitted to be employed by, or to have an interest in, a business that is in direct competition with the Company or its subsidiaries. A conflict of interest, or the appearance of a conflict in this area, can be avoided by adherence to the following: [Related to private work by employees] (1) Employees seeking to hold employment outside the Company are responsible for assuring that: (a) such employment does not interfere with Company job performance, including working overtime as required, (b) there is no conflict with or reflection upon the Company's services, and (c) customers and the public clearly understand that the Company is not involved or responsible for the work or services performed. (2) Employees considering outside work should consult their supervisors. (3) Employees must not accept money or other remuneration for advice or work done for customers if such service is normally supplied by the Company.

Temple-Inland

The Company expects each employee to devote full time and attention to Company business at all times. Outside employment or other business interest could involve a conflict of interest and must be approved by management. The nature of any outside employment or other business interest must be reported in the annual questionnaire and the department head shall indicate whether he has approved any activity which is reported.

United Banks of Colorado

Employees are not permitted to engage in outside employment or business ventures that interfere or conflict with the satisfactory fulfillment of their responsibilities to the Bank. Employees should not engage in business ventures where the primary purpose is competition with the Bank. It is improper for a trust employee to serve as personal representative, trustee or guardian of an estate, trust or guardianship, unless such appointments result from close personal relationships. Bank employees generally may accept customary honorariums from trade associations, schools or the like, when such honorariums are not earned in the ordinary course of employment.

Dominion Bankshares

An employee should not be employed by or advise any business which in its principal activity competes directly with the Corporation. Employment outside of the Corporation by employees is generally discouraged, and is prohibited if it might subject the Corporation to criticism or adverse publicity, impair the individual's mental or physical efficiency with the Corporation, encroach significantly on DBC's working time, or involve services generally rendered by DBC or by such individual while with the Corporation. Outside employment of officers must have the prior approval of the appropriate Chief Executive Officer or Chief Operating Officer.

First Union

Prior approval of the Committee is required before you may accept a position as officer or director of a corporation, or any nonprofit organization which may borrow from the bank, or become a member of a business partnership, with the exception of a corporation, partnership, or business owned by you or your immediate family. Normally, the Committee will not approve an employee's serving as director of a corporation which has a borrowing relationship with First Union. For example, if an employee is a member of the board of directors of a company or organization which has a line of credit from a First Union Bank, the employee/director could not act in the best interest in the relationship because of the competing duties and loyalties as a director of the borrowing company.

Boatmen's Bankshares

Employees should seek approval of their Chief Executive Officer before accepting directorships or officerships in outside business organizations. An employee serving as a director or officer in an outside organization should avoid involvement in any business decision that presents a potential conflict between Boatmen's and the organization.

TIME RECORDING, LABOR CHARGES, AND WORK SCHEDULES

EG&G

Many of you are asked to record the time spent each day on each job on which you worked. This record is vitally important. It is to be a true and honest record of the hours you spent on each job. In addition to being records of your attendance and hours worked for the purpose of computing your pay, time records are often the basis for billing our customers. Falsifying time records is fraudulent, and may be looked upon as a criminal offense. You are responsible for the accuracy of your individual time records. Your supervisor is certain to discuss this particular issue with you in greater detail and will describe the time-keeping procedures to be followed at your location. If [there are] problems with . . . time record-keeping system, [a] supervisor or manager [is to be consulted].

Litton

Time cards maintained and submitted by each Litton employee are a record of the company, just as other financial records. Each employee must be informed of management's commitment to accurate labor charging. Inaccurate labor charging is a violation of law, as well as a violation of these Standards. Such a practice further prevents the proper monitoring and control of costs. Each employee is to be informed of the procedures that must be utilized for acceptable labor charging and of management's commitment to assure accurate labor charging.

Cincinnati Bell

Personal responsibility isn't only a matter of honesty with Company funds and property, it is a matter of being honest with minutes and hours, as well as property. It means doing a conscientious day's work for a day's pay, which includes keeping absence to a minimum, coming in on time, and restricting personal telephone calls during working time. Our Company and our customers both suffer unless we accept the personal responsibility for the proper use of work time.

SAFECO

SAFECO's normal working week is less than 40 hours. You should be able to complete company business during normal working hours. If overtime is necessary, and if you are covered by wage and hour regulations, the overtime must be requested and authorized by your supervisor before you begin it. Your supervisor plans the work day expecting that you'll be on the job at the start of the day. If you're late, it puts a burden on everyone else. Punctuality and regular attendance are important factors when considering raises and promotions. Tardiness and absentee records are included in your personal record.

AllTel

Our normal working week generally has been five days; however, since we must furnish service around the clock, 24 hours a day, seven days a week, some of our jobs involve Saturday and Sunday work and evening and night hours. You may be required to work longer hours, additional days or be called out (i.e., overtime) when circumstances warrant.

Premier

Many jobs in the organization require different work schedules. An employee's work schedule will depend on the department to which he/she is assigned and the function of the position within the department. In some areas, supervisors have implemented "flextime" schedules that allow variable work hours with an adjustment of the starting and ending time. Your supervisor will inform you of the hours for your specific department. Under the Wage-Hour guidelines, hours for which compensation will be due are those established hours in which employees are actively engaged in work. Employees who report to the bank outside of normal, established working hours are considered to be "waiting to be engaged in work." Such time is not compensable. Employees waiting to be engaged in work who perform such duties as answering telephones, typing, etc., must be compensated for their efforts and, therefore, to preserve their status of "waiting to be engaged in work," should leave the work area and report back at the established work time.

McDonnell-Douglas

You have a clear obligation to use productively the time that MDC pays for. Your work hours should be devoted to activities directly related to MDC's business or to activities authorized by your supervisor. Unauthorized selling, trading, or bartering merchandise to others on company premises is not permitted. Neither is participation in or soliciting for organized or commercial lotteries or other gambling activities or the conduct of a personal business on company time permitted. The distribution of personal notices, pamphlets, advertising matter, or any other kind of personal literature during work time or in any work area and the engaging in informal games of chance for money are discouraged.

EMPLOYEE CONTACTS WITH THE MEDIA

First Union

Even though the Corporation has a policy of maintaining good media relations and tries to respond to all media questions, there is much information about the Corporation, its activities and employees which should not be made available to the public for various reasons. You can understand why neither the public nor the news media has a right to know everything which is known to employees of the Corporation. For instance, a business has a responsibility not to divulge information to the public about its customers. Also, such information could be valuable to a competitor. For these and other reasons, you should be mindful of your duty to the Corporation and its stockholders. If an inquiry is made of you about First Union or its businesses by the news media, you should seek the advice of Corporate Communications. You have a right to refuse to answer questions concerning the Corporation and there should be no adverse implications either to you or to the Corporation because of any refusal to answer. A simple way to decline to respond to questions concerning the Corporation is to say that "First Union Corporation has a department responsible for inquiries like this and I recommend you talk directly with them."

Control Data

News media contacts and responses must be made only through a public relations specialist. Failure to observe this simple policy can cause tremendous damage to the Company and spread misinformation. If a reporter asks you a question, explain that it is Control Data's policy to respond to media inquiries through its public relations staff, and refer that reporter to your Control Data public relations specialist. A list of public relations specialists is available from Corporate Public Relations. Control Data exercises particular caution when considering release of information of a sensitive or material nature, the disclosure of which could influence the judgment of investors to buy, sell or hold Control Data securities.

PPG

Public acceptance is an essential requirement for any business or social institution in a democracy. That acceptance must be earned; it does not come about automatically. Winning public understanding of PPG's objectives requires an ongoing effort to communicate with the various publics who come into contact with the Company. In addition to our own personnel, shareholders, customers and suppliers, these include public officials, residents of PPG plant communities, the financial community, various trade or professional groups and the general public. To foster this understanding, it is in the best interests of PPG to provide non-proprietary information about its products and activities to the various news media, which are often the major conduits of information about the Company to its various constituencies. In order to make sure that news released about the Company is accurate, timely and consistent, each PPG business group has developed policies for approving news related to is own facilities. As a general rule, individuals who receive inquiries from news media should refer them to the facility's senior manager for reply, consistent with whatever business group news policies may be in place. Corporate-wide guidelines for releasing news about the Company outside of the United States are provided in PPG's *Global Communications Policy*. Procedures for clearing news for release with the United States may be found in PPG's *Corporate External News Policy, U.S.* The Company's *Crisis Public Information Plan* outlines the requirements for clearing emergency-related news information worldwide.

Upjohn

All the editorial and reportorial contact on behalf of the Company with the news media serving the Upjohn Company's worldwide publics must be conducted or approved by the Public Relations Division.

PROTECTION AND USE OF THE FIRM'S EQUIPMENT, SUPPLIES, AND FUNDS

FMC

FMC has many valued assets, including its employees, physical property, proprietary trade secrets and confidential information. Protecting these assets against loss, theft and misuse is everyone's responsibility. Company property may not be used for personal benefit, nor may it be sold, loaned, given away or disposed of, without proper authorization. FMC assets must be used for proper purposes during and following employment with the company. Improper use includes unauthorized personal appropriation or use of FMC assets, data or resources, including computer equipment, software and data. Any individual aware of the loss or misuse of assets should report it to the security office or a supervisor. Supervisors receiving such reports will handle them in a careful and thorough manner.

Investigations will be conducted confidentially and in a way that will avoid recrimination.

Northeast Utilities

Protection of Company property—including information, tools, and materials, services and funds—is vital to our business. How well we prevent their negligent or fraudulent misuse or theft affects our ability to perform our job, the rates our customers pay for service and our Company's earnings. Company property should not be used for personal benefit or for any other improper purpose. It should not be sold, loaned, given away or otherwise disposed of, regardless of condition or value, except with proper authorization. Employees are personally accountable for the safekeeping of Company funds and associated records and materials over which they may have control. Anyone spending Company monies (or personal monies that will be reimbursed) must be sure that the Company receives full value in return. Anyone who approves or certifies the correctness of a voucher or bill for goods or services must verify that the purchases are proper and the amounts charged are accurate and consistent with the goods or services ordered. If there are ever questions about the appropriate use of Company funds or property, you should speak to your supervisor and the Human Resources Group.

Sara Lee

An employer shall not use or allow others to use funds, employees, facilities, materials, or equipment of Sara Lee ("Sara Lee property") for personal purposes which are unrelated to , or not intended to further, the businesses of Sara Lee, unless (1) prior written approval is obtained from the executive of Sara Lee who is accountable and responsible for the Sara Lee property proposed to be used ("responsible executive"), and (2) the employee promptly reimburses Sara Lee for its incremental costs incurred as a result of the personal use of the Sara Lee property. The responsible executive shall give such approval only under extraordinary circumstances and then only if such use of the Sara Lee property shall not disrupt or interfere with the business activities of Sara Lee, will not diminish or impair its value of the Sara Lee property and is for a legal and proper purpose.

Weyerhaeuser

When transferred, granted leave, or terminated, no employee shall remove from a work location any office equipment, company credit cards, keys, files, computer systems or other materials designated as company property without permission of the employee's supervisor.

Centel

Supplies and equipment purchased by Centel and the products of its employees' efforts belong to it and are to be used solely for its purposes. Safeguarding such property from loss, damage or theft is the responsibility of every employee. Centel property and property of its customers must not be taken for personal use or gain, or given away, sold or traded without proper authorization.

Employees who have responsibility to receive or disburse money have a special obligation to follow established procedures to ensure proper use and recording of funds. These procedures are designed to protect employees as well as Centel's assets. All receipts and expenditures must be fully and properly accounted for and recorded in Centel's records. Employee certification and supervisory approval of expenditures should be given only when the amounts are correct and proper. It makes no difference whether the payment is for a small item, such as personal reimbursement for travel expense on Centel business, or a substantial payment to a vendor or contractor. Employees who prepare records and reports are obligated, ethically and legally, to assure such documents are accurate and complete, safeguarded from loss or destruction, retained for specified periods and maintained in confidence.

Employees must not willfully or knowingly falsify, alter, remove or destroy records required to be maintained by law or Centel policy. Records shall not be delivered to any person other than to other Centel employees who need such records to perform their jobs or in response to legal process. All employees are bonded under a comprehensive fidelity bond which protects Centel against losses due to fraud or dishonesty by employees. This does not free employees from liability. An employee discovered to have committed a dishonest act will lose bonding and may be subject to disciplinary action or dismissal.

Philip Morris

Generally speaking, the use of corporate aircraft is limited to directors and officers of the Company and to other employees who are authorized by the responsible corporate or operating company officer. In appropriate cases, individuals representing entities with which the Company has a business relationship may use corporate aircraft but only where such an individual is an additional passenger and the responsible corporate or operating company officer approves it in advance. Under no circumstances should corporate aircraft be made available for hire to outsiders. Because of possible tax and other penalties under federal law, corporate aircraft should not be made available to employ government agencies with which the Company has a business relationship or other elected or appointed public officials without the prior approval of the responsible corporate or operating company officer and the office of the General Counsel of the Company.

Puget Sound

The Company acquires equipment for the purpose of directly serving customers or providing necessary support services in its operations. To protect both interests of our investors and our customers, strict accountability of all our assets and expenses is absolutely necessary. Employees are expected to take adequate precautions for the protection of Company assets.

Guidelines. 1. Employees are expected to provide reasonable care for Company property and equipment including use, maintenance, safety, and protection from theft or vandalism. 2. Company property and equipment are not to be used for employees' personal benefit, other than that covered in formal programs such as recreational facilities or Company cars. This prohibition includes items such as vehicles, construction equipment, tools, and audio-visual equipment. In situations where inappropriate use might be inferred, prior written authorization is required from a Company officer or division director stating the specific business or community service purpose. 3. Items of Company property should not be disposed of, regardless of value, without proper authorization and auditable accounting. 4. Inappropriate personal use of Company telephones, office machines, materials, services or supplies will be considered a form of theft and is not acceptable.

Zenith

Preventing the loss, damage, misuse or theft of company property, computer systems, records and funds is a matter of personal responsibility which employees must accept as part of their job. Company property is to be used exclusively for conducting business and should not be used personally, sold or given away without proper authorization. Property of vendors, customers, or the government should be protected as if it were company property. The misuse, theft, damage or destruction of Zenith's computer hardware, software or data (on tape, disk backup or within the computer system) as well as procedures and documentation is a violation of the Code of Conduct Policy. Company procedures for disbursing, receiving and reporting funds are designed to protect the employee as well as safeguard the company's assets and must be adhered to.

Southwestern Bell

Protection of company property and services is vital to our businesses. How well we protect them from theft, fraud, or negligent misuse affects the rates or prices our customers pay and our companies' earnings. Furnishing services to be used for illegal purposes is prohibited. When an employee has knowledge that such service is being furnished, or discovers or suspects that an unauthorized connection has been made to company facilities, the information should be promptly reported to his/her supervisor or to Security personnel.

Company property should not be used for personal benefit, or any other improper purpose. Except with proper authorization, it should not be sold, loaned, given away or otherwise disposed of, regardless of condition or value. The use of telephone service for personal use, both at home and at work, should be in accordance with company instructions. Concession telephone service, for example, is for reasonable use by you and members of your immediate household; unauthorized personal calls should not be made from or charged to company official stations, switchboards, testboards, terminals or other facility locations, nor should coin telephone upper housing keys be used to place calls in an unauthorized manner.

Pacific Power

Pacific's policy is to make available to all employees any company discounts with suppliers or other businesses which may be passed on to employees. However, employees should not use Pacific's name or purchasing power to obtain personal discounts or rebates unless the discounts are made available to all employees.

IBM

IBM equipment, systems, facilities and supplies must be used only for conducting IBM's business or for purposes authorized by management. Personal items that you consider private should not be kept in offices, work spaces, desks, credenzas or file cabinets; IBM management may gain access to these areas when required. Employees should not search for or retrieve articles from another employee's work space without prior approval of management.

Chapter 8

FUNDAMENTAL HONESTY

To profit and survive over the long term, a firm must be able to rely on the fundamental honesty of executives, managers, employees, stockholders, suppliers, and others. Yet, the sums of money and the types of goods that businesses handle leave the firm wide open to a basic human frailty, greed. Fraud, theft, and other forms of dishonesty born of individual greed can cost a business significant portions of its income—or, in the case of a small firm, its entire existence. An internal sense of trust, so important for growth and success, also can be broken or ruined by the actions of one or a few dishonest employees.

While guarding against dishonesty, a firm must set a strong example of honesty for its managers and employees by complying with all laws and regulations where it does business. Arguably, a company that encourages its managers and employees to circumvent laws and regulations in the name of profitability also encourages them to steal from, and defraud, their employer.

Virtually the only defenses a firm can muster against those who would steal or defraud are strict internal controls, careful and vigilant management, an unswerving emphasis on honesty at all levels, and an appeal to each person's sense of right and wrong through the code of business conduct.

The examples below show several approaches to the matters of fundamental honesty and compliance with laws.

HONESTY AND COMPLIANCE WITH LAWS

Williams

The Company is committed to being a good corporate citizen of all states and countries in which it does business. Because of this commitment, it is the policy of the Company to comply in all respects with all laws and regulations that are applicable to its business, at all government levels in the United States and abroad.

The sections which follow deal with specific laws and regulations and outline general guidelines for compliance therewith because of their particular importance to the Company's business activities. It should be understood, however, that the special emphasis on these laws and regulations does not limit the general admonition that all applicable laws and regulations are to be complied with.

The laws and regulations of the states and countries in which the Company does business form the framework around which its operations are built. To comply in all respects with both the spirit and the letter of those laws will best serve the interests of the Company, its employees and shareholders.

Inevitably a company operating on an international scale, such as this one, will encounter laws and customs applicable in one country which conflict with the laws of another. For example, the laws of one country may encourage or even require business practices which in this country are specifically prohibited. This being the case, every employee should be prepared to recognize such a situation by knowing the laws and obeying them strictly. Questions regarding the legality of a proposed action should be referred to the general counsel of The Williams Companies for consideration. The Board of Directors or the executive officers of The Williams Companies, after consultation with the general counsel, should then be relied upon for resolution of the matter.

Aetna

Our business requires the handling of or accounting for thousands of transactions each business day. We have strict rules to guard against fraud or dishonesty and to serve as guidelines for handling such problems when they occur.

The Corporate Audit Department's Security Control Section handles the investigation of any fraud or act of dishonesty. If you detect or suspect fraud or dishonesty on the part of any employee or agent of Aetna, any affiliated company or partnership, any supplier, borrower or other person with whom the Company deals, you should report it immediately to one of the persons listed in the supplement at the end of this book. They will see that the appropriate people are notified and that internal and external investigations are coordinated.

In the event that evidence of a fraud or crime against the Company is established, any involved Aetna employee or agent is subject to termination, and business relationships with others may be severed pending on the severity of the offense. Security Control will review the evidence with the Law Department in establishing its case.

Prosecution will be initiated when practical either in the name of the Company after review with the Law Department, or by referral by Security Control to an appropriate law enforcement agency.

Recovery of any loss suffered by the Company as a result of fraud, dishonesty or crime will be made where possible.

The handling of each case of fraud or dishonesty must, of course, be different. However, observe these general guidelines: [1] Don't discuss matters involving possible criminal conduct of an employee with anyone who is not authorized to investigate such conduct. Until the matter is resolved, you may be risking charges of libel or slander. [2] Don't terminate an employee suspected or proven guilty of fraud or dishonesty without agreement of Security Control. [3] Don't promise not to report a crime to law enforcement authorities to encourage the return of stolen funds or for any other reason. Such conduct, however well intentioned, may be viewed as extortion. [4] Don't attempt to destroy evidence of suspected criminal activity. Such attempted destruction may violate state or federal law and result in criminal penalties for the individual. [5] Give all reasonable help to any law enforcement agency prosecuting a criminal complaint. Such assistance will be coordinated through the Corporate Audit Department.

BB&T

It is the policy of the Corporation that all officers and employees will abide by all applicable laws, regulations, rulings, orders, and policy statements and other similar provisions which govern the operation of the Corporation. The Corporation will not tolerate any violation or intent to violate either the letter or the spirit of such provisions.

NWNL

As stated above, the Company is committed to compliance with laws and regulations affecting the Company's operations. Because laws and regulations are subject to interpretation by courts and administrative agencies and because the application thereof may vary according to the facts of a particular situation, it is not always possible for either the Company or its employees to know with any certainty what is required for lawful compliance. In such circumstances it is expected that employees will use common sense and good faith in attempting to comply with such laws and regulations and that advice of legal counsel will be obtained where possible.

Home Insurance Companies

While we must compete vigorously to maximize profits, we must at the same time do so in strict compliance with all laws and regulations applicable to our activities. Employees should not take any action on behalf of the Company which the employee knows or believes violates any applicable law or regulation.

AIG

If, in conducting business for AIG, an employee becomes aware of any conduct, illegal or otherwise, which may be detrimental to AIG, on the part of any person, it is the employee's duty to inform his or her supervisor.

Temple-Inland

The Company has a permanent commitment to recognition of the public interest. The activities of the Company and each employee are expected to be in full compliance with all applicable laws and regulations.

CRIMINAL ACTS

U.S. Bancorp

You will face termination and/or criminal penalties if you: [1] Accept a fee, gift or commission in exchange for extending credit. [2] Corruptly solicit, demand, or accept anything of value (except Bancorp Compensation) intending to be influenced or rewarded in connection with the business of Bancorp. [3] Steal, embezzle or misapply Bancorp funds or assets. [4] Threaten violence to hasten the repayment of a loan (extortion). [5] Make false entries of records or knowingly mispost accounts. [6] Knowingly make loans to examiners from the Federal Reserve or the Comptroller of the Currency. [7] Commit other criminal acts related to your employment by Bancorp.

If you become aware of criminal acts by other employees, you must report this fact to your immediate supervisor, region, division or Bancorp's Auditor. Failure to disclose such knowledge could make you an accessory to the crime.

Chapter 9

PROTECTING PROPRIETARY
AND CONFIDENTIAL
INFORMATION

In the last decade, the United States' and other industrial nations' economies have increasingly relied on knowledge, rather than natural resources or commodities, to add value to their products and services. Knowledge-intensive industries, in contrast to traditional resource-based businesses, have developed at a rapid pace. As a result, according to S.R.I. International's Donn Parker, proprietary information is the "new gold of the market place."

Firms of any size should now anticipate the need for protection against misappropriation of its intellectual property, including patents, copyrights, trademarks, confidential business information and trade secrets. Thefts of trade secrets, one form of intellectual property, alone cost American firms $20 billion a year, according to August Bequai, counsel to the American Society for Industrial Security.

Protecting competitively advantageous information is vital, because intellectual property is expensive and time-consuming to develop. Moreover, intellectual-property protection, whether by patent, copyright, trademark, trade secrecy law or by restrictive covenants, encourages further innovation. Firms holding such rights can move forward with enhancements and new projects with better assurance their investment is secure from thefts or infringements.

"Patents," according to Thomas I. O'Brien, Union Carbide's Chief Patent Counsel, "are an incentive to invention, an encouragement to investment in the commercialization of new technology, and a promoter of technology transfer both within the country as well as to and from other countries." Patents are issued by the U.S. Patent and Trademark Office and comprise three specific types of intellectual property: utility, plant, and design. If the inventor wishes to maintain the secrecy of his creation, that person (or firm) can exclude others from using it. Moreover, the inventor has a "negative right" to exclude another from constructing or employing the invention in return for placing the information in the public domain.

Copyright protection, a species of intellectual property, is exclusively federal and exists in an original work of authorship that is established in a tangible medium of expression from which it can be comprehended. Copyright protects the expression against copying and other specific acts; however, copyright does not protect a method of operation or an idea. The distinction between idea and expression defines the "boundary between the domain of the patent and that of copyright."

A trademark, first used by members of medieval Europe merchant guilds, is a distinctive mark of authenticity, whether a name, symbol, device, or configuration, through which the product of a particular manufacturer or the vendible commodity of a merchant may be differentiated from those of others. Three other types of protected marks are: service marks such as "Shell Oil"; certification marks such as the "Real" seal on dairy products or the "PG" symbol on movies; and the collective marks used by members of an association, such as "American Bar Association." In order to maintain trademark and other mark protection, an owner must use it and prosecute any infringement.

Confidential business information, though less classified than a trade secret, has been accorded protection by the courts. One important requirement for the firm or person to demonstrate that the information falls within the public's protection is that the material has been confidentially disclosed with the clear understanding that it was protected. Moreover, even though the information is within the public domain, if the recipient of the material reaps any value from his disclosure of it, he may be liable for damages under the legal theory of unjust enrichment.

A commonly accepted definition of trade secret is "any formula, pattern, device, or compilation of information that is used in one's business, and which gives him an opportunity to obtain an advantage over competitors who do not know or use it." For example, a trade secret may be a formula for a chemical compound, a process of manufacturing, treating or preserving materials, or a pattern for a machine or other device. Many trade secrets are protected by the Uniform Trade Secrets Act, which a number of states, including California, Connecticut, Delaware and Minnesota, have adopted. Under the Act, the court can enjoin either actual or threatened misappropriation of a trade secret, compel affirmative acts to protect a trade secret such as the return of documents, and condition future use of a trade secret upon payment of a royalty when an injunction appears unreasonable. Damages for actual losses as a result of the misappropriation also lie under the Act, as well as any unjust enrichment not calculated in the actual-losses portion of the damages.

Under common law, it is not necessary for an employer to rely on a written agreement with an employee to protect the firm's confidential information and trade secrets, since there often exists an employee duty not to use or disclose such material. Yet, restrictive covenants not to compete and not to disclose provide additional protection to employers. Courts enforce such covenants because, in the case of a former employee, he is under a duty, regardless of contract, not to disclose or use in his new employment those special skills, techniques, or knowledge of which he confidentially acquired in his previous employment.

A firm should not wait to promulgate an effective, comprehensive protection plan until a misappropriation or controversy over proprietary and confidential information occurs. A well-administered code section which protects the firm's intellectual property is not, however, a guarantee that such misappropriation will never transpire. However, it lessens the risk of loss and the damage when such misuse occurs. Toward this end, the firm must have the support of its employees to effectively administer its policy. The following excerpts can provide helpful guidelines for firms drawing up their own codes of conduct.

PROPRIETARY INFORMATION

IBM

IBM has a large variety of assets. Many are of great value to IBM's competitiveness and its success as a business. They include not only our extremely valuable proprietary information, but also our physical assets. IBM proprietary information includes intellectual property, typically the product of the ideas and hard work of many talented IBM people. It also includes the confidential data entrusted to many employees in connection with their jobs.

Protecting all of these assets is very important. Their loss, theft or misuse jeapordizes the future of IBM. For this reason, you are personally responsible not only for helping to protect the company's assets in general. Here is where your awareness of security procedures can play a critical role. You should be alert to any situations or incidents that could lead to the loss, misuse or theft of company property. And you should report all such situations to the security department or your manager as soon as they come to your attention. What types of assets should you be concerned about protecting? And what are your responsibilities in this regard?

Proprietary information is information that is the property of IBM and is usually classified under the IBM classification system. Such information includes the business, financial, marketing, and service plans associated with products. It also includes personnel information, medical records, and salary data. Other proprietary information includes designs; engineering and manufacturing know-how and proccesses; IBM business and product plans with outside vendors and a variety of internal data bases; and patent applications and copyrighted material such as software. Much of this information is called intellectual property, and represents the product of the ideas and efforts of many of your fellow employees. Also, it has required substantial investments by IBM in planning, research and development. Obviously, if competitors could secure proprietary information such as product design specifications without making the same substantial investment in research and engineering, they would be getting a free ride on IBM's investment. Pricing information and marketing plans are also highly useful to competitors.

The value of this proprietary information is well known to many people in the information industry. Besides competitors, they include industry and security analysts, members of the press, consultants, customers, and other so-called "IBM watchers." Some of these individuals will obtain information any way they can. No matter what the circumstances, IBM alone is entitled to determine who may possess its proprietary information and what use may be made of it, except for specific legal requirements such as the publication of certain reports.

As an IBM employee, you probably have access to information that the company considers proprietary. Given the widespread interest in IBM—and the increasingly competitive nature of the industry—the chances are you probably have contact with someone interested in acquiring information in your possession. So it's very important not to use or disclose proprietary information except as authorized by IBM and to provide adequate safeguards to prevent loss of such information. The unintentional disclosure of proprietary information can be just as harmful as intentional disclosure.

To avoid unintentional disclosure, never discuss with any unauthorized person information that has not been made public by IBM. This information includes unannounced products, prices, earnings, procurement plans, business volumes and capital requirements. Also included are: confidential product performance data; marketing and service strategies; business plans; and other confidential information. Furthermore, you should not discuss confidential information even with authorized IBM employees if you are in the presence of others who are not authorized—for example, at a trade show reception or in a public area such as an airplane. This also applies to discussions with family members or with friends, who might innocently or inadvertently pass the information on to someone else.

Finally, keep in mind that harmful disclosure may start with the smallest leak of bits of information. Such fragments of information from other sources to form a fairly complete picture. If someone outside the company asks you questions, either directly or through another person, do not attempt to answer them unless you are certain you are authorized to do so. If you are not authorized, refer the person to the appropriate source within the company. For example, if you are approached by security analysts or investors, you should refer them to your local communications manager or to the Office of the Treasurer. Similarly, unless you have been authorized to talk to reporters, or to anyone else writing about or otherwise covering the company or the industry, direct the person to the information specialist in your communications department. If you do not know what functional area the questioner should be referred to, ask your manager. Besides your obligation not to disclose any IBM confidential information to anyone outside the company, you are also required as an employee to use such information only in connection with IBM's business. These obligations apply whether or not you developed the information yourself. And they apply by law in virtually all countries where IBM does business.

Monsanto

Proprietary information developed or acquired by Monsanto and not freely available to others is a valuable asset that must be protected against theft or inadvertent loss. Improper disclosure could destroy the value of such information to Monsanto and substantially weaken our competitive position. Various types of proprietary information include trade secrets, as well as technical, financial and business information, which Monsanto either wishes to keep confidential or is under an obligation to keep confidential. For example, such proprietary information may concern research results, manufacturing techniques, cost data, marketing strategies, financial budgets and long range plans.

For protection of proprietary information, Monsanto must and does rely primarily on the loyalty, integrity, good faith and alertness of its employees. The understanding of this relationship is confirmed by requesting execution, at the time of employment, of an employment agreement containing a confidentiality provision. Upon leaving Monsanto, the obligation to safeguard Monsanto's proprietary information continues.

The disclosure of Monsanto's proprietary information to persons outside Monsanto must be limited to those who have a strict "need to know"; that is, Monsanto's need for the outside parties to know. Any such disclosure must be made under conditions which impose an absolute obligation on the outside parties neither to disclose nor use the information in an unauthorized manner. Even within Monsanto, the disclosure of proprietary information should be limited to those Monsanto employees who have a need for the information in order to fully perform their jobs. Policies and guidelines for protecting proprietary information are set forth in Monsanto's Information Protection Plan, which is available throughout Monsanto at all locations.

The Director, Corporate Security is available to assist employees in evaluating the security adequacy of their activities. Questions about the legal aspects of protecting proprietary information should be referred to the Patent and/or Law Departments. From time to time, suggestions pertaining to activities of Monsanto such as new products and processes, improvements in present operations and products, slogans, advertising themes, and the like are received from persons not employed by Monsanto.

Although Monsanto has used the ideas of others under appropriate circumstances, there is always potential danger in accepting or discussing unsolicited suggestions made by outsiders. The same or similar idea may already be under development within the company. Upon completing development of our own idea, the outsider may feel that our new activity is based on the unsolicited suggestion. Legal claims against Monsanto may then result. All suggestions or proposals received from outsiders, whether or not pertaining to our business activities, should be immediately referred to the Patent Department without any review, consideration or even acknowledgement by the recipient. After screening and reaching a proper understanding with the submitter, the suggestion will be forwarded to the appropriate technical and/or business group to pursue.

PATENTS, DISCOVERIES, INVENTIONS, AND OTHER INTELLECTUAL PROPERTY

United Telecom

The company's strength and growth potential depend on our ability to stay ahead of the competition in key technologies and to plan and implement our business initiatives. All employees have a direct interest in contributing to the development and protection of United Telecom's technologies, know-how, skills and innovations. All innovations developed or created by employees in the course of their employment, whether during or after working hours, belong to the company and should not be used for personal gain.

Intellectual assets are valuable and can be protected under laws governing patents, copyrights, trademarks and trade secrets. No employee should take any action (e.g., unauthorized disclosure) that could diminish the company's ability to protect intellectual assets. Special effort is required to protect proprietary (trade secret) information. Proprietary information includes financial information (e.g., profit margins, financing plans), organizational information (e.g., personnel data, expansion plans), marketing information (e.g., new product developments, customer lists, advertising plans), and technical information (e.g., R&D reports, service records) and so forth. Unauthorized disclosure of information, whether deliberate or inadvertent, could destroy its value and give unfair advantage to others. When you leave the company, all documents and records containing proprietary or national security information must be returned to the company. Even after your employment ends, you have a continuing obligation to safeguard all such information.

In the conduct of our business, we have occasion to receive and use proprietary information of others. We must use this information only in accordance with the agreements under which we have received it. It is company policy to honor copyrights and to respect the trade secrets of others. You should not engage in unauthorized copying or reveal or use any trade secrets of a former employer in connection with your United Telecom employment.

COPYRIGHT MATERIAL

IBM

In most cases, the copyrights in employee generated works of authorship such as manuals and computer programs are automatically owned by IBM through operation of law. In other cases, title to the copyrights is given to IBM by contractual provisions. IBM considers it important to limit the distribution of copyrightable material within IBM to that in which the copyright is owned by or appropriately licensed to IBM. To assure that material not owned by IBM is appropriately licensed, IBM may request a license from you before you will be permitted to place copyrightable material into or on any IBM owned distribution channel, including internal mail and electronic channels such as conferencing disks, VM or PROFS. This license may be requested whether you or IBM actually owns the material. If there is a question of ownership, you should consult your manager before you distribute material in IBM through any channel. Your manager may consult the legal and the intellectual property law departments to determine whether you will be permitted to place the material in the particular distribution channel.

CONFIDENTIAL INFORMATION

Ashland

One of Ashland's most valuable assets is its body of business information. The widespread use of computer terminals and computer systems has caused this information to be accessible by many employees. Failure to adequately protect this corporate information can lead to the loss of highly confidential data that place Ashland at a disadvantage in the marketplace. Each employee must take steps to protect information that has been entrusted to him. Documents containing sensitive data should be handled carefully during working hours and must be properly secured at the end of the business day. Particular attention must be paid to the security of data stored on the computer systems. You must maintain the secrecy of your password and lock the equipment when not in use. If you observe individuals that you do not recognize using terminals in your area, immediately report this to your supervisor.

Bank of America

BankAmerica monitors its conduct through its managers and their administration of our system of internal controls, and through the Board of Directors' Audit and Examination Committee, which has responsibility for the internal and external audit process. You are expected to comply with all control procedures, cooperate fully in the audit process, and be truthful with all managers and auditors. Employees in, or applicants for, positions in sensitive or high loss exposure areas of the company may be required to submit to a personal security screening to ensure that they do not pose an unreasonable risk to the company's interests.

To protect the company's property and premises, and to protect the safety and security of our employees and customers, we reserve the right to take necessary action. Such action may include, but is not limited to, the right to review your work, work area, desk, or locker, as well as to inspect or search the following: company premises and/or property, personal property of employees, as well as other persons entering or leaving company premises, or any personal property found or maintained on company premises.

(Personal property includes, but is not limited to, purses, packages, briefcases, and the contents of an employee's pockets.) If you refuse to permit or cooperate in any inspection of company property or premises and/or of personal property found, maintained, or brought on or off company premises, you may be subject to disciplinary action, including dismissal. If you have a conflict with any policy or procedure because of your own personal standards, you should discuss the matter with your manager or Personnel Relations. Until the issue is resolved, you are required to comply, even if you feel it is inconsistent with your standards.

SECURITY AND CONFIDENTIALITY

Rockwell

Information is the lifeblood of any corporation. Much of the information concerning Rockwell's business activities is confidential, and its disclosure to others could seriously damage the company's interests. Many Rockwell employees are exposed to confidential information. This is especially true if an employee uses or helps develop proprietary techniques, technologies or software, or works on proprietary or classified projects. We should never disclose confidential or proprietary information regarding the company or its affairs to anyone without first obtaining proper management approval.

As a government contractor, we have a special responsibility to safeguard classified material. When working on government programs or contracts, we must always ensure that confidential information is disclosed and handled in strict compliance with the rules applicable to such material. We also have a personal and professional obligation to protect confidential and proprietary information provided by our customers and suppliers. They expect this from us and we expect the same from them.

Questions and Answers:

Q: A customer's employee has given me copies of internal memoranda relating to a proposed procurement. I know this violates the customer's policy—what should I do?

A: You should report the matter immediately to security, or, if your location does not have that organization, to your location controller. You should not make copies of that material or make it available to others. If you have any reason to believe classified material is being given to you in an unauthorized way, promptness in making disclosure to the company and seeking guidance is essential.

Q: I have worked on important new technology in the course of my work for the company. Am I free to publish technical papers or give talks on the new technology without any approvals?

A: No. Such technology belongs to the company. You should review your proposed publication or presentation with, and obtain advance approval from, both your management and the Patent Department to make sure that Rockwell's intellectual property rights are properly safeguarded.

Q: A good friend and former fellow employee has asked me to let him see some documents we jointly worked on when he was with the company. May I give him a copy or let him see my copy?

A: No, unless you have reviewed the request with the Legal Department and have received its approval.

Q: I know classification markings are required on the first and last pages of a document and the front and back covers. What should I do if some of the interior pages need to be removed?

A: By removing some of the interior pages from the original document, you have in essence created another document. It must be marked in the same manner with the same classifications as the original document.

Q: I know that before I release classified information to anyone, I must verify that the individual has the proper clearance level and the need-to-know. How do I determine that, if the person is not from my organization?

A: An individual's clearance level can only be verified by the Security Office. This includes government personnel, company employees from other locations, and employees from other companies. . . .

E-Systems

E-Systems is engaged in many significant projects essential to the defense of our country. Many of these projects are classified. The safeguarding of vital information and equipment used in connection with these classified projects is of the utmost importance. All employees who are involved in classified programs will observe all the rules and regulations concerning the handling and transmission of classified information. Any employee believing that classified information or equipment is being handled in a manner which violates applicable requirements must report such information immediately to his or her supervisor or the head of security at the facility involved.

AGREEMENTS REGARDING CONFIDENTIAL INFORMATION AND INTELLECTUAL PROPERTY

IBM

When you joined IBM, you should have been required to sign an agreement that sets out specific obligations you have as an employee, relating to the treatment of confidential information. Also under the agreement, when you are employed in a managerial, technical, engineering, product planning, programming, scientific or other professional capacity, you assign to IBM the rights to any ideas and inventions that you develop if they are in an area of the company's business. Subject to the laws of each country, this obligation applies no matter where or when—at work or after hours—such intellectual property is created. The existence of this intellectual property must be reported to IBM, and the property must be protected like any other proprietary information of the company. However, if you believe that your idea or invention falls outside the area of IBM's business interests, you may ask IBM for a written disclaimer of ownership.

Weyerhaeuser

Each manager of employees who will have or have had access to the company's trade secrets has the obligation to arrange for entry and exit interviews of those employees so that new, newly promoted or terminating employees will understand their obligations with respect to the company's trade secrets.

IBM

If you leave the company for any reason, including retirement, you may not disclose or misuse IBM confidential information. Also, IBM's ownership of intellectual property that you created while you were an IBM employee continues after you leave the company.

ESPIONAGE AND SABOTAGE

Southwestern Bell

The importance of preventing disclosure of any company information that could be of value to saboteurs and espionage agents, including those engaged in industrial espionage, cannot be overstated. Such information includes security procedures, marketing plans and strategies, new business ventures, product development information, location of physical plant facilities, circuit layout information, emergency rerouting and service restoration procedures, and classified national security information. As mentioned in the section on proprietary information, access to classified national security information is restricted to those having proper government clearance and a "need to know." Any attempt by an unauthorized person to obtain sensitive information, or gain access to secured company locations, should be reported at once to Security personnel.

Chapter 10

INTERNAL COMMUNICATIONS

Clear channels of communication within a firm are vital for success in today's globally competitive, electronically interconnected markets. Executives, managers, and employees must be able to get the right messages and information to each other as quickly and as accurately as possible. So it is not surprising that many leading firms now include an ethical commitment to good internal communications in their code of business conduct. As the model codes below illustrate, communications within a firm must always be two-way.

COMMUNICATIONS

Walt Disney

One of the most valuable and important skills of the [Walt] Disney leader is his ability to effectively communicate. All of the positive human relations techniques available today are virtually useless without effective communication. Since communication means getting ideas across and finding out what other people have to say, we stress the following points in the Disney Way of Leadership. Communicate clearly . . . get your message across. Let your employees know how they're doing. Encourage upward and downward communications. Listen to what employees have to say. Keep an open door and an open mind. Tell employees how they fit in . . . explain the big picture. Let your employees feel like they belong. Communication should be direct, open and honest.

TECO

It is our policy, whether communicating with our fellow employees or with the public, to tell the truth at all times. The chief operating officers at each company are responsible for releasing any information that the public has a right to know.

The Corporate Communications Department provides staff support for communications with the public, employees, shareholders, and Customers, and handles inquiries from the news media.

SAFECO

. . . In addition to education and training, SAFECO is committed to keeping everyone in the company well informed. Through a variety of advanced communications techniques, employees are advised on industry trends, company plans, programs and results, and other such information of interest. Communication is a two-way street. It's important for you to let your supervisors know what you're thinking and what your plans are. Your supervisor will be available for discussions as you see the need and in addition to this, each employee participates in an annual Performance Appraisal which gives a scheduled opportunity to express career interests and get the guidance needed to further those interests. Open communication is important. We believe in it, we further it. We are very concerned about being fair with employees and very anxious to do the right thing. If you ever are concerned that we aren't being fair, or doing the right thing, please see your supervisor, or the Personnel Department, or anyone else in management at SAFECO you think might be able to help. We promise to listen carefully and give you the best possible response we can.

PPG

The achievement of PPG's performance goals depends on a well-informed, well-motivated workforce. That, in turn, requires effective, candid, two-way communications throughout the organization. Every PPG associate is expected to take part in that process by passing along important information and by offering suggestions which will benefit the operations of the Company. This includes the prompt reporting of problems and violations or Company procedures to the appropriate supervisory personnel.

Likewise, every supervisor is expected to convey timely information about Company plans, performance, goals and policies to the people who report to him or her. Additionally, every PPG associate has the right to information related to their own performance, compensation and benefits as well as to other general and individual information. Additional details can be found in the Company's Employee Information Practices Policy statement. The essential points of that document are summarized in PPG Employee Communications Policy and Guidelines.

Chapter 11

EQUAL EMPLOYMENT AND AFFIRMATIVE ACTION

In the ideal free-enterprise model, the positive growth of any economy results from using and enhancing the abilities of all persons to their fullest extent. Merit, rather than irrelevant factors such as race, sex, religion or national origin, are the most important considerations in the system of distributing economic rewards.

The real world, of course, does not behave like the ideal model. The business world mirrors the views, conditionings, values, and prejudices of executives, managers, employees, stockholders, suppliers, and customers alike. Despite countless legal actions, legislations, and social protests in recent decades, many prejudices and inequities remain, and will continue to influence interpersonal relationships in the workplace.

Today, numerous federal statutes, executive orders, and regulations prohibit employment discrimination because of age, race, color, sex, religion, national origin, handicap or status as a veteran. And many firms address these issues in their codes of conduct. Often, however, it is not an easy task. Codes written one year sometimes have to be updated the next—or sooner—as new laws and rulings emerge from the legislative and judicial systems. At the same time, the composition of the American workforce is changing, with more women, handicapped persons, and older workers on the job. In the midst of these changes, courts likely will stay busy through the 1990s with cases involving allegations of employment discrimination, sexual harassment, or violations of equal opportunity statutes.

Comparable worth is another equal-rights issue that many firms may face in the 1990s. Comparable worth, which has its roots in the 1963 Equal Pay Act, is far removed from the notion of equal pay for equal work. Sean DeForest, in an article in *Personnel* entitled "How Can Comparable Worth Be Achieved," defined the concept as "requiring equal pay for employees whose work is of comparable value even if their jobs are totally different from each other." In 1981, while expressly stating it was not endorsing the comparable-worth doctrine, the United States Supreme Court ruled in *County of Washington v. Gunther* that female jail matrons, who received only 70% of the salary of male guards, had suffered discrimination even though their jobs were dissimilar from those of male guards. Recently, at least a dozen states have enacted statutes requiring public and private employers to pay equally for comparable worth, and many more were considering such legislation.

The following examples provide useful models that can be customized to suit a firm's needs for codes which address nondiscrimination in employment and sales, equal employment opportunities, affirmative action, preferential treatment, reverse discrimination, comparable worth, and other issues.

NONDISCRIMINATION

Bethlehem

Bethlehem is firmly committed to a policy of nondiscrimination in employment and to the cause of equal employment and advancement opportunity for all. Bethlehem fills its job requirements by selecting from the available labor force those applicants best qualified to perform the work in safety to themselves and others. It is Bethlehem's policy not to discriminate against any employee or applicant for employment because of race, color, religion, sex, age, national origin, or handicap. In addition, it is Bethlehem's policy to refuse to enter into any contract or agreement which would have the effect of discriminating against United States persons or firms on the basis of race, color, religion, sex, age, national origin or handicap.

Summit

Staff members must deal with customers, prospects, suppliers and other employees without any discrimination because or race, creed, sex, national origin, marital status, age or related criteria. All business decisions shall be considered uniformly on their own merits.

First Virginia

All customers, applicants for employment, and employees must be treated fairly. Employees and directors should avoid discriminating against any person due to race, creed, religion, color, age, sex, marital status, ancestry, national origin or physical or mental handicap. All directors and employees must follow the provisions of the Corporation's and/or affiliate's affirmative action and fair credit programs, which are developed and documented, from time to time, to assure fulfillment of this policy.

Sara Lee

The evaluation of applicants for employment by Sara Lee shall be based on the needs of Sara Lee and the ability and relevant business experience of the applicant. No employee in a position to hire or discharge, or influence the hiring or discharging of, employees shall refuse to hire any individual or discharge an employee or discriminate against an employee with respect to his or her evaluation, advancement, compensation, duties or other conditions of employment or career development because of his or her race, color, religion, sex, age, national origin or handicap.

EQUAL EMPLOYMENT OPPORTUNITIES

Olin

Olin is an equal opportunity employer. Its policy is that all employment practices, including recruiting, hiring, promotion, benefits, compensation, transfers and termination, will be based on performance and qualifications without regard for race, color, creed, religion, national origin, sex or age.

SCE&G (Scana)

The Company's employment policy is to provide equal employment opportunity to all employees regardless of race, color, religion, sex, age or national origin. This policy applies to all employment practices including (but not limited to) recruiting, hiring, training, compensation, benefits, transfers, promotions, layoffs and terminations. The Company is also committed to taking affirmative action steps to achieve its goal of equal employment opportunity for all persons. The affirmative action policy applies to (but is not limited to) recruitment, hiring, training, and promotion practices without regard to race, color, religion, sex, age or national origin.

The Vice President-Personnel and Corporate Communications has the following responsibilities: [1] Developing and implementing the Company-wide Affirmative Action program. [2] Serving as a liaison to senior management, keeping them informed of the progress of the Affirmative Action program. [3] Formulating affirmative action goals for each department based on annual manpower projections, and presenting the goals to senior management for approval and to company officers for implementation. Company officers are responsible for achieving departmental affirmative action goals by exercising the following principles: [1] Ensuring that management employees who make employment decisions or recommendations comply fully with this policy. [2] Ensuring that employees are given development opportunities and promotions without regard to race, color, religion, sex, age or national origin. [3] Making every effort to maintain desirable equal employment opportunity/affirmative action percentages in their organization units.

General Motors

The matter of discrimination in employment has been the subject of a substantial body of legislation and regulation at the federal, state, and local levels in the United States. General Motors is committed to a policy of equal opportunity employment. Members of management are expected to discharge their responsibilities not only in conformity with the law governing this subject but also in a manner fully consistent with the objectives and intent of the Corporation policy.

That policy finds expression in the following statement:

"Operating as it does on a nationwide basis, General Motors Corporation offers employment opportunities to many people in many different locations throughout the United States.

"The policy of the Corporation is to extend these opportunities to qualified applicants and employees on an equal basis regardless of an individual's age, race, color, sex, religion or national origin.

"Hiring and employment practices and procedures implementing this policy are the responsibility of the employing units. However, these practices, procedures, and decisions are to be at all times, in conformity with the Corporation Equal Opportunity Employment Policy."

Members of management also are expected to adhere to Corporation policies regarding the employment of qualified handicapped individuals, disabled veterans and veterans of the Vietnam era.

The policy applies to the work environment as well as to matters of hiring and promotion. Abuse of the dignity of any person or group through ethnic, racist or sexist slurs, or through derogatory or objectionable conduct, is unacceptable behavior. It is expected that all employees will respect the rights, privacy, and integrity of all persons in order to maintain an atmosphere free from any type of intimidation or harassment including sexual harassment. On a worldwide basis, General Motors expects its employees to support its equal opportunity objectives and its efforts to pursue the goals of equal opportunity in employment.

Panhandle Eastern

Panhandle Eastern Corporation recognizes its responsibility to all citizens and, in order to insure equal opportunity to all employees and to all applicants seeking employment, pledges that it will not discriminate against any person because of race, color, religion, age, handicap, sex or national origin. All Panhandle Eastern Companies will take affirmative action to insure that applicants for employment as well as present employees are treated fairly without regard to race, color, religion, age, handicap, sex or national origin. The foregoing policy and affirmative action pledge applies also to the employment of qualified disabled veterans and Vietnam era veterans. Such action shall include employment, upgrading, promotion, transfer, recruitment advertising, layoff or termination, rates of pay or other forms of compensation, and selection for training. Each Company, if required, will develop an Affirmative Action Plan containing specific recruiting procedures and employment goals in accordance with existing law, executive orders, and regulations. Each Company will designate an Affirmative Action Officer who is responsible for the implementation of the Affirmative Action Plan within that organization.

Overall Corporate responsibility for Equal Employment Opportunity and

Affirmative Action compliance is assigned to the Vice President-Administration. It will be the responsibility of the Vice President-Administration to audit the Equal Employment practices and procedures and the Affirmative Action Plans of each Company for the purpose of insuring compliance and continued implementation of this policy. The Vice President-Administration will report quarterly to the Chief Executive Officer with a detailed summary of progress.

Rite Aid

Rite Aid is an equal opportunity employer and shall make employment and promotion decisions based on qualifications for the job responsibilities without regard to race, color, religion, national origin, handicap, sex, or age. Personnel in supervisory positions are prohibited from making demands on employees under their supervision that are clearly unrelated to job performance or that are unreasonable, unlawful, or immoral.

Fort Howard

Fort Howard Corporation is dedicated to the goal of providing equal employment for all persons without regard to race, color, religion, sex, national origin, age or handicap, or status as a disabled Vietnam era veteran. The Corporation insists that all employees refrain from any act which is designed to cause unlawful employment discrimination in hiring, placement, transfer, demotion, promotion, recruiting, or use of employee benefits or facilities.

Universal

Universal is an Equal Employment Opportunity Employer. This means that there shall be no discrimination on the basis of race, sex, national origin, religion, age, etc., in any phase of our employment practices which include applicant flow, hiring, layoffs, promotions, etc. Our Human Resources Department at both Universal and Lawyers Title have developed and maintain expertise in this area. It is hoped that any employee who believes that he or she has been aggrieved will feel free to discuss his or her problem with a member of the Human Resources Department. It is also our policy to take affirmative action to insure that minorities, women, Vietnam veterans and handicapped persons are not discriminated against and to insure that our Equal Employment Opportunity Policy is observed.

Texas Instruments

Ethical and moral responsibilities go far beyond the specific situations described in these statements. These responsibilities are involved in everything we do, both on and off the job. We all want to be proud of TI and the people with whom we work. The basic virtues of kindness, courtesy, and integrity are the elements that provide the framework for a pleasant working environment. The hours we spend at work are more satisfying and rewarding when we demonstrate respect for all associates regardless of gender, age, creed, racial background, religion, handicap, national origin, or status in TI's organization. TI is committed to being an equal opportunity employer. It is TI policy to support this objective through hiring, promotion, transfer, and all other actions that affect TI employees or prospective employees.

Public Service Indiana

We believe in equal opportunity for all employees and candidates for employment. Individuals are selected and placed on the basis of qualifications for the work to be performed. We strive to permit each employee to achieve his or her full potential.

NCNB

NCNB is committed to recruiting and hiring qualified applicants without regard to race, religion, color, sex, age, handicap or national origin. Additionally, these factors will not affect employees with regard to wages, salaries, benefits and opportunities for advancement, including upgrading, training, promotion and transfer. Questions concerning NCNB's affirmative action policy should be directed to the affirmative action officer in the Corporate Personnel Division.

Jostens

The Company, an Equal Opportunity and an Affirmative Action employer, believes it is vital to the successful conduct of its business and to basic human dignity and welfare to promote economic, social, and educational opportunities for all. It is the Company's policy, therefore, to affirmatively recruit, hire, train, compensate, promote, assign, transfer, lay off, recall and terminate employees based on their abilities, achievements and job-related experience without regard to race, color, religion, age, sex, marital status, national origin, veteran status or physical handicap. Further, the Company will maintain all facilities on a non-segregated basis.

AFFIRMATIVE ACTION PROGRAMS

Goodyear

Title VII of the Civil Rights Act of 1964 makes it an unlawful employment practice to fail or refuse to hire, or to discharge or otherwise discriminate against any individual with respect to his compensation, terms, conditions or privileges of employment because of race, color, religion, sex or national origin. It is unlawful to limit, segregate or classify employees in any way that would tend to deprive any individual of employment opportunities or otherwise adversely affect their status as an employee because of race, color, religion, sex or national origin. Executive Orders . . . further enunciate the National Policy advanced by Title VII in specifying that no federal contractor shall discriminate against employees or applicants for employment on the basis of race, color, religion, sex, or national origin. Under these provisions, the Company is required to take affirmative action to assure the absence of discrimination throughout the total employment process and further will post for all employees its Policy on non-discrimination.

Under these laws, jobs cannot be designated as male or female. If a person is qualified for any job, he or she must be considered for it. All managers will assume responsibility for seeing that this Policy is carried out in their respective departments. To accomplish an effective affirmative action program, the management and employees are committed to a set of specific and result-oriented goals and timetables to which good-faith efforts will be directed to eliminate any under-utilization of minorities and women throughout the Goodyear organization.

The Vice President Human Resources is responsible for the coordination of the Company's Affirmative Action Program. The direct responsibility for the implementation of this policy has been assigned to the Director, Equal Employment Opportunity. All assistance and support necessary for the control and execution of commitments made in the Affirmative Action Program shall be made available to that office.

EMPLOYMENT OF THE HANDICAPPED

SCE&G (Scana)

(A Policy Memorandum from the President and CEO of Scana).

It is a Company policy to provide equal employment opportunities for qualified handicapped individuals. The Company does not discriminate because of physical or mental handicaps. This policy applies to *all* employment practices including recruiting, hiring, training, compensation, benefits, transfers, promotions, layoffs, and terminations. Further, affirmative action steps are taken to employ and advance qualified handicapped individuals at all levels of employment. The Vice President-Personnel and Corporate Communications is responsible for developing and implementing the Company-wide plan for equal employment opportunities for the handicapped and its accompanying Affirmative Action Program. The Personnel Department enlists the assistance of all recruiting sources to find qualified handicapped individuals. The records of handicapped employees are reviewed periodically to determine whether their skills are being fully used.

Company employment practices are reviewed periodically to determine the effectiveness of the equal employment opportunities plan for the handicapped. The Personnel Department also prepares a monthly report for the Vice President-Personnel and Corporate Communications showing the number of handicapped individuals employed. An annual report is prepared, for individual senior management staff members, which reflects the total number of handicapped individuals employed for the year, highlights the accomplishments, and suggests remedies for deficiencies. This policy is communicated to employees, applicants, labor unions, subcontractors, and the public. This Company makes reasonable efforts to accommodate the limitations of handicapped employees or applicants, investigates complaints made by handicapped individuals regarding employment practices, and takes appropriate action.

Chapter 12

SEXUAL AND NON-SEXUAL HARASSMENT

At the Boston office of Goldman Sachs, a leading investment-banking firm, Kristine Utley was the only female sales associate in the money-market department. In a lawsuit she filed in 1987, Utley charged that the firm's environment was "hostile, intimidating and sexist." She alleged that the sexual harassment at Goldman included memos that announced the hiring of new female employees, with each memo containing a photograph of a naked pinup. Utley also described literature, routinely circulated at Goldman, containing sexist jokes. For example, the query "Why is beer better than a woman?" included the rejoinders, "a beer doesn't get jealous when you grab another beer" and "a beer always goes down easy." Meanwhile, at another firm's meeting of department heads, male managers tossed about a condom and made provocative comments in the presence of two female department heads.

Despite considerable progress in breaking down barriers to employment, many employees, primarily women, still encounter discrimination on the job in the form of sexual harassment. Men, too, have been harassed, and will be more prone to sexual harassment as greater numbers of women occupy supervisory and managerial positions. Moreover, homosexual harassment occurs, with equally distressing consequences to the victim.

One of the most significant changes in the labor market in the past decade has been the rising influx of women into the labor force. Some 60% of new employees entering the workforce are female. By the year 2000, more than 66% of new entrants will be women, and the problem of sexual harassment likely will be exacerbated. Some observers consider sexual harassment as tantamount to "corporate rape" and point to a multitude of cases in which male supervisors have offered jobs and promotions to women as inducements for sexual favors. In 1985, for example, 7,273 sexual-harassment complaints were filed with the Equal Employment Opportunity Commission (EEOC) for review, a prerequisite before a plaintiff can file a federal-court action under Title VII of the 1964 Civil Rights Act.

Consequently, firms that refuse to try to eliminate sexual harassment face lawsuits, disastrous public relations, negative publicity, and loss of business. For example, a 1989 *Forbes* survey indicates that in California, settlements for sexual harassment cases have averaged $300,000. For firms, the cost of harassments in monetary and personnel terms can be staggering. According to a Civil Service study, the federal government spent an estimated $267 million from 1985 to 1987 as a result of harassment. The money went (1) to replace harassed employees who had quit their jobs; (2) to pay sick leave to those who took absences to avoid harassments at work; and (3) to compensate for reduced productivity. In the private sector, meanwhile, the costs and losses from sexual and non-sexual harassments are much greater.

Non-sexual harassment in the workplace can be as demeaning, insidious, and destructive as sexual harassment. Like sexual harassment, non-sexual harassment inhibits productivity and morale and firms should never tolerate it. Examples of non-sexual harassment are the use of profane, abusive, or demeaning language; disorderly conduct such as fighting; causing physical harm to another; intimidation; any activity or speech that disrupts other employees; slurs or jokes in bad taste; and any activity or speech that discriminates against any employee on the basis of race, color, religion, sex, national origin, ancestry, marital status, age, handicap, or veteran status. Title VII and other statutory and constitutional protections have been extended to victims of nearly every type of non-sexual harassment, which are comparable to sexually offensive environment cases because, unlike quid pro quo harassment, the supervisor or manager does not use his authority to demand some act from the employee.

A firm's sole protection against liability is the prevention of harassment. And a working environment that is as free of harassments as possible is one that encourages greater productivity. By addressing sexual and non-sexual harassment in its code of business conduct, a firm can more effectively prevent or combat expensive lawsuits and negative publicity that could adversely affect sales of its goods and services. At the same time, the firm is better able to recruit talented persons of all races and sexes who want assurance that everyone has an opportunity for success.

The following excerpts from business codes of conduct show how several leading firms have addressed the sensitive issue of preventing harassments, including sexual harassment, in the workplace.

TREATMENT OF EMPLOYEES

BankAmerica

Our policy is that the workplace should be free of harassment. Harassment includes such things as: verbal harassment (e.g., derogatory comments, jokes, slurs); physical harassment (e.g., unwanted physical contact, assault); visual harassment (e.g., derogatory posters, cartoons or drawings); or sexual harassment (e.g., an unwanted or unwelcome sexual advance which is verbal, physical, or creates an offensive or hostile working environment). You should not tolerate such treatment. It is up to you to promptly notify management or go directly to Personnel Relations is you are being harassed. Where evidence of harassment is found, disciplinary action up to and including termination may result.

Scana

In order to maintain a professional environment, all employees are treated with respect and courtesy. The Corporation prohibits employee harassment because of race, sex, religion, national origin, age, handicap or similar distinction. Employees should report violations of this policy through the Corporate Grievance Procedure as outlined in [a procedure memorandum] . . . . All such reports are confidential and will receive a thorough and impartial investigation. Any employee violating this policy will be subject to disciplinary action, including dismissal, commensurate with the seriousness of misconduct. Questions concerning this policy can be directed to the Personnel Department.

First Wachovia

It is Wachovia's policy that an atmosphere of tension created either by racial, ethnic or religious remarks or by verbal or physical conduct, advances or threats of a sexual nature, will not be tolerated. Where any such verbal or physical conduct interferes with any individual's performance or creates an intimidating, hostile or offensive work environment, the offended individual should notify a supervisor or Personnel Officer so the appropriate corrective action can be taken.

Sara Lee

No employee, male or female, shall harass another employee by (1) making unwelcome or unsolicited sexual advances or requests for sexual favors, either explicitly or implicitly as a condition of an employee's continued employment with Sara Lee, (2) making submission to or rejection of such conduct the basis for employment decisions affecting the employee's evaluation, advancement, compensation, duties or other conditions of employment or career development or (3) creating an intimidating, hostile or offensive working environment by such conduct.

Premier

It is the policy of Premier to maintain a working environment free of all forms of sexual harassment. Sexually harassing conduct will result in disciplinary action, up to and including dismissal. Specifically, no supervisor shall threaten or insinuate, either explicitly or implicitly, that an employee's refusal to submit to sexual advances will adversely affect an employee's job, evaluation, wages, advancement, assigned duties, working schedule, or any other condition of employment or career development. Other sexual harassing conduct in the workplace, whether committed by supervisors or non-supervisory personnel, is also prohibited. Such acts include: repeated propositions, continued or repeated verbal abuse of a sexual nature, graphic verbal commentaries about an individual's body, sexual and degrading words used to describe an individual, and the display of suggestive objects or pictures.

It is the responsibility of any employee who is subjected to sexual harassment to inform the appropriate manager and Human Resources of the facts regarding such harassment so that appropriate corrective action may be taken. An employee who reports an incident of sexual harassment to management will be informed that an investigation of the alleged sexual harassment will be conducted and that appropriate corrective action will be taken by management.

Burlington Northern

The Company does not condone in the workplace sexual harassment or discrimination based on race, color, religion, age, sex, national origin, or handicap, or any other basis prohibited by applicable state law. No director, officer, or employee shall conduct himself or herself in a way that constitutes, or could be interpreted as discrimination or sexual harassment. Each employee is protected from sexual harssment by law and is expected to discuss with management any situation which could be interpreted as sexual harassment. This unlawful activity is a form of sex discrimination and will not be tolerated in the Company's workforce. Sexual harassment is defined to include (1) unwelcomed and repeated physical or verbal gestures of a sexual nature; or (2) making employment conditional upon providing sexual favors. One of our objectives is to provide each employee in the Company with an optimal work environment. Therefore, offensive or hostile working conditions created by sexual harassment cannot be allowed.

Each member of management has the responsibility to be aware of any behavior that could be interpreted as sexual harassment and take immediate steps to stop these actions. In addition, any complaints alleging sexual harassment are to be handled in a timely fashion . . . .

Central Bankshares of the South

No employee shall, by words or actions, sexually harass any other employee or in any way contribute to the creation of a workplace environment which may be perceived as sexually hostile. Because the acts which may constitute impermissible sexual harassment range from conditioning employment upon sexual cooperation to using sexually offensive language in the workplace, you are urged to exercise good judgment in your dealings with other employees. A professional attitude toward your job and your fellow employees is the best safeguard against any type of sexual discrimination or harassment.

AmeriFirst

Every AmeriFirst staff member is expected to maintain a high standard of personal honor and integrity; and every staff member has the right to expect similar standards of fellow workers. Staff members are required to avoid conduct toward a member of the opposite sex which could reasonably be construed as sexual harassment. If any staff member feels they have been sujected to sexual harassment, the staff member has an obligation to report the facts in accordance with the procedures as specified in . . . this policy or the Equity Procedure as described in [section] of the Personnel Manual.

ITT

Sexual harassment has no place in a professional business environment and will not be tolerated within the ITT System. You are responsible for taking measures designed to ensure that no one under your supervision is subjected to sexual harassment in any form.

Olin

The corporation does not condone and will not tolerate any form of sexual harassment, defined as any unwelcome sexual advances, requests for sexual favors and other verbal or physical conduct of a sexual nature, particularly where such harassment has the purpose or effect of in any manner interfering with an employee's employment relationship with the corporation or creating an intimidating, hostile or offensive working environment.

Chapter 13

SUBSTANCE ABUSE IN THE WORKPLACE

An imposing sign greets shoppers, employees, and job applicants alike at the main entrance of Home Depot stores in Florida. The sign's message is plain and direct: "NOTICE. We test all applicants for illegal drug use. If you use drugs, don't bother to apply."

Home Depot's stern warning is, in many ways, a sign of the times. Drug and alcohol abuse have become pervasive influences in the workplace. For example, according to Bureau of Labor Statistics data released in 1989, 3.9 million American employees in the private sector were screened for drugs, and 11.9% of them—more than 464,000—tested positive.

Alcohol figured prominently in the disastrous oil spill that occurred in Alaska's Prince William Sound after the tanker *Exxon Valdez* ran aground in 1989. Investigators found high levels of alcohol in the blood of the ship's captain, as well as in the blood of a Coast Guard radar operator assigned to cover the area where the spill occurred.

In recent years, many disquieting examples of narcotics abuse in the workplace have been discovered. For example, within two hours of employment at a nuclear power plant, an undercover investigator was able to purchase cocaine from a fellow employee. After a few month's investigation, eight employees were arrested for selling narcotics at the nuclear plant.

The illicit use of drugs and alcohol on the job has become as common as the coffee break—and it is costing American business dearly: billions of dollars annually, or about $800 for every employee. The annual loss in productivity from drug abuse alone is estimated at between $34 billion and $60 billion, and the estimated productivity losses from alcohol abuse is estimated at more than $50 billion.

There are further—and substantial—losses to businesses affected by drug and alcohol abuse among employees and managers. These losses are less easily quantified than production losses, but they include higher medical expenses, increased theft, poorer decision-making at all levels, more accidents and injuries, adverse effects on employees' morale, wasted material, work errors, poor product quality, and the necessity to train new workers to replace those lost to drug or alcohol abuse.

As a result, since drug and alcohol testing is legal in the private sector, firms are attacking the substance abuse problem by implementing testing and employee-assistance programs. Although a majority of firms have not yet implemented drug and alcohol testing programs, there is a pronounced upward trend. In 1983, only 3% of U.S. companies employed drug testing of any kind. By 1989, more than one-third of all American firms had established testing programs. Forty-nine percent of America's largest firms, including one-half of Fortune 500 firms, have either or both of these programs. IBM, which President Bush has singled out as a model for drug screening, began testing all job applicants in 1984. In 1986, IBM began testing employees who exhibited "unexplained changes in behavior" in the workplace.

A firm's code of conduct or ethics should include coverage of substance abuse in the workplace. These guidelines are necessary to safeguard the employer from lawsuits and to try to dissuade employees from engaging in drug or alcohol abuse on the job and away from the workplace, as well.

Additionally, many firms' codes also advise employees of programs inside or outside the company that offer relief from drugs, alcohol and other burdens that may affect job performance.

The following excerpts illustrate how some leading firms have addressed substance abuse, treatment programs, and conditions for employment in their respective codes. These excerpts can be used as guides for creating new or updated codes.

SUBSTANCE ABUSE, TREATMENT, AND CONDITIONS FOR EMPLOYMENT

Kimberly-Clark

In its code of conduct, Kimberly-Clark states that it is:
. . . committed to the health and fitness of our employees. We have pioneered programs to prevent illness by encouraging employees to manage their own health and fitness. We are also a leader in establishing a health management program to evaluate employees' health risks through medical screening and by prescribing exercise and educational activities to decrease these risks.

The possession, use, distribution or sale of illegal drugs on company premises and the use of alcoholic beverages by employees while performing their job responsibilities is prohibited except when the use of alcoholic beverages has been authorized at a company sponsored event.

We realize that problems stemming from drug and alcohol abuse, family and marital conflict, depression, stress, and financial and legal burdens may affect job performance. In response to these concerns, we have established confidential employee assistance programs for all United States and Canadian employees.

PPG

Every PPG associate, as a fundamental tenet of employment, owes the Company his or her best efforts on the job. PPG's people are its most valuable, as well as its most costly assets. The care, diligence and creative energy which individuals employed by PPG are expected to provide requires that every associate exercise reasonable care in matters concerning their personal health and well-being.

Deliberate abuse or neglect of the individual's health diminishes that person's value to the Company and therefore undermines the basis of this implicit arrangement. Accordingly, it is contrary to policy for anyone employed by the Company to impair their capabilities on the through the use of alcohol, drugs or other intoxicants. In addition to diminishing an employee's own work capability, the use of these substances can seriously jeopardize the safety of others and the welfare of the business. As a result, drug abuse is a matter of legitimate concern to PPG.

BankAmerica

BankAmerica strives to provide a safe work environment for its employees, as well as a safe business environment for its customers and clients. Therefore, the presence or use of illegal drugs or unauthorized alcohol on company premises will *not* be tolerated.

Illegal drugs, for the purpose of this policy, include drugs that are not legally obtainable but are used for illegal purposes. The sale, purchase, transfer, distribution, use, or possession of illegal drugs, as defined above, by anyone on company premises or conducting company business, is prohibited. Violation of this policy may result in dismissal.

Whenever the use of any drug, including alcohol, affects your job performance or safety, or interferes with the job performance or safety of others, BankAmerica may take disciplinary action, including dismissal. When non-prescribed or physician-directed drugs adversely affect an employee's job performance or the safety of others, it is in the best interest of the employee, co-workers, and the company that time off or other job arrangements be made, if possible.

BankAmerica also prohibits the unauthorized use or presence of alcoholic beverages on company premises. Employees who violate this policy may be subject to disciplinary action, including dismissal. The use or presence of alcoholic beverages on company premises may be approved by management *only* for the entertainment of customers or special business-related events.

BankAmerica reserves the right to take necessary action to maintain a safe work environment free of drugs and alcohol. Such action may include, but is not limited to, the right to inspect or search the following: company premises and/or property, personal property of employees, as well as other persons entering or leaving company premises, or any personal property found or maintained on company premises. (Personal property includes, but is not limited to, purses, packages, briefcases, and the contents of an employee's pockets.)

You are required to cooperate in company inspections, as well as to disclose personal items, as a condition of employment. Therefore, if you refuse to permit or cooperate in any inspection of company property or premises and/or of personal property found, maintained, or brought on or off company premises, you may be subject to disciplinary action, including dismissal.

U.S. Bancorp

While there is concern for the employee's well-being, Bancorp's concern with alcohol and drug-related problems is limited to their effect upon work performance, which includes the maintenance of a positive image in the community. Employees who suspect they have an alcohol, or drug-related problem, even in its early stages, are encouraged to call the Employee Relations Department or the Employee Assistance Program for confidential assistance.

Disciplinary action, including termination for the first offense, may result from the non-medical use of or activity with drugs, possession of alcohol, non-medical drugs or related paraphernalia during work hours or on Bancorp premises, or being under the influence of alcohol or the non-medical use of drugs during working hours, on or off Bancorp premises. Bancorp reserves the right to inspect all property brought onto its premises.

Ameritech

The use of any drug or controlled substance, including alcohol, interfering with safe and efficient job performance, is a matter of Company concern and will be dealt with in an appropriate manner.

The Company recognizes that drug or alcohol misuse is a serious problem, and has a rehabilitation program in the Illinois Bell Medical Department. Employees cooperating in a clinically supervised rehabilitation program may be eligible for benefits.

Possession, use, or working under the influence of alcohol or illegally obtained drugs on the job or on Company premises may be a cause for dismissal. In addition, dismissal may result from the improper selling of controlled substances to employees or others, whether on or off the job.

W.W. Grainger

Improper use of narcotics and other controlled substances, commonly referred to as illegal drugs, has become a significant problem to businesses, employees, and society in general. Their sale, use, and abuse, when connected to the conduct of business and the work environment, can threaten the safety, morale, and public image of both you and your Company. Because of our strong concerns in this area, we have established the following policy regarding illegal drugs:

1. No person will be hired who is known to be a promoter, user, or seller of illegal drugs.

2. Possession or use of illegal drugs on Company premises or during working hours, including break or meal periods, or working under the influence of illegal drugs, is strictly prohibited. Violation of this policy is cause for immediate disciplinary action, up to and including discharge.

3. An employee who is found to be a seller or involved in the sale, solicitation, or dealing of illegal drugs will be subject to immediate discharge from the Company.

It is the Company's policy to discourage the use of alcoholic beverages during business hours, including lunch. The possession or use of alcoholic beverages on Company premises, except for authorized functions, is prohibited. Reporting to work or performing one's job assignments under the influence of alcohol is cause for immediate disciplinary action, up to and including discharge.

DRUG AND ALCOHOL TESTING

Philips Industries, Inc.

(A) Pre-employment Testing. Consistent with the commitment to provide a drug- and alcohol-free work environment, Philips Industries, Inc., at its discretion, may require job applicants to submit to a pre-employment drug and alcohol screen. (B) Voluntary testing may be appropriate regarding routine physical examination, such as annual physicals, return to work physicals, and other job related circumstances. (C) Individual testing shall be required when there is reasonable suspicion that drugs or alcohol is affecting job performance and conduct in the workplace. (D) Any random, or surprise testing on a wholesale basis would be rarely used, and must be preceded by clear evidence of probable abuse by a large number of individuals within the group. (E) Employers engaged in the operation of vehicles, who as part of their transportation duties are required to be physically certified under DOT regulations, shall have an alcohol and controlled substance screen as a mandatory part of such physical examination. A negative result is required as a condition of continued employment.

All individuals to be tested must be advised of the purpose and possible consequences of the particular test. Every effort shall be made to insure confidentiality of test results.

REHABILITATION

Panhandle Eastern

The Panhandle Eastern Companies will seek to aid in the rehabilitation of employees who suffer from drug and alcohol abuse by: [1] Recognizing alcoholism and drug abuse as conditions which are treatable and which only the affected employee, with appropriate assistance, can control. [2] Offering employees with either of these conditions assistance in treatment and rehabilitation. [3] Recognizing that any action contemplated by the Companies in alcoholism or drug abuse cases should have the dual objectives of restoring the individual to a condition of health and usefulness to himself and his family and to restore his job performance to an acceptable level. [4] Relating continuation of employment to the taking of corrective action by the employee. Refusal to accept diagnosis and treatment or continued failure to respond to treatment will result in appropriate action by the employing Company, including possible termination.

Chapter 14

WORKPLACE SAFETY, CONSUMER PROTECTION, AND PRODUCT QUALITY

In the past two decades, safety in the workplace, consumer protection, and product quality have become serious national issues in the United States. The reasons are not hard to discern, when you consider a few statistics and trends.

For example, despite 20 years of workplace safety enforcement by the Occupational Safety and Health Administration (OSHA), many deaths and disabling injuries still occur on the job. Estimates of the combined number of fatalities and injuries each year vary, however. They range from the Bureau of Labor Statistics' (BLS) figure of 5.75 million employees to the National Institute of Occupational Safety and Health (NIOSH) tally of more than 10 million. The economic costs of workplace injuries and deaths, meanwhile, are staggering. For example, losses from workplace accidents have increased from about $8 billion in 1970 to about $50 billion in 1990.

Each year, 20 million Americans suffer injuries and about 30,000 die as a result of consumer-product incidents. Another 5 million persons are injured and about 30,000 are killed each year in vehicular accidents.

Also each year, about 110,000 product-liability suits are tried in federal district courts, and product quality is a key focal point in many of these battles.

Meanwhile, the issue of consumer protection gained widespread attention in the 1960s, and three decades later, consumer distrust of business persists. In one recent public-opinion survey, only 19% of the respondents agreed that business attempts to strike a fair balance between profits and the public interest.

Despite the creation of numerous laws and government agencies to regulate business conduct, the American public clearly has grown more and more dissatisfied with the response to the need for better workplace safety, more consumer protection, and higher-quality products. As one commentator noted in 1989: "Increasingly, people see grave risks in the most basic elements of their lives: their food, their water, even the air they breathe." That concern, of course, stays with them while they work, shop for consumer goods, or judge the quality of what they have purchased.

Faced with these statistics, mounting concerns, and rising number of lawsuits, firms in the 1990s must make stronger, clearer commitments to safety on the job, protection of consumers, and the quality of the goods and services they produce. Obviously, labor and management must cooperate to promote a safer, healthier work environment, and both must realize that it is individual attitudes and psychology, as much as safe equipment and work areas, that helps reduce accidents. Better consumer protection, meanwhile, will require a higher awareness of, and adherence to, a substantial number of laws, regulations, and guidelines that regulate business and protect consumers from unsavory or unfair practices in the marketplace. And a renewed emphasis on higher product quality is vital.

One important place to address these issues is in the firm's code of business conduct. Along with ethical responses, of course, the ways firms face these issues also will be shaped by federal and state laws and regulatory agencies. For example, the Occupational Safety and Health Administration, located in the Department of Labor, has broad legislative and executive powers to establish and enforce standards related to health and safety in the workplace through workplace inspections, citations and monetary penalties; to institute required record-keeping procedures for employers to implement; and to collaborate with the states in developing their respective health and safety programs. The National Institute for Occupational Safety and Health, meanwhile, is an agency in the Department of Health and Human Services that (1) conducts research to promulgate health and safety standards and regulation through OSHA, (2) provides education and training programs, and (3) can inspect workplaces and gather evidence and testimony from employers and employees. Furthermore, the Occupational Safety and Health Review Commission (OSHRC), an independent agency consisting of three commissioners—appointed by the president—and 45 administrative-law judges, has the mission to handle appeals from employers concerning violations and penalties resulting from OSHA inspections. Under the Consumer Products Safety Act of 1972, the federal Consumer Product Safety Commission is empowered to issue and enforce safety standards relating to safe performance, composition, contents, design, construction, finish, or packaging of more than 10,000 consumer products. Further the commission has authority, in case of a potential danger in a product's use, to require that the product be "marked with or accompanied by clear and adequate warnings or instructions," and is empowered to declare that the product is a banned hazardous product, if the commission deems the public is not adequately protected.

Other regulatory agencies focus on specific products and goods. For example, the National Highway Traffic Safety Administration establishes standards for motor-vehicle safety, fuel economy and emission standards, while the Food and Drug Administration serves to protect the public against impure and unsafe foods, drugs, and cosmetics and regulates hazards involved with medical devices and radiation.

Firms of the 1990s must address the issue of workplace safety, consumer protection and product quality with comprehensive guidelines in their codes of business conduct. The following excerpts reflect how some leading firms have tackled these complex issues in their codes.

HEALTH AND SAFETY IN THE WORKPLACE

Westinghouse

Westinghouse recognizes its responsibility to provide employees a safe and healthful workplace and proper facilities to help the employees do the job effectively.

It is the policy of Westinghouse to: [1] Provide safe and healthful working environments and to reduce occupational injuries and illness. [2] Install and maintain all facilities and equipment in accordance with recognized and accepted standards essential to the protection of employees. [3] Reduce to the extent reasonably possible, the use of materials, procedures or processes that expose employees to substances that are potentially toxic, flammable or radioactive, or to other potentially hazardous conditions. [4] Provide not only the employee medical services required by law but also additional medical services that are consistent with circumstances of each organizational unit, reflect good medical practice, and that may be reasonably be expected to benefit the employee and Westinghouse. [5] Assure compliance by all locations with both the spirit and intent of national, international, state and local legislation and governmental regulations providing for occupational health and safety.

PPG

Assuring the health and safety of PPG personnel is a top corporate priority, worldwide. PPG's strategy for achieving that objective is to provide safe and healthful conditions on the job, to protect our plant communities against undesirable effects resulting from industrial processes, and to promote safety off the job for our associates and their families.

An important component of this strategy is assuring that both our own personnel and those living near us are clearly informed about the nature of the materials used at our facility. This includes briefing Company personnel on appropriate safety and preventive measures as well as alerting them to the appropriate emergency steps in the event of accidental contact with those materials. The exact nature of such hazard communications will vary with each facility and reflect its unique operating circumstances.

It is PPG's goal to completely eliminate the incidence of work-related illness or injury. To achieve that goal, the Company has developed a series of emergency response procedures as well as corporate-wide policies related to the safe operation of PPG's equipment, the proper handling of materials, limits on exposure to potentially hazardous substances, and other matters affecting employee health and safety on the job.

Coors

Coors Industries will conduct its business in such a manner that employees, potential employees and the community will consider it a desirable employer for which to work. Wages, salaries and benefits will be competitive. A work environment will be maintained that demands excellence and rewards accomplishment. Operations will be conducted with the highest regard for employee health and safety.

Meridian

Every effort is made by Meridian to provide all employees with a work environment which is comfortable, pleasant, and secure. It is the intent of the management of Meridian to detect, eliminate, or correct conditions which do not promote that kind of environment. However, employees are also responsible to themselves to provide for their own safety and to be aware of potential hazards and the Company or department's procedures in the event a threatening situation should occur. Employees should call the supervisor's attention to conditions which create an unsafe environment. The cooperation of all employees in the Company's safety effort will assist immeasurably in accomplishing the Company's safety goals.

BellSouth

While the company is obligated to furnish a safe working environment, employees are responsible for following all company safety and health rules. This ensures compliance with all rules, regulations, and orders issued under the Occupational Safety and Health Act (OSHA) of 1970 that apply to an individual employee's actions and conduct.

All employees must: [1] wear the required personal protection equipment on the job, including mandatory use of seat belts while driving or riding in any company vehicle; [2] report hazardous conditions to ensure that deficiencies are corrected promptly; [3] report to their immediate supervisor or another management employee any job-related injury or illness on the same day that such injury or illness occurs; [4] know emergency procedures and telephone numbers that are applicable for their building. These procedures and telephone numbers will be furnished to employees by their supervisors.

Any questions regarding employees' obligation under company health and safety rules should be referred to their supervisors. Employees guilty of violating these procedures may be subject to disciplinary action which could include dismissal.

Olin

Olin's policy is to provide a safe workplace for its employees and to insist on safe work practices. Employees who endanger the safety of themselves, other employees, or neighbors of Olin property will be disciplined or discharged. In addition, Olin charges all of its employees to comply with all applicable federal, state and local laws and regulations relating to the protection of the environment.

Cincinnati Bell

The Company has a responsibility to provide a work environment in which safe operations can be achieved in accomplishing all phases of work. Employees have a responsibility to exercise care and to perform work operations in accordance with the Company's safety rules and regulations. Employees who violate safety practices pose a threat not only to themselves, but also to other employees and the public.

In using Company vehicles or vehicles rented for Company purposes, safe driving practices and all traffic laws are to be observed. Under no circumstances is such a vehicle to be operated while the driver is under the influence of alcohol, drugs, or controlled substances. Also in our work on customer premises or on streets, alleys and highways, we are to show respect for the rights and safety of the public.

Allied-Signal

It is the policy of this Corporation to design, manufacture and distribute all products, and to handle and dispose of all materials, safely and without creating unacceptable risks to health, safety or the environment. We will stop manufacturing or distributing any product, or carrying out any operation, whose environmental risks or costs are unacceptable.

We will adhere to all applicable environmental laws and regulations. Where laws do not exist or are not adequately protective, we will adopt our own standards.

To carry out this policy, managers will: [1] Identify and control any hazards stemming from operations or products. [2] Conduct prevention and control programs to safeguard employees and the public. [3] Conduct research about the health, safety and environmental effects of materials handled in the Corporation, and share promptly any significant findings with others, such as employees, suppliers, customers, government agencies or the scientific community. [4] Work with government and other organizations to develop realistic laws, regulations and standards to protect the public.

Every employee is expected to adhere to the spirit as well as the letter of this policy. Employees have a special obligation to advise management promptly of any adverse situation that comes to their attention.

International Paper

It is long-standing policy at International Paper to comply with all laws and regulations concerning the environment and the workplace. Federal, state and local laws—which can include civil or criminal liabilities—may be enforced against operating managers who had actual knowledge of a violation and failed to correct it. Likewise, any employee who delays or fails to pass on to his or her supervisor information regarding possible environmental violations which could create a significant risk to health or the environment may also be liable. Additionally, substantial fines and other penalties can be assessed against International Paper.

Accordingly, if you are in a position to affect environmental or workplace compliance in any way, it is essential that you become familiar with the permits, laws, and regulations which apply to the operations in which you are involved, and that you comply with them. If you have any questions in this regard, promptly consult your manager or the Corporate Environmental Department, the Health Department, or the Industrial Hygiene Department.

WORKPLACE SMOKING POLICY

Bank of America

In all locations, employees must not smoke while serving customers or while working in areas visible to the public during normal business hours. Smoking is also prohibited in areas where records or supplies—such as cleaning fluids, other flammable liquids, or equipment—would be exposed to hazard from fire, ashes, or smoke; and where combustible fumes can collect—such as in garage, maintenance and storage areas—and all other areas where smoking would create a safety hazard.

In addition, smoking is prohibited in libraries, medical facilities, elevators, stairwells, copy rooms, and *any areas* where smoking is prohibited by local ordinance.

In areas with local ordinances regulating smoking in the workplace, managers are expected to find a reasonable accommodation between the non-smoker and the smoker in BankAmerica buildings and facilities. When the preferences of the non-smoker and the smoker conflict, and a reasonable accommodation is not possible, non-smokers will be given preference and smoking will be prohibited in that work area. In cases where smoking is prohibited in the work area, efforts will be made to accommodate smoking in a non-work area.

Disciplinary action may be taken, as necessary, to ensure adherence to smoking policies.

PUBLIC SAFETY

Florida Progress

The safety of the public and our employees is of paramount importance. In support of this belief, we will: Adhere to the philosophy that no part of the service we render shall ever become so important that it will endanger the life of an employee [and] Sponsor safety programs that emphasize the importance of safety to our employees and the general public.

PRODUCT SAFETY AND QUALITY

Goodyear

Once again you are reminded of our Company Policy on Product Quality & Safety. Our jobs—and the well-being of our Company—are closely related to our ability to provide products that are not only useful but are durable, reliable and dependable.

There are a number of public laws that define our obligations. The most important to Goodyear is the National Traffic and Motor Vehicle Safety Act, which regulates tires and all other products that are used on motor vehicles. Another important law is the Consumer Product Safety Act which regulates nearly all consumer products including many items of merchandise sold through our company-owned stores. These laws make it illegal for Goodyear and its subsidiaries to make or sell a product that is unsafe.

No matter what your job is—salesman or secretary, repairman or researcher, tire builder or trainee—you share the responsibility of immediately reporting to your superior whenever you know—or even suspect—that a Goodyear product is unsafe or inferior.

The rule of thumb is this: If you have the slightest doubt, report it to your superior, who, in turn, has the responsibility of reporting the information to the Quality Assurance Manager having direct responsibility for the product in question. The Quality Assurance Manager must report such an event to the Office of Product Quality and Safety in Akron. A safety-related defect is admittedly difficult to define. A generally accepted rule is that a product defect that creates a risk of injury to anyone is considered a safety-related defect.

The Office of Product Quality and Safety was established to insure compliance to corporate requirements, customer specification, and government regulatory standards.

Our obligation does not end at the Nation's borders. If we import a product, it is subject to U.S. product safety laws the moment it arrives in the United States. We must be as scrupulous abroad as we are at home in observing any foreign product safety law that affects our international sales or manufacturing operations.

In all our relationships, we strive to act as responsible corporate citizens in matters or product quality and safety.

You are directed to give complete dedication to this policy.

Westinghouse

Westinghouse recognizes its responsibility to provide safe products that meet its customers' needs. Acceptance of this responsibility is essential to preserve the confidence of customers, retain their business, compete successfully in the marketplace and insure compliance with laws, regulations and standards governing product safety.

It is the continuing policy of Westinghouse to provide products which: [1] Meet applicable laws and regulations and industry standards. [2] Are safe for their normally intended uses. [3] Are properly labeled and accompanied by appropriate instruction materials.

The quality of Westinghouse products, services and operations affects our reputation, productivity, profitability and market position. The Westinghouse goal is to be the total quality leader for the products and services we offer and to create the conditions that allow and encourage each employee to do every job right the first time.

PPG

Assuring the safety of our products and minimizing the risk of product-related injury to our customers is critical to PPG's welfare, wherever we operate. Those products which enter the food chain, are typically required by law to undergo extensive safety testing. PPG is committed to conducting those tests in full compliance with the spirit as well as the letter of the law.

As a matter of policy, PPG will not manufacture or market any product which is incapable of being handled safely. In the case of those products which carry significant risks of injury from mishandling, clear and relevant safety information must be provided with the product. We are committed to protecting our customers and our Company against the harmful consequences of unsafe products or product packaging. Therefore every PPG product is to be appropriately labeled in relation to any reasonably foreseeable hazard that the product may pose to people, property or to the environment. Additionally, no one employed by PPG shall authorize the shipment of a product known to be defective, unsafe or unsuited for its intended use.

Each PPG business unit has developed safety policies and procedures related to its own operations. Additionally, PPG's corporate *Product Safety Policy* provides detailed guidelines to assure company-wide consistency in the handling of similar products.

Proctor & Gamble

Company documents have detailed the general principles of our product safety policy. In brief: . . . our products shall be safe for humans and the environment when used as intended and under conditions of reasonable foreseeable misuse; . . . our safety testing program must provide practical assurance of safety for the products we sell; . . . our programs must be based on an expanding scientific understanding of our products and their components, and input from leading consultants shall be used to ensure that latest scientific judgment is reflected in both our research and our safety conclusions; . . . any research involving animals shall be done only when no equally predictive alternative testing methods are available, or when required by law, and then such testing will be conducted under professional supervision so as to provide for the humane treatment of all animals and to minimize the numbers used; . . . findings which contribute to the world's scientific knowledge will be submitted for publication to leading journals.

In the conduct of safety research, it is essential that we adhere to high professional standards for such research in order to assure the Company and the consumer of the best possible safety judgments.

All employees associated with safety research have a responsibility to see that experiments meet the highest scientific standards of design, conduct, documentation and reporting.

Of equal importance is the responsibility of both manager and scientist to ensure that all responsible views are included in the evaluation of safety data. Managers must avoid actions which in any way discourage or tend to suppress the free exchange of views.

JC Penney

Products sold by the Company must not only meet all applicable safety standards set by law, they must also meet our often more stringent Company standards. It is Company policy not to handle knowingly any defective product and to minimize as much as possible hazards from products which inherently entail some risks. The reputation and success of our Company has been built upon the performance of our products. Our customers have a right to expect that our products will not endanger their health or safety in any way.

Unisys

Unisys is committed to developing, manufacturing and delivering quality products which meet all contractual obligations and Unisys quality standards. We will not deliver products that: (1) are made from lower quality materials than those ordered, (2) are not properly tested, (3) contain foreign-made materials when domestic materials are specified, or (4) otherwise fail to meet contract specifications.

Parker-Hannifin

Strict product integrity is necessary for Parker to achieve its quality objectives and to maintain its reputation for quality products. All Parker products must conform to all the requirements, specifications, and standards required by internal or outside customers. It is Parker policy to never willfully conceal defective work or material, intentionally falsify records or make false certifications of claims regarding its products. In some instances, particularly in connection with Government contracts or subcontracts, it is necessary for employees to make specific product certifications, generate records and supply other information or statements concerning product integrity. It is unlawful to intentionally falsify such records for the purpose of misleading or defrauding the Government or any other customer.

All employees are responsible to insuring the integrity of the Parker products under their control and for the accuracy of the documentation supporting product integrity. Incidents of suspected intentional concealment of defective work or material or falsification of records should be immediately reported to supervision.

Colgate Palmolive

We set the highest standards for our products. We are committed to ensuring that consumers can continue to trust Colgate products for their reliability, quality and superior performance. In addition, to serve the more than 3.5 billion people in the markets where we do business, we must constantly strive to produce our products in the most efficient way possible so that they are affordable to the greatest number of consumers.

Products sold by Colgate must not only meet all safety standards set by law but also our often more stringent Company standards. We participate in programs to provide prompt assistance to consumers in case of product tampering or misuse. Consumer health, safety and well being are of paramount concern to us.

We can best achieve our objectives and serve the needs of consumers by following a consistent, fair and sensitive program of consumer communication.

We recognize the importance of anticipating and assuring responsiveness to consumer needs and preferences in our products. We also believe that consumer opinions, concerns and inquiries communicated to the Company regarding our products are important sources of information. Consumer needs are constantly changing. So we must continually listen to what people want and use our creativity to satisfy these changing needs.

When a consumer expresses dissatisfaction, we address the problem promptly, courteously and fairly and make every reasonable effort to sustain or regain the consumer's goodwill and his or her continued purchase of Colgate products.

Weyerhaeuser

Products produced, marketed and/or distributed by any elements of the company must conform to the standards for such product established by independent industry associations and grading bureaus, customs of the trade, or agreed upon customer specifications. Products which fail to meet such standards or specifications will not be knowingly cleared for sale or distribution unless the customer is specifically told the product is off-grade.

INSPECTION AND TESTING

TRW

Product inspection and testing is the lifeblood of our operations, whether for spacecraft, electronics, or computer software. Those involved in the inspection and testing process must: make sure our products and services meet all contractual specifications and inspection criteria; perform all tests required by contract or otherwise necessary to ensure that all products delivered meet all contractual requirements; and provide the customer with documentation that is complete and accurate.

Remember the customer has a right to expect, and the company has an obligation to ensure, that all products meet all contractual requirements.

Sun Microsystems

To reduce delivery times to our customers and lower inventory levels, Sun has adopted just-in-time and total quality-control production programs. Sun's suppliers play a key role in the success of these programs, whose goal is to certify a supplier's product as receivable at Sun with a minimum amount of inspection and/or testing.

Sun's development process ensures that as Sun reaches production volumes, each supplier reaches a defect-free status. To maintain this objective requires a Defect Free Program that constantly reduces the defect rate of Sun products. Key elements in this program are: [1] Prompt corrective action to eliminate defects that Sun and the supplier have verified that affect the functionality and/or reliability of the product. [2] Ongoing documentation of critical process points in the supplier's manufacturing process to ensure continued process control. [3] Ongoing reliability testing of production samples.

Upjohn

Any employee who believes that a side effect or potential adverse drug reaction associated with an Upjohn product or product candidate may need corporate attention should bring his or her concerns to the attention of the Senior Vice President for Scientific Administration.

Eaton

Quality is more than just a high priority at Eaton—it is one of the cornerstones of our corporate reputation. Eaton is committed to producing high quality products and services. Making quality a high priority in your daily work is an important component of individual integrity.

Our quality program includes a well-developed series of quality guidelines that focus on fault prevention rather than detection; a full commitment to Statistical Process Control by the company and its suppliers; training programs to reach every level of the company; continuous monitoring to ensure that the process works effectively; and survey teams to provide feedback. A commitment to quality also requires that Eaton products be designed and manufactured to meet our obligations to our customers. That includes making sure that all inspection and testing is complete and correctly performed, and that all record documents containing those results are accurate, truthful and properly maintained.

As a corporation, we are committed to providing our customers with quality products. It is individual dedication to excellence that permits us to honor that commitment.

If you have questions about your ethical responsibilities in this area, ask your supervisor.

Chapter 15

ETHICS IN MARKETING AND ADVERTISING

Many successful companies, such as Hewlett Packard, Delta and 3M, share a common devotion: excellence in design and application of their marketing concepts. In these companies, marketing is concerned not merely with selling, but with satisfying customers' needs.

"Marketing," according to noted commentator Philip Kotler, "is a social and managerial process by which individuals and groups obtain what they need and want through creating and exchanging products and value with others." The importance of marketing has grown as society has become more affluent. The fact that marketing visibility contributes enormously to customer patronage also presents a risk. When marketers and firms engage in deceptive or questionable practices, they also jeopardize company image, goodwill, and ultimately their existence. Critics assert that marketing contrives consumer demand, and that production creates, rather than satisfies, the urgency of wants. Moreover, as another prod to marketers' proper conduct, government is an omnipresent force, ready to be directed by political forces to further regulate the marketing system.

Advertising—the use of media to present products and services—is an essential and visible element in marketing. In 1989, firms spent more than $128 billion, up from $102 billion in 1986, on advertising in the United States.

Because of the public's concern for an economic system that efficiently communicates accurate and complete information about products and services, government regularly intervenes in the marketing and advertising, and the Food and Drug Administration prohibits the distribution of misbranded, unsafe or adulterated food and drugs.

In a survey reported in *Harvard Business Review*, substantial majorities of the respondents indicated that firms should eliminate untruthful or misleading ads (91% of respondents), establish and enforce a code of ethics (65%), upgrade the intellectual level of ads (62%), and increase the information content of ads (59%).

One vehicle a firm can use to address these concerns is its code of business conduct. Measures can be added to ensure proper marketing activities. These measures should spell out the firm's ethical and policy stances on important issues such as: proper marketing practices; refraining from unfair use of corporate size; selling and marketing; marketing relationships; selling against competitive orders; and accurate advertising and promotion.

PROPER MARKETING PRACTICES

Allied-Signal

The Company expects integrity in the conduct of all aspects of marketing. For example, employees are expected to: [1] Communicate clearly with customers to ensure understanding of contractual obligations. [2] Ensure that oral and written proposals relay clear and precise information on performance, cost and schedules. [3] Ensure that normal marketing practices such as data gathering and dissemination are proper and legal. No employee shall attempt to obtain or use classified Government or sensitive procurement information from any source where there is reason to believe the release of such information is unauthorized. [4] Ensure that all marketing expenditures are job related, necessary and prudent.

Boeing

The Boeing products and services must be marketed on their merits. The use of deceptive or misleading statements, or attempts to induce individuals to place their personal interests above those of the companies or organizations they represent, is a violation of Company policy. Attempts to improperly restrict competition, induce a competitor or customer to breach a contract with a third party, or secure an unfair competitive advantage, or activities that may violate any laws or regulations or embarrass or damage the reputation of The Boeing Company, are prohibited.

Proper marketing practices must emphasize the quality, service, price, and similar competitive factors of the Company's products and services. They should focus on providing accurate information to our customers to enable them to make informed decisions, and must in no way be designed to induce employees or representatives of our customers to place their personal interests above the interests of the firms or organization they represent. Marketing activities that could cause embarrassment to The Boeing Company, its employees, or its customers also are prohibited as a matter of Company policy, regardless of the justifications for such activities. To this end, employees of the Company may use only legal, ethical, and proper methods to maintain markets for the Company's products and services and to secure additional business.

Lockheed

All marketing and related practices that infringe on business ethics or could cause embarrassment to Lockheed are strictly forbidden, and violations will not be tolerated. Employees are responsible for adhering to ethical behavior, regardless of any perceived justification for deliberate infractions.

REFRAINING FROM UNFAIR USE OF SIZE

IBM

IBM has achieved its size through legitimate business success over many years. And there is certainly no need to apologize for it. That said, you should never use the fact of IBM's size to intimidate or threaten another person or organization. In other words, do not throw IBM's weight around in dealing with other companies, organizations or the public. However, there is nothing wrong with citing legitimate advantages that accrue from our size—as long as such assertions are accurate and free from misleading statements. For example, it is permissible to discuss the advantages that derive from large-scale buying, selling, servicing and manufacturing. Whenever you are discussing any aspects of our size, you should make sure that your statements are accurate and relevant, and not misleading. For example, you may discuss IBM's national service coverage or the broad range of our product offerings as long as such references are accurate and relevant in demonstrating IBM's capability to meet a particular customer's need.

SELLING AND MARKETING

Boise Cascade

The company's marketing practices emphasize the quality, service, price, and competitive factors of the company's products and services. Accurate information about the company's products and services or those of our competitors may be provided to our customers to enable them to compare our products and services to the products and services of our competitors. It is not ethical business practice and, in fact, may be illegal to falsely criticize a competitor's products or services. From a practical as well as an ethical viewpoint, marketing that emphasizes the positive aspects of our products and services rather than the negative aspects of a competitor's is normally more successful. Of course, employees must not engage in illegal or improper methods to maintain or obtain markets for the company. Realistic proposals on performance, cost, and scheduling should be submitted to customers based upon our understanding of their requirements, and the company's contractual obligations should be clearly defined. The company will honor its commitments and will expect customers to honor theirs.

Pioneer Hi-Bred

The third point in our formula is: "We try to advertise and sell our product vigorously but without misrepresentation." It has always been a source of great satisfaction to us to know that we really do have something to talk about when we advertise and sell Pioneer products. Some high pressure salesmen have learned how to sell practically worthless products. All of us have watched the glib talkers at the state fair sell fancy gadgets for peeling potatoes or for increasing gas mileage on your car. Thanks to the science and application of genetics, we have the kind of products that do not need that kind of salesmanship.

When we write a catalog or an ad for magazine, newspaper or radio, or when we are selling face to face, we want to picture our products as they are, without misrepresentation. It may be easier to get the order today by overselling, but future business will come much harder. For instance, for many years Pioneer catalogs have rated the various Pioneer varieties for important economic characteristics. Each variety has its strong points and its weaknesses. All are shown. We are willing to admit that the perfect variety is yet to be developed and that any variety of ours has a weakness. Over much of the Corn Belt, we are selling seed corn to nearly one-half of the farmers. We sell it year in and year out. Farmers recommend us to their children. We are recommended to farmers moving into the community. Our long time success in selling Pioneer products is in large part due, we believe, to our policy of advertising vigorously but without misrepresentation.

MARKETING RELATIONSHIPS

Eaton

Eaton supports vigorous competition. We believe that enduring customer relationships are based on integrity and trust. We seek to gain advantage over competitors only through superior research, engineering, manufacturing and marketing. It is our intention to win business through excellent products and services, never through unethical or questionable business practices.

It is contrary to Eaton's policy to pursue any business that would require you to engage in unethical or illegal activity to gain it. Likewise, customers should not be given preferential treatment—such as unauthorized services or special contract terms—unless they are approved in advance by management. Our marketing activities must not entice representatives of customers to place their own personal interests above those of the organizations they represent. In commercial business areas, for example, it would violate company policy to give an expensive gift to a contact at a customer company—even if the budget can handle it. And, in our government business areas, we cannot offer or give *anything* of value to government employees. Take care not to make any deceptive or misleading statement. All information we provide about Eaton products and services should be factual.

On defense-related projects, be particularly alert to soliciting, accepting or possessing classified information for which you are not authorized. Simply put, don't do it. If you are authorized to have access to classified information, know and follow the rules for handling such information to the letter. Basic honesty is the key to ethical behavior. Trustworthiness in the marketplace is essential to building solid and lasting relationships with either commercial or government customers. If you have questions about your ethical responsibilities in this area, ask your supervisor.

SELLING AGAINST COMPETITIVE ORDERS

IBM

If a competitor already has a firm order from a customer for an application, it is IBM practice not to market IBM products or services for that application before it is installed. What is a "firm order"? Letters of intent, free trials, conditional agreements and similar arrangements usually are not considered firm orders; unconditional contracts are. Generally, if a firm order does not exist, you may sell to that customer. However, this is a complicated subject, and as a result it is often difficult to determine if a firm order actually exists. When a situation is unclear, seek advice from your marketing practices, business practices or legal department.

ACCURATE ADVERTISING AND PROMOTION

Proctor & Gamble

In every country in which we operate, Proctor & Gamble expects the advertising and promotion of its brands to be effective with consumers, but also to be truthful and in good taste. These are essential tenets of our dedication to consumers and essential to gaining and keeping their continuing loyalty to our brands. The principle of honesty is paramount. It is a basic operating principle of the Company and should never be compromised.

Simply put, neither deceptive advertising nor questionable promotional activity can ever be justified, regardless of potential short-term business gains. Since "good taste" is essentially a subjective matter, thoughtful judgment and attention are necessary to avoid advertising or promotional activity that is likely to offend the public's sense of decency. Of course, the public's "taste" changes with the passage of time. We must stay abreast of such changes in order to make good decisions in these matters. Good taste and honesty—both in fact and in spirit—are imperative. Employees should never compromise either.

Colgate Palmolive

One of the most important aspects of our business is advertising our products. Advertising should be creative and competitive but at the same time honest and not misleading. Our advertising must avoid any stereotyping of individuals based on factors such as age, sex, race or religion. Advertising creates more than a product image. It creates our reputation for reliability, dependability and trustworthiness. In addition, we exercise care in the selection of the programs on which our television commercials air. We do not permit our commercials to be shown on programs which make gratuitous or excessive use of violence or sex or are antisocial or in bad taste.

We observe standards of commercial fairness in devising, using and selecting advertising and trademarks, so that our products succeed on the strength of their own quality and reputation, rather than by imitation or trading on the good will of competitors. Commercial fairness implies: Strict adherence to local legal requirements respecting trademark infringement and unfair competition [and] avoiding copying of well-known trademarks, slogans, advertising themes and graphics used by multinational companies outside of your locality.

JC Penney

Advertising used by the Company is legally required to be true and not deceptive in any manner. All product claims must be substantiated by supporting data before they are made. We must be careful to assure that the Penney customer is not disappointed by claims for our products which are not supported by performance. The purpose of our advertising has always been to emphasize the quality of our products and the fairness of our prices. We believe that a properly informed customer will be a loyal Penney customer.

Texas Instruments

TI's reputation for integrity is a priceless asset and the result of continuous effort by all of us. The truth, well told, must be the objective of all of our promotional efforts. A momentary advantage gained through even slight misrepresentation or exaggeration can jeopardize our future success. This applies to our personal discussions with others about TI as well as to our promotional effort. TI's reputation is completely in our hands, to be enhanced or damaged by the nature of our actions.

Wells Fargo

Wells Fargo makes clear and accurate statements in its marketing and advertising. Advertising and marketing brochures contain sufficient information to enable informed decisions to be made. Whenever features, terms or prices are presented, the presentation is not misleading.

Chapter 16

COMPLIANCE WITH ANTITRUST LAWS

As society has become more complex, government rule-making, in the form of statutes, regulations, and ordinances, has become more pervasive. Laws that apply to all members of society, such as prohibitions against defamation, slander, murder, and larceny, also apply to employees of businesses. Other laws, such as antitrust statutes, apply to individuals and firms in the context of employment and their economic activities.

The objectives of antitrust laws are to foster free enterprise, the hallmark of the American economic system, by protecting and nurturing business competition. The antitrust laws help ensure that the results of market forces are not adulterated by unfair and predatory business practices. By protecting vigorous competition in purchasing and selling, fair competition laws have allowed the business sector to flourish. Even though such laws enhance the firm's chance for success, almost every leading corporation has violated the law at one time or another, often because of ignorance and poor judgment by managers and employees.

In the minds of many business people, antitrust laws apply only to the activities of huge firms. Yet, there are very few areas of economic activity that are beyond the potential reach of antitrust laws. These regulations can affect anything from the operation of a local restaurant to the business dealings of foreign firms acting at the behest of their governments. Antitrust regulation has become a prominent feature of every manager's environment.

There are four major antitrust and trade-regulation laws: the Sherman Act, Clayton Act, Federal Trade Commission Act, and Robinson-Patman Act. Additionally, most states have enacted antitrust and trade-regulation statutes that mirror the federal acts. State laws regulate behavior in intrastate commerce while federal laws regulate behavior in interstate commerce. In most cases, the state laws are generally satisfied by compliance with federal laws.

Antitrust violations can result in very serious consequences. First of all, criminal violations of the Sherman Act are felonies, punishable, in the case of a corporation, by fines up to $1 million for each offense; and, in the case of an individual, by fines up to $100,000, and by a prison term as long as three years for each offense. Second, all firms, customers, competitors, or other persons who suffer injury by a Sherman Act violation, or by certain Clayton Act violations, may recover treble damages, essentially three times the amount of any actual damage. Third, violations of the laws or FTC regulations usually result in sanctions, including injunctions, which are enforced by monetary penalties and contempt of court proceedings, and divestments. The scope of the injunctions, usually broad, can impair a firm's ability to remain competitive in a market or industry.

Every manager and employee must know enough about applicable laws to determine when it is appropriate to seek advice from more knowledgeable individuals, such as the firm's legal advisers.

Almost every firm, especially those that market products and services in any manner, face potential exposure under antitrust laws and must develop antitrust compliance programs.

The following excerpts show how some major firms have attempted to encourage compliance with the antitrust laws of the United States through their codes of business conduct. The example from Becton Dickinson is particularly notable because it contains basic definitions of the major antitrust laws, as well as descriptions of how they apply to the firm's business environment.

ANTITRUST COMPLIANCE

Becton Dickinson

The antitrust laws are among the most important ever enacted in the United States in terms of setting the rules of commerce in a free economy within a free society. Their purpose is to assure fair competition within a truly competitive marketplace.

These laws arose from the experience of the American people with growth, monopoly practices and powers of huge business organizations (the "trusts") that fixed prices, forced smaller companies out of business, and dominated entire markets.

The Sherman Act of 1890 was the first major attempt in any nation to define free enterprise in terms of fair play among all competitors.

Other laws followed the Sherman Act, most notably the Clayton and Federal Trade Commission Acts of 1914 and the Robinson-Patman Act of 1936.

Many other laws, amendments, judicial interpretations, and rulings have given these laws widespread application.

Despite numerous individual and special reservations over aspects of the antitrust laws, most people in business—as indeed in other sectors—agree that the United States needs antitrust laws to maintain free and fair competition.

It is particularly important that every Becton Dickinson employee engaged in the sales and marketing activities of our products and knows the basic provisions of these laws. Consult freely with the Law Department in every instance where you may need advice on the applicability of the antitrust laws to your own work and dealings with suppliers and customers.

Every Becton Dickinson employee, however, should know the force and meaning of the antitrust laws—because, despite their special relevance to the sales and marketing people, they apply to all of us.

These laws, as other laws, evolve over time in terms of what they really mean, and how they really affect specific business operations. So it's a good idea to keep in close touch with the Law Department—if only to remain abreast of the latest interpretation of how the laws apply in any given instance.

SMALL TALK EQUALS BIG TROUBLE

You're just one of many people attending a trade association meeting or convention. You're talking over trade problems with a number of other people—which is natural enough and indeed one of the prime purposes of the trade get-together in the first place.

Sometime after the trade conversation meeting, let's just suppose that Becton Dickinson and one or more other companies had decided, independently and separately of one another, to discontinue selling to a particular troublesome customer.

Suppose then that the customer sued and, in the course of the lawsuit, it became known that you, the Becton Dickinson representative at that trade association meeting, had talked about this particular customer with the representatives of the other company or companies that had discontinued selling to him.

That trade association might well be construed as a conspiracy directed against the customer: a violation of the anti-trust laws.

The penalty for such a violation could be substantial. So could the resulting embarrassment and damage to reputation of everyone concerned.

Moral: Be extra careful when talking with competitors, suppliers, customers, indeed, with anyone, if your words may raise even the slightest suspicion (however unfounded in fact) of conspiracy, unfair tactics, favored treatment for certain customers or suppliers, or price fixing.

THE SHERMAN ACT OF 1890

This first antitrust law prohibits any contract, combination, or conspiracy that unreasonably restrains trade or commerce. It also forbids the attempted or actual monopolization of any business, either independently or in combination with others.

Penalties for violation of the Sherman Act are severe and have been imposed many times over the years. These include civil liability for damages as well as criminal prosecution.

Fines can reach $1 million for a corporate defendant and $100,000 for an individual.

Jail sentences may be for as long as three years for serious violations of the law.

Unreal as it may seem, high-ranking corporate executives (among others) have gone to the penitentiary and paid huge fines for Sherman Act violations. Some of these individuals had never been found guilty of any previous transgression—not even a traffic ticket.

Section One of the Act forbids any contract, combination, or conspiracy that unreasonably restrains trade or commerce.

Such an agreement may be with a competitor, a supplier, a customer, or indeed with anyone. The agreement need not be in writing or formalized in any way. It may be proven by circumstantial evidence alone.

The effect of such an agreement must be an unreasonable restraint upon competition. The courts have found certain practices to be *per se* unreasonable: in other words, in violation of the law even if those accused plead a sound business reason for the practice. Some of these *per se* illegal practices include: [1] *Agreements to fix prices*. These are illegal, whether between or among competitors or between a seller and its customers to fix the customer's resale price. [2] *Group boycotts*. A company can refuse to deal with a customer or supplier or someone else on its own accord—if it has no monopolistic purpose in mind. But it cannot agree with its competitors or coerce others to refuse to deal with another company. [3] *Tying arrangements*. A "tie-in" is usually defined as an arrangement where the seller won't sell a particular product or products unless the buyer purchases another product or products from the seller.

Other practices—while not illegal *per se*—may be found to be unreasonable, hence illegal, unless there are special circumstances. Such practices include: [1] *Territorial or customer restrictions*. Here a manufacturer restricts where and to whom a buyer may resell the manufacturer's products. [2] *Exclusive dealing arrangements*. Here both buyer and supplier agree to deal exclusively with each other for an unreasonable period of time.

Section Two of the Act forbids the monopolization and even the attempted monopolization of a market. No agreement, written or spoken, is necessary. What *is* necessary is for a company to have the power to control market prices or to exclude competition—if it can be shown the company has willfully attained or used that power unfairly.

It is not illegal to have attained a monopoly position through a superior product, business acumen, or an historical accident.

Note that a company need not control 100% of a market to be in violation of the law. Seventy-five percent or less may be enough to constitute a monopoly within the meaning of the Act.

This section also forbids abusive practices by companies that have lawfully achieved a monopoly position.

Indeed, certain practices which would otherwise be perfectly legal may be illegal if maintained by a company having monopolistic power.

An example of this would be lowering prices to below cost to drive smaller companies from the market. A lowering of price would not be illegal if it were done to help build up a small market share.

THE CLAYTON ACT OF 1914

The Clayton Act prohibits certain acts or practices which are reasonably likely to lessen competition—even though no harm to competition has been caused up to the time when the law is invoked against an alleged violator.

Section Three of the Act deals specifically with the practices of "tie-in" sales and exclusive dealing arrangements, which were discussed above under the Sherman Anti-Trust Act.

Section Seven of the Act prohibits mergers and acquisitions whose effect may be to substantially lessen competition or to tend to create a monopoly.

In the case of acquisitions exceeding a certain size, the Federal Trade Commission and the Department of Justice must be notified in advance, so that these agencies may review the proposed consolidations prior to their closing.

THE ROBINSON-PATMAN ACT OF 1936

This Act makes it unlawful to discriminate in prices charged to different purchasers of the same product, where the effect may tend to substantially lessen competition or help to create a monopoly.

This does not require that all customers be charged the same price under all circumstances.

A seller, for example, may charge different prices to different levels of trade, e.g., to wholesalers, retailers, hospitals or to buyers who are not in competition with one another.

There are other limited exceptions. Different prices may be charged where a lower price results from cost savings the seller achieves from dealing in large quantities or in special selling or distribution processes.

A seller may offer a lower price to meet—but not beat—an equally low price offered by a competitor.

And volume discounts are lawful if, as a practical matter, they are available to all customers, not just a select few.

A warning, however: These conditions, exceptions, and circumstances are highly technical and require expert advice before any deviation from the general rule. Therefore, as a general practice, never vary from our established selling price without first consulting the Law Department.

FEDERAL TRADE COMMISSION ACT OF 1914

A final important antitrust law, the Federal Trade Commission Act, prohibits unfair methods of competition and unfair or deceptive trade practices.

The growing body of law prohibiting unfair competition follows common-sense standards of fair play for the most part—but it's a good idea to consult our Law Department whenever you encounter a practice that gives you pause or that may otherwise seem unusual.

A growing list of trade practices found unlawful includes the following: [1] Making false claims about what your product can do or about what your competitor's product cannot do. [2] Making false claims of price reductions. [3] Giving deceptive guarantees containing hidden conditions. [4] Failing to disclose a product's country of origin.

Few people, indeed, anywhere in our society, would dispute the need for rules like these.

In our own case, we have an old and respected name to protect—so it's most unlikely anyone at Becton Dickinson would fall afoul of this law. We believe in the continuing worth of the old adage: honesty is the best policy. The name of Becton Dickinson, after all, is an integral part of our products—which is just what integrity means.

Martin Marietta

Generally speaking, antitrust laws of the United States prohibit agreements or actions "in restraint of trade"—restrictive practices that may reduce competition without providing beneficial effects to consumers. Among those agreements and activities found to be clear violations are agreement or understandings among competitors to fix or control prices; to boycott specified suppliers or customers; to allocate products, territories, or markets; or to limit the production or sale of products or product lines. Such agreements are against public policy and against the policy of Martin Marietta. Employees should never engage in discussions of such matters with representatives of other companies. Employees should report any instance in which such discussions are initiated by other companies.

U.S. antitrust laws also apply to international operations and transactions related to imports to, or exports from, the United States. Moreover, the international activities of the Corporation could be subject to antitrust laws of foreign nations or organizations such as the European Economic Community.

Because of the complexity of antitrust laws, it is imperative that advice be sought on any question regarding this subject.

Sundstrand

The U.S. antitrust laws prohibit agreements and activities that may have the effect of reducing competition without providing counter balancing benefits to consumers. Agreements and activities which are prohibited include: [1] agreements with competitors to fix or control pricing, [2] agreements with competitors to allocate products, markets or territories, [3] agreements to boycott certain customers or suppliers, [4] agreements to refrain from or limit the manufacture, sale, or production of any product, or [5] reciprocal purchase arrangements or tie-ins.

It is Sundstrand's policy to adhere to the antitrust laws. Accordingly, agreements with competitors regarding pricing, terms or conditions of sale, or allocation of products, business markets, customers or territories are prohibited. It is also against Sundstrand policy to discuss or correspond directly or indirectly with any competitor regarding plans or contemplated actions of Sundstrand or pricing, terms or conditions of sales.

Since the U.S. antitrust laws may be applied to international operations and transactions and since there are laws of other nations or organizations such as the European Economic Community which deal with subjects covered by the U.S. antitrust laws, you must seek the advice of the Corporate Law Department when questions covering international activities arise.

Exxon

It is the policy of Exxon Corporation that all of its directors and employees shall, in carrying out their duties to the Corporation, rigidly comply with the antitrust laws of the United States and with those of any other country or group of countries which are applicable to the Corporation's business.

No director or employee should assume that the Corporation's interest ever requires otherwise. Moreover, no one in the Corporation has authority to give any order or direction that would result in a violation of this policy.

It is recognized that on occasion there may be legitimate doubt as to the proper interpretation of the law. In such circumstances it is required that the directors and employees refer the case through appropriate channels to the Law Department for an opinion.

ITT

Each of you who is an executive doing business in U.S. domestic or foreign commerce has had the scope and meaning of the U.S. antitrust laws explained to you by ITT legal counsel.

The objective of these laws is to promote vigorous competition in open markets. You are aware that any conduct with competitors, tending either to "fix" prices, or to agree directly or indirectly about the nature, extent or means of competition in any market for goods or services is prohibited. Contracts with competitors should be undertaken only after consultation with legal counsel.

Violation of the U.S. antitrust laws is a serious offense and can result in severe disciplinary action including discharge, fines and imprisonment. You and those reporting to you are responsible for full compliance with these antitrust laws . . . those doing business outside the United States must comply with the applicable antitrust laws of various other countries and of the European Economic Community. You should obtain legal advice from ITT legal counsel as to issues arising under those laws.

Aetna

Aetna's policy is to comply fully with all laws relating to trade practices: state and federal antitrust laws, state unfair trade practice laws and various non-discrimination statutes.

Compliance with the antitrust laws is so important that the Company now has a specific antitrust compliance program which has been presented to many employees, ranging up to and through senior management. Group presentations are still made as demand warrants. A film ("The Price") which is part of the program graphically demonstrates the difficulties employees can create for themselves when antitrust laws are violated.

To help you understand more fully the trade practices you should follow, we've set out below an overview of the basic legal prohibitions and Aetna's corporate policy.

State anti-trust laws typically mirror federal antitrust laws. The chief difference is that state laws concern intrastate commerce (activities wholly within a single state) while federal laws concern interstate commerce (activities involving two or more states). Among the practices that violate the antitrust laws are: **price fixing, agreements to divide markets, group boycotts and refusals to deal, tie-in sales, reciprocity,** monopolization and attempted monopolization, certain exchanges of price and other sensitive competitive information among competitors, exclusive dealing, price discrimination, unfair competition, deceptive practices (particularly in advertising), commercial bribery, commercial espionage, anti-competitive mergers, acquisitions and joint ventures [and] certain interlocking directorates.

The bold-face items are so inherently anti-competitive that, once their existence is established, they are presumed illegal without further inquiry. Criminal prosecution is an increased possibility for any of these offenses, especially if price fixing is suspected. State unfair trade practice laws overlap, to some extent, both federal and state antitrust laws. Typically they prohibit such things as: misrepresentation and false advertising of insurance policies, misrepresentation on applications, secret rebates, unlawful discrimination, issuance or circulation of false literature, willful circulation of false statements or rumors about insurance institutions, unfair claim settlement practices, misrepresentations and incomplete comparison of policy terms and benefits, and "twisting" . . . .

Chapter 17

MANAGING COMPUTER-BASED INFORMATION SYSTEMS

Computers—from the biggest superprocessors to the smallest laptops—have transformed business from an age of automation to an age of information. Today, one of the central focuses of management is managing information as a vital resource.

Firms today can gather and utilize tremendous amounts of information at speeds scarcely imagined just a few decades ago. And in many companies, virtually everyone, from the chief executive officer to the chief custodian has access to personal computers or computer terminals, as well as a wealth of software and data that is vital to the operations of the firm. Computers and computer-based information systems (CBIS) literally have become the lifeblood of many companies. Computer systems have proven to be highly successful at enhancing operational efficiency, increasing decision-making effectiveness, improving competitive positions, identifying new opportunities, adding customers, providing better service, and improving the quality of products.

Computer networks for handling information have become so extensive that almost $1 trillion is transmitted among financial institutions every workday, an amount that is equal to 25% of the United States' gross national product.

Consequently, hardware, software, and electronic data all represent important assets that must be effectively managed and carefully protected. At the same time, the speed, ease of access, and information-storage capabilities of a CBIS raise a variety of ethical questions and conduct decisions that firms must address in their codes of business conduct.

The code of the Association of Computing Machinery (ACM) or the code of the Data Processing Management Association (DPMA) can serve as a starting point for developing a firm's code for its computer professionals. Although CBISs will continue to be increasingly distributed among non-professionals, the firm's computer professionals will remain the backbone and center of expertise for the entire firm for many years to come. Therefore, it is vital that these professionals conduct themselves in a socially, legally, and ethically responsible manner.

The following excerpts present several leading firms' approaches to the increasingly complex needs of those who must manage computer-based information systems. Obviously, not all issues related to computers can be illustrated here. But the ones covered effectively in these model codes include: (1) proper use of computer systems; (2) computer security and password protection; (3) use of information about employees; (4) company ownership of information resources; (5) ownership of employee-developed software; and (6) using the software of others.

PROPER USE OF COMPUTER SYSTEMS

AT&T

Computer systems and the information they contain, control, transmit or process are essential for AT&T's daily operations. They help provide products and services to customers, maintain vital records, collect revenues, and process information necessary for internal operations and development. Employees are responsible for ensuring that computer systems and information they contain are adequately safeguarded against damage, alteration, theft, fraudulent manipulation, and unauthorized access or disclosure. Though the data is processed and stored in a computer may appear to be intangible, it still must be protected as a Company asset, and properly identified and safeguarded according to its proprietary and/or critical nature. Passwords or other procedures used to access or transmit computerized data must be selected, controlled and safeguarded to ensure that Company data is adequately protected. Ultimately, each employee is responsible for the security of information accessed or modified under his or her password or access procedure. Also, as a user or manager of corporate data or computer resources, each employee must strictly adhere to the specific security measures and controls that have been established.

Along with the responsibility for safeguarding the information in Company data bases, employees are responsible for: Obeying U.S. copyright laws and Company policy regarding the reproduction of copyrighted software [and] using licensed computer software only as permitted by the specific license. Any personal or other non-business use of a Company data communication system or computer system (mainframe, micro, mini or personal computer) that's not expressly sanctioned by supervision is forbidden. Violations or suspected violations of computer security measures or controls should be reported to the AT&T Corporate Security Organization.

Southwestern Bell

Computer systems are essential for the daily operations of all Southwestern Bell Corporation companies. They help provide telecommunications services to customers, maintain records of company activities, assets and revenues, and process information necessary for internal operations. Accordingly, it is imperative that the hardware, software and data processed by computers and stored in them and elsewhere be adequately safeguarded against damage, alteration, theft, fraudulent manipulation and unauthorized access to, and disclosure of, company information. Though information processed and stored in a computer may appear to be intangible, this does not lessen the need for all employees to protect such information. Data stored and accessed in internal computer systems and outside vendor-provided data services is company property. This data and the computer/communications resources utilized to access and use it are to be used for properly authorized company business purposes only.

Office automation systems and microcomputers allow data to be easily moved between offices, and between the office and home. The portable storage devices and data used in these systems must be physically and logically (access controlled) secured. These devices and systems and magnetic media are to be used for company business purposes only. Each employee must adhere strictly to the specific security measures of internal controls that have been established for . . . guarding the integrity and validity of computer systems. These may vary, however, depending on the characteristics of a particular system, the sensitivity and privacy or its data files and its importance to company business. Violations or suspected violations of computer security measures . . . should be reported at once to Security personnel.

Boeing

Material, equipment, and information (including computer hardware and software) of the Company and its customers and suppliers shall be used only for the purposes required by the Company. Company managers and employees having custody of such items are responsible: 1. For ensuring that materials and equipment will remain on Company-controlled property. Exceptions may be authorized by a functional head, program general manager, or equivalent when the use in other locations is clearly in the Company's interest. 2. For ensuring that proper measures are taken for the storage and safeguarding of information or knowledge, and for precluding unauthorized access, use or removal by any means (e.g, physical removal, or use or removal by remote communications) in any form (e.g., electrical, optical, magnetic, or hard copy form).

Approval from the customer or supplier, as appropriate, must be obtained when the use of customer or supplier materials, equipment, or information is involved. Misappropriation or unauthorized use by any employee of Company-owned or other business-related materials, equipment, or information for personal purposes, or uses not in the interset of the Company, customer, or supplier, will be considered a violation of Company policy.

Aetna

Management has the responsibility to ensure that computer resources are used to further Aetna's business. You should not allow computers to be used for amusement or other trivial purposes since that is a misuse of a valuable company asset. Private benefit or gain is strictly prohibited. Misappropriation, destruction, misuse, abuse or unauthorized modification of computer resources are offenses for which dismissal will be considered. Malicious and abusive acts directed to computer resources subject the Company to the risk of loss of its processing capability with severe consequences to the business. As soon as you detect or suspect such activity, report it to your security officer listed below. The officer will see that appropriate people are notified and initiate the internal and external investigations. Follow the guidelines for handling fraud or dishonesty.

BellSouth

Computer hardware, software, and data must be safeguarded from damage, alteration, theft, fraudulent manipulation, and unauthorized access to and disclosure of company information. Employees must adhere to specific security measures and internal controls for each computer system for which they are authorized access, and should avoid any personal use of computer hardware or software, except as specified in company or departmental guidelines.

Each employee using licensed software is responsible for understanding and adhering to the terms of the licensing agreement. The right to use software is limited to authorized employees for company business. Copies of software and associated materials may be made only as specified in the licensing agreement. Employees must not sell, transfer, or otherwise make available to any unauthorized person any software products, documentation or copies thereof. Violations or suspected violations of computer security measures or controls should be reported at once to the security organization or other appropriate group. Employees guilty of misuse of company computer hardware of software may be subject to disciplinary action which could include dismissal.

COMPUTER SECURITY AND PASSWORD PROTECTION

Crestar

Crestar relies heavily on computers to meet its operation, financial and informational requirements. It is essential that all corporate and customer data created, processed or stored on Crestar computer systems (including microcomputers) be treated as confidential and protected from misuse.

Aetna (Passwords)

Passwords are the customary means to control access to computer systems. In most cases, a password is unique and known only to the individual authorized to use it. It authenticates the individual's identity and validates that the access is authorized. When properly administered, password control provides accountability for each access and for the manner access, once gained, is used. Accordingly, since passwords are essential safeguards of vital assets, employees who, without authority, disclose their own passwords to others or who possess or attempt to obtain the passwords of others may be charged with or suspected of improper computer use and are subject to disciplinary measures.

Any unauthorized disclosure of a password, even accidental occurrences, should be reported to appropriate security officer . . . .

Aetna (Computer Security)

Managers are responsible for identifying and protecting all computer resources within their control and for assuring that their employees understand their obligation to protect these resources and use them for proper business purposes. Various aspects of resource protection must be addressed in meeting this responsibility.

Physical Security requires a safe work environment, the ability to deter and contain emergencies such as fire, and the ability to deter theft and to restrict access to sensitive work areas. While physical security at Aetna is generally handled by Home Office Properties and Risk Management, if your work depends on small business computers or terminals, you should consider how you would meet various contingencies that would prevent your use of the equipment.

Contingency plans ensure appropriate responses to emergencies so that critical business operations and data may be quickly restored on backup facilities or by alternative processing methods. For example, you should ensure that critical data or business records are periodically copied and archived in a secure location. Controls ensure accountability for actions, integrity of data, exclusive use of authorized operating procedures and detection of variances. They are equally important for small computer users.

Data security is vital to protect against misappropriation or loss of vital information and involves password controls and other protective measures. Data and text can be produced and copied with great speed. This increases the risk of misappropriation or improper disclosure. You should ensure that data (whether in computerized or printed form) private to an individual or confidential to the business are not easily compromised by disclosure or misappropriation. For example, sensitive computer printouts should be attended when producing sensitive output, such as employee appraisals.

Using personal business computers to process or produce sensitive information is a matter of particular concern, because the storage medium, floppy disks, can be easily appropriated or quickly copied. You should store disks containing sensitive information in a locked location when not in use. If you have questions concerning your security and control responsibilities, or desire guidance in meeting them appropriately, contact the appropriate security officer . . . .

USE OF INFORMATION ABOUT EMPLOYEES

General Motors

General Motors has established the following policy of fair information practices relative to the collection, maintenance and use of personal employee information throughout the Corporation. General Motors collects personally identifiable employee information for a variety of business reasons such as proper administration of labor agreements, benefit programs and other business functions or to comply with a law or government regulation. Only such information as is relevant and necessary in the performance of those functions should be collected by General Motors employing units. For example, no records should be gathered or maintained concerning an employee's non-employment related associations, political activities, publications or communications unless such information is submitted in writing to the employing unit by the employee, and is required for a particular business function.

Access to personal information within General Motors should be limited to those persons having a legitimate need for such information in the performance of their job responsibilities. Personally identifiable employee information is not to be disclosed outside the Corporation by employing units without the employee's consent with the exception of: (a) verification of employment for credit approval purposes, (b) information on employment dates for employment reference checks, (c) information which an employee's collective bargaining representative is properly entitled to have, and (d) information required to be disclosed by law or court order. Further, all information collected in conjunction with the Corporation's annual Conflict of Interest Survey of selected employees should be maintained separately from personnel records.

Upon written request to the personnel office, employees will be provided an opportunity to inspect documents contained in their personnel files in accordance with established procedures.

Upjohn

Company policies governing the management of information for all Company operations is contained in the *Information Management Policy Manual*, which is available through the Director of Information Resource Management.

Information Security (confidentiality, internal control, integrity, and recovery) is vital for all Company information. Compliance with the Company's information security and classification policy is the responsibility of all employees. Any employee who suspects that information security has been or is being threatened should direct his or her concerns to the Director of Information Resource Management.

Panhandle Eastern

It is the policy of the Panhandle Eastern Corporation to maintain a responsive, cost effective information processing effort for each of the Companies as well as for the Corporation as a whole. A cooperative effort by all affected parties is required to achieve this goal. Panhandle Eastern Corporation has established a Central Processing Facility (CPF) with the necessary software, hardware and personnel expertise for remote access use by any of the Companies. Each Company using the CPF shall in all ways cooperate and coordinate their individual system development efforts with management of the CPF management. Cooperation shall extend to the acquisition of information and word processing equipment under central CPF contracts. Application software will be developed or purchased as required by each Company; however, coordination will be maintained with the management of the CPF to insure that where such application software is useful to other Panhandle Eastern Companies the most effective application can be obtained.

Those companies having independent information/word processing capability will coordinate with the management of the CPF as to hardware and software acquisition to achieve the policy objective set out herein. Each Company will plan and develop application software responsive to its needs. Such planning will be documented and shared with management of the CPF so that overall planning required for future systems and modifications will be achieved in accordance with the policy objective set out herein.

It will be the responsibility of the management of the CPF, as well as of the information systems management of each Panhandle Eastern Company, to stay abreast of improvements in computer technology and related areas and to coordinate any significant changes in hardware or software systems in order to avoid any adverse impact on any party.

COMPANY OWNERSHIP OF INFORMATION RESOURCES

Aetna

The Company's computer resources are Company assets. Computer programs developed by employees, within the scope of their employment and using Aetna's computer resources, are the property of the Company. All rights to such programs reside exclusively with the Company.

Not all computer programs used within the Company are owned by the Company. Many are proprietary products licensed from program supply firms which, to preserve their proprietary rights, impose copyright or contractual obligations on the Company. To ensure that the Company meets its obligations, you should treat all programs, program documentation and related materials as property of the Company, and treat them as trade secrets. You should not, for example, make any program, any copy of any program, or any program documentation available for use by anyone outside the Company or by any Company employee for personal purposes.

TECO

The company's information resources are valuable company assets. Information systems and the hardware, software and data processed by computers and stored by them are critical to the management, marketing and operations of the company. Our investment in these systems and the data they process is substantial and must be carefully safeguarded. These systems must be protected against damage, theft, fraudulent manipulation and unauthorized access to, and disclosure of, company information.

Computer programs developed by us, within the scope of our employment and using the company's computer resources, are the property of the company. All rights to such programs are held exclusively by the company. Not all software programs used by TECO are owned by the company. Many are proprietary products licensed from program supply firms which, to protect their proprietary rights, impose copyright or contractual obligations on the company.

Therefore, to ensure the company meets it obligations and does not violate copyright law or subject itself to a lawsuit, we may not copy software programs without the permission of the firm that owns the rights to the program. In addition, we must not make any program, any copy of a program, or any program documentation available for use by anyone outside the company or by any employee for personal purposes. Our computer facilities are provided for company projects and are not to be used for any unauthorized purpose.

OWNERSHIP OF EMPLOYEE-DEVELOPED SOFTWARE

Control Data

Many Control Data employees write software programs at their homes. These programs may not be related to the employee's job—but may still be in the area of Control Data's business. For situations like this, Control Data has a policy that is designed to protect the interests of the employee and the Company. The policy includes a procedure under which employees may submit software for possible licensing through Control Data. The policy also offers a process by which employees can request that Control Data release whatever rights it may have in the software. For more information, you should ask your manager for a copy of this policy.

USING THE SOFTWARE OF OTHERS

Texas Instruments

Much of the software used at TI was created and copyrighted by other companies and may be subject to nondisclosure restrictions. TI does not usually own software created by other companies, but receives and uses the software under a license agreement. It is TI policy to comply with license agreements which govern the use of software. Reproducing software without authorization may violate these agreements and the U.S. Copyright Act. No TIer should make copies, resell or transfer software created by another company unless it is authorized under the applicable software license agreement.

IBM

Special care should be taken in acquiring software from others. As intellectual property, software is often protected by copyright or as a trade secret or as confidential information. Such software includes computer programs, data bases and related documentation. Before you accept software or sign a license agreement, you must follow established procedures. The terms and conditions of such license agreement—such as provisions not to copy or distribute programs—must be strictly followed.

Also, if you acquire software for your personally owned equipment, you should not copy any part of such software in any development work you do for IBM, place such software on any IBM owned computer system or generally bring such software onto IBM premises.

Chapter 18

ETHICAL DUTIES OF
ACCOUNTANTS

Management must have accurate accounting methods, as well as accurate information, if it is to make well-advised decisions regarding cash-flow, asset deployment, market entry, product pricing, taxation and other tactics. At the same time, management must be able to depend on a firm's accountants to perform their jobs in an ethical and honest manner.

In virtually every firm, upper management establishes the organization's tone that determines whether the honest and ethical actions of managers will or will not be subjugated to drives for growth and greater profit. To instill and maintain a culture of honesty, firms of all sizes, whether publicly traded or privately held, should promulgate and enforce internal controls to assure that deceptive financial accounting and reporting will be detected and prevented. Written codes of conduct should (1) establish procedures to monitor and enforce compliance, and (2) protect employees from reprisal for revealing fraud and errors in financial reporting. Before the creation of the Securities and Exchange Commission (SEC) in 1934, incidents of deceptive financial reporting were commonplace and generally conducted without sanctions. The Federal Trade Commission, which regulated firms before the birth of the SEC, had no formal disclosure requirements. Some firms manipulated earnings and stock prices by gross adjustments of depreciation charges. For example, American Can (now Primerica) charged $500,000 in depreciation in 1912 and raised that figure fivefold in 1913 to hold profits constant before cutting depreciation to $1 million in 1914 to double profits, thereby causing the stock price to inflate from $11 to $50.

Today, accountants are much more independent and conscious of their duty to accurately and fairly report financial affairs to the public. Still, there are problems and a need for better compliance with codes of conduct. A recent study of allegedly fraudulent activities in publicly traded firms revealed that 87% of the frauds were accomplished through the use of misleading financial information, that high-level management was involved in 66% of the alleged frauds, and that 45% of the cases entailed breakdowns in the firms' internal-control systems.

Growing expectations that public accountants should aggresively serve the public interest have led to a substantial increase in lawsuits filed against accountants and in the size of damages sought. For instance, in 1989, British partners in Arthur Young agreed to pay $42.5 million to settle claims of negligence in that firm's audits of the former Johnson Matthey Bankers Ltd. in 1982 and 1983.

The organized accounting profession began in the United States with the establishment of the American Institute of Certified Public Accountants (AICPA) in 1887. Throughout its history, the AICPA has implemented numerous rules that govern its membership, and it has refined the process for promulgating accounting standards. While CPAs provide tax and management advisory service, their primary function is auditing.

Through the auditing process, the public-accounting profession attests or provides assurance as to the fairness and dependability of financial statements. Originally, the independent auditor's primary function was the discovery of theft, bookkeeping discrepancies, and other indicators of proper or improper management for the client's benefit. Today, however, the audit's most important mission is the unbiased reporting of the firm's financial condition for the benefit of third parties.

The following examples from codes of conduct show how some firms have addressed a number of key issues associated with financial accounting and reporting, as well as the various legal and ethical duties that surround these activities.

MAINTAINING THE INTEGRITY OF ACCOUNTING RECORDS AND REPORTS

Eaton

While only a few of us have responsibility for maintaining accounting records, many Eaton employees have responsibilities that affect the company's record-keeping functions. For example, the data from a time card may become the basis for Eaton charges to customers. Specific rules apply. Be accurate! Only the true and actual number of hours worked must be reported. Never shift costs to other customers or inappropriate work order numbers—this is strictly prohibited.

Another crucial type of reporting that many employees regularly encounter concerns business expenses. They must be documented and recorded accurately. For those of you who have direct responsibility for keeping the company's official records, your job requires maintaining Eaton's books, records, accounts and financial statements in an accurate and auditable manner. Never make entries that intentionally conceal or disguise the true nature of any transaction. No funds or accounts should be established or maintained for purposes not fully and accurately disclosed. Unrecorded "off the books" funds or assets should not be established for any purpose. What all of this means is that each of us had a role in making certain that our records are accurately prepared and maintained in accordance with all applicable laws and regulations. If, at any time, you have reason to believe that some aspect of Eaton's record-keeping is not being conducted properly, report it directly to your supervisor or call the Eaton Ethics Line.

Mead

The integrity of Mead's financial and accounting records is a matter of vital concern to the corporation. To assure that such records are valid, accurate, and complete, Mead requires: that a strong and comprehensive system of internal accounting controls be maintained at all locations; that all transactions be executed, and access to assets be permitted, only in accordance with management's authorization; that all transactions be recorded accurately, fairly, and in sufficient detail so that financial statements can be prepared in accordance with generally accepted accounting principles; that there be no unrecorded or undisclosed funds or assets; that no false or intentionally misleading entries be made in the books and records of the company; that no relevant information be concealed from management or from Mead's internal auditors or independent accountants; that employees safeguard company assets and records under their control.

Union Carbide

The Corporation will fulfill all legal financial reporting obligations. These obligations include the requirements that no director, officer or other employee will falsify or cause to be falsified any book entry, record, or document, or will make any false or misleading statement to any internal or external auditor or accountant. A formal system of approvals and authorizations for financial operating decisions will be maintained throughout the Corporation. All authority for such decisions is subordinate to that vested in the Chief Executive Officer by the Board of Directors, who have the sole right to set the limits for any approval authority that may be delegated to others.

Olin

Olin and its affiliates are required to keep books, records and accounts that are in conformance with generally accepted accounting principles and that fairly and accurately reflect all transactions. The corporation must also employ a system of internal accounting controls that safeguard company assets and that provide an auditable record of financial transactions. To ensure compliance with these various laws and regulations, no undisclosed or unrecorded funds or assets will be established or maintained for any purpose, nor will any payments be made into unidentified or secret bank accounts. No false or contrived entries or statements may be made for any purpose in the books and records of the corporation. All reimbursed expenditures for travel, meals and entertainment must be fully documented and recorded.

Boston Edison

We must prepare all Company business data, records, and reports accurately and truthfully. These include such routine documents as time sheets, expense reports, test reports and production records. They also include accounting entries, cost estimates, contract proposals, and other presentations to management, regulators, customers and the public. It is important that those who rely on these records and reports have truthful and accurate information. The integrity of the Company's records is based upon the validity, accuracy and completeness with which they are prepared. If we prepare such information, or represent or certify its accuracy, we must be diligent in assuring its accuracy and integrity. If we are the custodians of such information, we must be sure it is released outside the Company only for proper purposes.

Ameritech

All reports, vouchers, bills, payroll and service records, measurement and performance records and other essential data should be prepared with care and honesty. Service and cost performance measurements, for example, are a key to the successful management of the business. Upon them are based the allocation of resources, assignment of personnel and implementation of special action programs. A false or misleading report or record of measurement data is considered as serious as falsifying vouchers, financial data, or records pertaining to Company funds or property. There is no excuse for a deliberately false or misleading report or record. Company accounts are maintained according to the rules of the Securities and Exchange Commission, Federal Communication Commission, and other state regulatory agencies. These agencies require that certain Company records be retained for specific periods of time. Other records and documents may have to be held in connection with court and regulatory proceedings, or for other business purposes. Records should therefore be destroyed only in accordance with these requirements and with Company authorization.

LEGAL AND ETHICAL DUTIES OF ACCOUNTANTS AND FIRMS

General Mills

General Mills has high standards for achieving operating and financial goals. These results must be achieved with the same high standards for accounting and financial reporting methods. Accounting and financial reporting practices must be fair and proper, in accordance with generally accepted accounting principles (GAAP), and using management's best judgments where necessary.

GMI does not condone practices that might lead to fraudulent financial reporting. While difficult to give an all-inclusive definition of fraudulent financial reporting, it is, in general, any intentional or reckless conduct, whether by act or omission, that results in materially misleading financial statements. Clear, open and frequent communication among all management levels and personnel on all significant financial and operation matters will substantially reduce the risk of problems in the accounting and financial reporting areas as well as help achieve operating goals. All management people are expected to be aware of these risks (see Controller's Memorandum #4B) and to communicate accordingly.

Kimberly-Clark

Reporting of financial information to stockholders and to the Securities and Exchange Commission requires the highest standards of fairness and honesty. The harm done to the company's reputation and to its investors by fraudulent or misleading reporting can be severe. Dishonest financial reporting can also result in civil or criminal penalties to the individuals involved or the company. Consequently, the reporting of any false or misleading information in internal or external financial reports is strictly prohibited.

GOVERNMENT REPORTING

Olin

There are serious civil and criminal penalties (both for the corporation and individual employees) associated with filing false or fraudulent reports or other false information with governments or their agencies, both here and abroad. Because even a genuine mistake can threaten relationships with government bodies, or cast a suspicion on the overall integrity of the corporation, employees must make every effort to ensure that any governmental reports they prepare or which fall under their purview are honest and accurate.

Chapter 19

EXPENSE ACCOUNTS, CREDIT CARDS, AND ENTERTAINING

Changes in business tax laws, stronger enforcement of certain tax codes by the Internal Revenue Service, and renewed drives for lower costs of doing business have caused companies to pay stricter attention to how their employees and managers handle expense accounts, credit cards, and entertainment of current or potential customers. Reflecting this stricter attention, many firms have added statements to their business codes of conduct that provide ethical and policy guidelines for employee expense accounts, credit card usage, and entertainment expenditures.

The following examples from three major companies can be used as guidelines when creating codes to address these sensitive areas.

GUIDELINES FOR EXPENSE ACCOUNTS, CREDIT CARDS, AND ENTERTAINING

Bank of America

You are required to be familiar with expense account guidelines and to follow them carefully when submitting expense accounts. You also are responsible for accurate submission of expense claims. Falsifying expenses, in any form or amount, or submitting false claims, is a misappropriation of company funds and constitutes grounds for discipline, including dismissal.

US West

Company credit cards are provided to employees for convenience in conducting company business. No personal expenses may be charged on company credit cards except as specifically authorized by company procedures. Any charged personal expenses must be paid promptly by the employee. Company credit cards should not be used to avoid preparing documentation for direct payment vendors. Where allowed by local law, charges on company credit cards for which a properly approved expense report has not been received at the time of an employee's termination of employment may be deducted from the employee's last paycheck. The company will pursue repayment by the employee of any amounts it has to pay on the employee's behalf.

NCNB

Entertaining customers and others outside the bank who have an effect on bank business is a normal part of business life. Here are some guidelines on ethical issues related to entertainment: [1] Reasonable entertainment is appropriate and reimbursable by the company. Detailed expense reporting is required, including the names of the people entertained, the occasion and the business purpose of the entertainment. [2] You may entertain customers and others in your home, but be certain that it is justified and when filing for reimbursement document the event with a guest list, relationships to NCNB and purposes of the entertainment. [3] When entertaining government officials, you should be sure that the hospitality you show them is reasonable. A good test in determining reasonableness is to ask yourself whether NCNB or the government official would be embarrassed if the full details of the relationship, whether a gift or an evening's entertainment, were described in the newspaper. [4] You should never circumvent the policies related to gift and entertainment of government officials through contributions to third parties, such as customers, vendors or consultants, or through the use of your own personal funds. Both are violations of NCNB policy.

Chapter 20

INSIDER TRADING AND SECURITIES LAWS

Illegal insider trading refers to the buying or selling of securities by a person who has obtained non-public information and who employs it to gain a profit at the expense of others.

Persons who periodically obtain information of this sort include a firm's executives, directors and large shareholders. But managers, employees, securities dealers, and investors sometimes attempt to make quick profits from inside information, as well.

No other form of business conduct, with the exception of price fixing, has raised the public's moral disapproval and brought such disgrace to the offenders as improper use of non-public information. With increased enforcement of securities laws by the federal government in recent years, a number of former high fliers on Wall Street have been convicted, sentenced to prison, and fined for insider trading, and several investment firms have paid heavy penalties for their involvements in illegal trading, as well.

America's securities laws are intended to help maintain the public's confidence in the integrity of the financial markets and in the individual investor's ability to secure a fair return on investment. The prices of the vast majority of securities reflect available public information about companies and the economy. By publishing and enforcing business-conduct guidelines to deter securities fraud, firms can help assure the public that fairness and efficiency generally rule in the securities and financial markets.

FEDERAL SECURITIES ACT OF 1933 AND SECURITIES EXCHANGE ACT OF 1934

Becton Dickinson

These laws regulate the issuance of and trading in corporate securities. The Securities and Exchange Commission (SEC) has issued extensive rules and regulations covering all aspects of these activities. The most important provisions of these laws for most employees are the prohibitions against trading in shares of a corporation's stock on the basis of undisclosed, unpublicized inside information. The idea is to prevent "insiders" from using their special knowledge to advance their own financial interests at an advantage over and conceivably at the expense of members of the general public who may not have that information.

If the information is publicly known, there is no special advantage to the insider. The price of the securities would then "reflect" that publicly known information: a stock would rise, presumably, on favorable information about the corporation and would go down if the information were unfavorable.

Anyone whose relationship with Becton Dickinson provides access to important information about the Company not available to the public—and who uses that information to buy or sell securities or to influence friends or family to do so, could be in violation of the federal securities laws and subject to fines and imprisonment.

Such restrictions on "insider trading" have been broadly applied by the SEC, which has prosecuted many cases on the strength of them.

Let's assume an instance where you might become entangled with these laws. Suppose Becton Dickinson had developed a new line of products, or had achieved a research breakthrough. The announcement of this might well increase the demand for—and hence the price of—Becton Dickinson shares. If you know of this information and bought the Company's shares on the strength of it before the news was made public, you could be in violation of federal securities laws.

If convicted, you would certainly lose your profit and your reputation—and, most likely, your job. You might even have to pay a heavy fine and/or spend some time in prison.

The best way to invest in the stock of Becton Dickinson is on a regular basis for the long-term. It's a good idea to avoid short-term trading that may raise questions concerning the use of inside information.

The issue of improper use of inside information about Becton Dickinson can even arise when you trade in another company's stock.

Suppose you had advance news of that research breakthrough and—instead of buying Becton Dickinson shares—you sold your shareholdings in a company that might be adversely affected by this breakthrough. That stock sale might violate the prohibition against insider trading.

You might be similarly in violation if the inside information is not about Becton Dickinson at all, but merely comes to your attention because of your position with the Company.

The whole idea here is that inside information gives you a "leg up" on the general public to gain profits or to avoid losses which you would otherwise incur.

So, taking unfair advantage of the general investing public in the ways described above could expose you, the Company, and, indeed, anyone else involved, in expensive, embarrassing, and damaging litigation which would hurt all concerned.

It's also good practice to avoid buying substantial shareholdings or other ownership of a competitor, supplier, or customer. Such an investment may create a potential conflict of interest. In addition, although you may not be aware of occurring developments, your investments may make it appear that you are profiting from inside information.

So it's prudent to avoid transactions where misunderstandings might crop up and cause real trouble for you.

JC Penney

The securities laws and rules of the securities exchanges affect a wide variety of the Company's activities. No associate may engage in, or permit any other Associate to engage in, any activity on behalf of the Company which he or she knows, or reasonably should know, is prohibited by the securities laws. Examples include the following: No false, misleading or deceptive statements may be made in connection with the purchase or sale of any security or in any report filed with the Securities and Exchange Commission, or distributed to any financial analyst or stockholder. Improper or premature disclosure of confidential information to outsiders or Associates who do not require the information to outsiders or Associates who do not require the information to perform their jobs must be avoided. In addition, no Associate may trade in securities of the Company when he or she has knowledge of material events affecting the Company which have not been made public.

TRADING IN COMPANY STOCK AND CONFIDENTIAL OR INSIDE INFORMATION

Bankers Trust

Generally, a fact is material if there is substantial likelihood that a reasonable investor would consider it important in making an investment decision. Examples of material information may include the following:

1. A proposal or agreement for a merger, acquisition or divestiture or for the sale or purchase of assets.

2. A proposal or agreement concerning a financial restructuring or an extraordinary borrowing.

3. A proposal to issue or redeem securities or a development with respect to a pending issuance or redemption of securities.

4. An increase or decrease in dividends.

5. Information or estimates about earnings or sales.

6. An expansion or contraction of operations.

7. Increases or declines in orders or information about major contracts.

8. The development of a new product or, in the case of an oil and gas or mining company, information about mineral deposits or discoveries.

9. The institution of, or a development in, litigation or a regulatory matter.

10. Liquidity problems, payment or covenant defaults or actions by creditors, customers or suppliers relating to the issuer's credit standing.

11. Management developments.

12. Information about future actions of government agencies.

13. Information from the Federal Reserve System such as information affecting interest rates.

This list is merely indicative of the types of information that could be considered material. Moreover, any given item of information must be considered in light of all the relevant circumstances in order to make a determination as to materiality. Except in obvious cases of trivial information, non-public information should be presumed to be material unless the Central Compliance Department has concluded otherwise.

Many employees of Bankers Trust will, from time to time, have material non-public information about Bankers Trust, and during such times they may not trade in Bankers Trust securities. (See below for additional restrictions on trading in Bankers Trust securities.)

Since Bankers Trust's activities as banker, underwriter, broker, financial advisor, and investment manager and in connection with securities research will also frequently result in our obtaining material non-public information about other companies, care should be exercised by every Bankers Trust employee to avoid violations of the legal and ethical constraints regarding insider trading or improper "tipping" with respect to other companies' securities.

The prohibition against insider trading applies to all persons connected with Bankers Trust worldwide, including consultants and temporary employees. It is the obligation of the responsible officers to ensure that consultants and non-professional employees understand the prohibition against insider trading and tipping. Consultants, temporary workers and other outside service organizations should sign a statement indicating their awareness and understanding of, and their agreement to comply with, our policies.

Insiders who possess material non-public information about an issuer of securities and other persons who have received such information from insiders are subject to the "abstain or disclose" rule. They may not trade or recommend securities affected by the material non-public information or pass the information to others. These prohibitions remain in effect until the information had been fully disclosed to the public. Specific rules about insider trading and tipping appear below.

As a general rule, insiders who possess material non-public information about an issuer of securities, and persons who have received material non-public information from insiders, may be subject to the "abstain or disclose" rule—that is, they may be required by the securities laws either to refrain from passing such information on to others and from trading in or recommending the purchase or sale of the corporation's securities, or to disclose such information to the investing public.

A similar rule may apply to loan sales under principles of common law fraud. In addition, there are particularly broad restrictions on the misuse of material non-public information in the context of tender offers.

While the securities laws generally provide that proper public disclosure of non-public information will free the party who possesses the information to trade in the affected securities, when Bankers Trust employees come into possession of material non-public information about clients, disclosure will often not be permissible because of our obligation of confidentiality to our clients. Thus, personnel in possession of material non-public information about clients will usually simply be barred from trading in the client's securities.

To be subject to the "abstain or disclose" rule, a person must be an insider or have received information from an insider. Corporate officers, directors, employees and advisors who have access to material non-public information are "insiders." Bankers, accountants, underwriters, lawyers or printers who receive confidential information from a corporate client will ordinarily be considered insiders as well. Even information not received directly from an insider may be subject to the rule if the person who trades on the basis of, or tips, such information, should have known that the information emanated from an insider or one who had a duty not to disclose it. For example, it may be illegal to trade or recommend securities on the basis of a rumor that is traceable to such a person. Moreover, in the context of a tender offer, it is illegal to trade or recommend securities on the basis of, or to pass on, any material non-public information emanating directly or indirectly from anyone connected with the target or the offeror.

Outboard Marine

While the Company believes that all of its employees should be able to invest and trade in the stock of the Company, certain Federal laws impose obligations on the Company and on employees who trade in the Company's stock. The reputation and credibility of the Company depends on compliance with these laws by all employees.

If any employee has any "material information" (which is any information concerning the Company which has not been publicly disclosed, but which, if publicly disclosed could reasonably be expected either to affect the price of the Company's stock, or be considered important by a reasonable investor with respect to such investor's decision to buy, sell or hold the Company's stock) then such employee cannot either buy or sell the Company's stock for such employee's own account, or "tip" others, whether inside or outside of the Company, to transact or otherwise take a course of action with respect to the Company's stock. Moreover, material information can also be information about an organization with which the Company has entered or is about to enter into a transaction. Any employee with such material information cannot buy, sell, "tip" or otherwise transact in the securities of the other organization.

The purpose of these rules are two-fold: (i) So that everyone in the market place is, as much as possible, on equal footing; that is, all investors have all of the same *material* information; and (ii) So that this *material* information about the Company or the party with whom the Company is transacting business can be made available to employees so that the employees can do such employee's job better, and not so that such employee can benefit personally by selfishly using the information.

American Express

The federal securities laws impose restriction on the manner in which employees of a company that has publicly-traded securities may buy and sell or otherwise deal in those securities. Moreover, in the interest of prudence and to preserve the public image of integrity of American Express Company, the Company has adopted additional policies in this area. This statement summarizes those legal restrictions and Company policies insofar as they apply to employees of American Express Company and its subsidiaries in general. Separate, more stringent rules apply to elected officers of American Express Company, which have been communicated separately to those officers.

It is illegal for any employee, regardless of title or rank, to engage in any transaction in any securities of the Company at a time when he or she knows of material information with respect to the Company not known to the general public. It is also illegal for a person with material non-public information to reveal that information to others for the purpose of assisting their trading activities. Securities of the Company include not only its common shares but also pay preferred shares or publicly-traded warrants that may be outstanding or put and call options on common shares. The definition of material information is highly subjective. The general test is whether or not such information would reasonably affect an investor's decision to buy, sell or hold securities of the Company. Examples of such information include: [1] the pendency of an acquisition or disposition of a substantial business; [2] financial results for the Company or any major segment of the Company that are better or worse than recent trends would lead one to expect; [3] an increase or decrease in dividends; or [4] a stock split.

If at any time you are planning to trade in Company securities and you have questions as to whether or not you possess information that precludes you from doing so, you should consult the Office of the Secretary of American Express Company, who will act as a clearing center for all such questions.

In addition to the foregoing restrictions on trading, the Company from time to time, pending the release of material information to the general public, imposes a ban on trading in Company securities by employees who are likely to have access to such information. Accordingly, as a matter of corporate policy and without regard to whether or not they actually possess material inside information, employees with such access are required to consult the Office of the Secretary prior to engaging in any transaction in securities of the Company to determine whether or not such a ban is in effect. The employees to whom this policy applies have been so notified by a separate communication from the Office of the Secretary.

Similarly, because of their inherently speculative nature, the Company believes that it is inappropriate for employees with access to inside information to engage in any transactions in put and call options on the Company's common shares other than options issued under the Company's employee stock option plans. Again, this policy applies without regard to whether or not the person involved is actually in possession of material non-public information, and extends to those employees who have been notified that these policy restrictions apply to them.

As a final matter, the Company believes that it is inconsistent with the American Express reputation for complete integrity for any employee to trade in the securities of another company on the basis of material non-public information about that company obtained as a result of the employee's affiliation with the Company. Examples of such information would include knowledge that the Company is evaluating an acquisition of such company or proposes to enter into a major commercial transaction with it. Additionally, courts have imposed criminal liability on persons who "misappropriate" and trade on the basis of material non-public information in these circumstances. Any questions in this area should be referred to the Office of the Secretary of American Express Company who, as in the foregoing cases, will consult with the General Counsel's Office, as appropriate.

These are matters that the Company takes very seriously, and, accordingly, violations of these policies and procedures may result in disciplinary actions, including, depending on the circumstances, the possibility of termination of employment.

AT&T

AT&T encourages employees to participate in the Company's future by investing in its securities. Various Company plans allow employees to acquire Company securities on a regular basis. These include the Dividend Reinvestment and Stock Purchase Plan, the AT&T Savings Plan for Salaried Employees, the AT&T Savings and Security Plan, and the Employee Stock Ownership Plan. Besides these plans, the Company also encourages long-term investment in its stocks and bonds.

However, in trading in Company securities, employees should be aware that it is improper and illegal, and could result in civil or criminal penalties, to buy or sell Company securities based on "inside information" which includes material information about the Company that is not yet public.

"Inside" material information can be anything that could have actual significance in an investor's decision, such as acquisition plans; dividends; earnings; new contracts, products, or discoveries; major regulatory, court or legislative events; and major management changes or other business plans. Such information should only be disclosed to those with a Company authorized "need to know."

Employees aware of such information prior to its being made public should not buy or sell Company securities until the information has been made public. Also, employees who invest in AT&T stock through Company plans should not transfer account balances or change their allotments or investment direction based on material inside information until it has been made public.

Similarly, employees should not trade in the securities of other companies based on material non-public information about these companies which they've learned as part of their job. For example, an employee who learns that another company is being considered for a major contract or a joint venture, may not use this information to trade in that company's securities.

Employees should keep any such information about AT&T or other companies secret and use it only for Company purposes. Inside information must be treated as Proprietary Restricted or Registered Information until its public release. Details that are not made public are still considered Proprietary. It is also illegal and unfair to "tip" others who may buy, sell, advise or report on such securities, even though the "tipper" does not.

Some types of legal trading could appear to be based on the misuse of inside information. To avoid even an appearance of impropriety, employees must not engage in short-term speculation in Company securities—that is, the purchase and sale on the open market within a six-month period—unless there are circumstances unrelated to the investment value of the securities. Such circumstances may involve having to sell recently purchased stock to pay unexpected medical bills.

Further, employees must not engage in any transaction where they stand to profit from short-term swings in the value of the Company securities. This includes "short sales"—selling borrowed securities which the seller hopes can be purchased at a lower price when they are due for delivery—and "put" and "call" options— publicly available "rights" to sell or buy securities within a certain number of months at a specified price.

Any questions about a proposed investment in securities of the Company, or of other companies, should be directed to the Law Department. Violations or suspected violations of Company policies on insider trading or short-term trading in securities must be promptly reported to the AT&T Corporate Security Organization.

Aetna

Rule 10b-5 under the Securities Exchange Act of 1934 prohibits certain fraudulent or deceitful practices, the making of materially false statements, and the omission of material information in connection with the purchase or sale of securities. It applies to Aetna employees who, as a result of their jobs, possess confidential information about the Company or about other companies with which Aetna does business. Therefore, adhere to the following guidelines in determining when it is appropriate for you to buy or sell Aetna securities, or securities of other companies.

[Re: transactions in Aetna securities] . . . Because of the substantial legal exposure involved, if your job is at class 80 or above, you **must** consult with one of the persons whose names are shown at the end of this Statement before you or any member of your immediate family or anyone sharing your home buys or sells any Aetna security, including Aetna's common stock, preferred stock, debt instruments, put and call options on Aetna's stock, and any interests you may have related to Aetna's Stock Option Plan.

Systematic purchases of Aetna stock for an account where you cannot control the timing of those purchases, such as the Company's Incentive Savings Plan, Stock Purchase Program, Dividend Reinvestment Plan or Management Incentive Plan do not normally present legal risks. However, Incentive Savings Plan transfers or accumulated values to and from the Common Stock Account are within your control and subject to the rules set forth below. If you are a Parent Company director or officer, special rules apply; check with one of the people listed at the end of this Statement before electing to have Aetna stock purchased for you under any such plan. For all purchases other than the systematic purchases described, the rules are as follows:

(1) **Materiality of Information**—It is important to assess whether non-public information to which you have access is "material." To do this, ask yourself, erring on the conservative side, whether the information should affect someone's decision to buy, hold or sell Aetna securities. If it could, then you must forego any transaction in Aetna securities until Aetna has disclosed this information to the public. Talk to one of the Law Department personnel named at the end of this Statement if you have any doubt.

The fact that you are generally more familiar with Aetna's operations than the average investor will not, in itself, prevent you from buying or selling the Company's securities.

(2) **Determining When Information Is "Public"**—Information is not fully disclosed until a reasonable time has passed after dissemination of that information to the public. You should allow two business days between the time information is sent to the news services and the time you place your buy or sell order, so the information can be absorbed by the financial markets.

For maximum safety, limit transactions in Aetna securities to times when it can reasonably be assumed that all significant, relevant information about the Company has been disclosed. The best times for trading in Aetna securities are the periods following distribution of earnings reports or the annual report to shareholders. Conversely, the periods shortly preceding those distributions are not desirable times to trade. This guideline is particularly important for anyone with frequent access to significant non-public information about the Company.

If you feel you must buy or sell Aetna securities at some time other than suggested above, confer first with one of the people listed at the end of this Statement to discuss whether there is any imminent disclosure of significant information which, in hindsight, might make it appear that you bought or sold with previous knowledge of such information.

(3) **Disclosure of Aetna Position**—Whenever you buy or sell Aetna securities,

tell the broker of your relationship with Aetna. If you do this, it can never be argued that you had "inside" status and deliberately withheld that fact.

(4) **Transactions by Family Members**—The rules governing your securities transactions apply equally to transactions by members of your immediate family and to anyone sharing your home. They also apply to your giving recommendations to others. Giving tips based on material, non-public information is prohibited, which suggests a need for discretion when discussing your work with friends or family members.

(5) **Monitoring of Compliance**—The Corporate Secretary's Office monitors compliance with these rules and policies. In addition, pursuant to stock exchange rules, special procedures have been established for employees seeking to open margin accounts with brokers which require the Company to consent to the opening of such accounts and which allow the Company to receive duplicate confirmations of trades for those accounts.

Trinova

Employees should preserve the confidentiality of, and not use for their personal benefit, information obtained in the course of the Company's business. Occasionally employees are made aware of inside information about the Company which if publicly available could affect the market price of the Company's securities or influence an outside investor's decision whether to buy or sell such securities. Accordingly, all information pertaining to the Company's sales, earnings, financial condition, major contracts and acquisitions or divestitures must be kept confidential until it is fully disclosed to the public.

Any employee who possesses material inside information about the Company may not buy or sell TRINOVA securities or recommend the purchase or sale of such securities to others until the information has been released to the public and enough time has elapsed to permit investor evaluation of the information. Any employee who possesses such information should review *any* proposed sale or purchase with TRINOVA's General Counsel before trading in the Company's securities.

The Company's trade secrets and technical know-how are among its most valuable assets. Each employee must maintain the confidentiality of this information and not disclose it at any time to competitors, customers or suppliers of the Company except as may be required in the ordinary course of the employee's duties on behalf of the Company.

Motorola

(a) A Motorola employee may not buy or sell, or recommend to others to buy or sell, any security or other interest in property based on knowledge derived from such person's employment. Employees should avoid transactions in the area of real estate which Motorola may be considering buying or selling or has decided to buy or sell. (b) A Motorola employee may not discuss confidential Motorola information to any person other than in the proper discharge of the employee's Motorola duties.

Baxter

Employees whose job grade Hay Points exceed 1200 are prohibited from writing call options or otherwise buying or selling options on Baxter stock and from engaging in other short term trading activities, such as short sales, with respect to Baxter stock. Short term trading activities and option transactions increase the potential for profit from improper use of inside information, and such activities by members of management may adversely affect investor confidence. Employees designated above shall not carry or place Baxter shares in street name without prior written notification to the General Counsel and shall report changes in street name holdings.

Ingersoll-Rand

While working for the Company, employees may, from time to time, become aware of, or be involved in, matters of a confidential or proprietary nature. These would include financial projections, potential acquisitions, or other information which could be used by the employee for personal gain or advantage. The Company expects it employees to maintain the highest degree of integrity and ethical standards by not divulging such information to third parties or utilizing it in any manner, including purchase or sale of securities, which would be improper. Since such use may also violate existing laws, employees will be expected to act scrupulously to avoid even the appearance of impropriety.

Michigan National Bank

All information obtained from the relationship between the bank and its customers, prospective customers and suppliers is confidential and shall be used solely for MNB banking purposes. The use of such information to further private interests of oneself or others is unethical and may violate applicable security laws, the National Bank Act and regulations promulgated under that Act. No information should be disclosed except as authorized by the customer or as required by statute or a court of competent jurisdiction.

Confidential informations may, in some instance, be considered "insider information" that, if used or disclosed, could subject the employee, the corporation, and a person outside the corporation to whom the information is communicated, to liability under federal securities laws. "Insider information" is material non-public information. The test of materiality is that the information is sufficiently important that it would be expected to affect the judgment of investors on whether to buy, sell or hold stock, and if generally known, to affect materially the market price of the stock. The courts have ruled that insider information must be publicly disclosed before anyone possessing it can trade in the securities concerned. This applies to trading MNB securities as well as the securities of any other company, if its stock is publicly traded.

Chapter 21

CORPORATE CITIZENSHIP AND RESPONSIBILITY TO SOCIETY

In many communities, firms play a unique and powerful role. They are major employers, major contributors to the local economy, major sources of contributions to charitable causes, and important sources of local civic pride. They act as magnets for attracting other businesses and new residential growth to the area. The firms' executives and managers often play leadership roles in community government, schools, churches, social organizations, and civic activities.

At the same time, a big firm may dominate—and some would argue—control the destiny of a small town or medium-sized community. It may unleash pollutants or hazardous wastes with long-term dangers to the citizens of the area. A firm that is newly relocated may quickly change the character of a town or bring it increased traffic and more demands on public services.

As a result, many firms stress the importance of good corporate citizenship and the business's responsibility to society in their codes of conduct. The models presented below show the approaches taken and issues addressed by several major companies.

CORPORATE RESPONSIBILITIES TO SOCIETY

Holiday

We believe that to be an industry leader we must also be community leaders, sharing corporate resources to improve the living and working environment for our employees and fellow citizens. We will focus corporate contributions on our home communities where we can have the most impact, and encourage active volunteer participation in all types of civic affairs by all the people of Holiday Corporation.

Wells Fargo

Wells Fargo is dedicated to seeking solutions for a wide range of social and community concerns. Wells Fargo continually monitors areas where it can have a beneficial impact as a lender, as a provider of services and as a corporate citizen.

Existing programs are regularly reviewed and refined. Following are some of the programs reflecting Wells Fargo's corporate philosophy.

Kimberly-Clark

Kimberly-Clark is committed to being a good corporate citizen and is taking all reasonable measures to control the environmental effects of its manufacturing and other operations. It will conform to applicable local, state or federal air, water and other environmental rules or regulations and will carefully assess the need for controls to meet and adequately protect the interests of the company and the public at large. All employees are expected to act as responsible citizens by adhering to workplace rules and regulations concerning the environment.

San Diego Gas and Electric

As an integral member of the communities in our service territory, we have a corporate responsibility to support and be active in them. For this reason, we will: (1) Keep the public, community leaders, local governments and the media informed of events or plans which significantly affect community interests, and will respond openly to their inquiries. (2) Evaluate and consider in our decision-making the impact of Company operations and facilities on the surrounding communities. (3) Support participation by employees in community leadership and volunteer activities consistent with their job responsibilities.

COMMUNITY INVOLVEMENT

Ashland

Ashland strives to be a responsible corporate citizen in the communities and areas in which it operates. In this effort, the company provides support to various educational, cultural and civic endeavors. Such support may involve gifts of time—such as participating in executive-in-residence programs, sponsoring Junior Achievement activities, serving on community or university boards—or money. Monetary contributions are made in four main categories, including education, health and welfare, culture and art, and civic causes. Funds are allocated on the basis of financial need, degree to which programs affect employees or their families, effectiveness of the program being considered, and the extent of benefits to the public.

Support of higher education through making grants to colleges and universities and matching employee gifts to these institutions receives primary emphasis.

In addition, Ashland supports the United Way and similar united fund appeals through payroll deduction of employee gifts and through matching employee donations. An equal opportunity employer, the company also supports equal opportunity by seeking out and purchasing materials and supplies from minority-owned businesses. A subsidiary, Equal Opportunity Finance, Inc., assists minority entrepreneurs in obtaining capital for their business ventures. The company also encourages employees to become active citizens in their communities. You should use your good judgment to assure that your participation doesn't conflict with your responsibilities to the company.

Lafarge

The prosperity of Lafarge Corporation is closely linked to the prosperity of the communities in which we operate; our resources and the talents of our employees can therefore play an active role in improving those communities. As a responsible community member, Lafarge Corporation will conduct all of its business in an environmentally sound manner.

PPG

PPG is a corporate resident of the many communities in which we operate facilities. We believe that it is important for the Company to be regarded as an asset to those communities. Local goodwill contributes to the kind of climate in which a plant can operate profitably. It also helps to shape favorable attitudes which form the basis of municipal, state and national law. Our goal is to secure public understanding and support for PPG activities at the local level. To a certain extent, favorable attitudes toward the Company will result from its economic contribution as an employer, a purchaser and a taxpayer. But beyond that, PPG recognizes the need to play an active and visible role in improving the community's welfare. This includes operating a safe and clean facility, cooperating closely with local health and safety services, participating in civic programs, and communicating with local citizens. One of the most important objectives of communicating with residents of PPG plant communities is making sure that effective emergency response programs are in place at each location.

Harris

We will be a responsible participant in the local, national and international communities in which we operate. We will stress good citizenship and corporate leadership, and conduct business in a professional manner that is both legal and ethical.

TECO

TECO has established a tradition of being a strong community supporter and a responsible corporate citizen. And, as employees, we are encouraged to be active, responsible citizens in the communities in which we live. We should, however, use good judgment in selecting our community activities to assure that our participation does not conflict with our responsibilities to the company or with the company's business interests.

CHARITABLE ACTIVITIES

Public Service—Indiana

In our role as a good corporate citizen, we support worthy charitable causes so far as prudent allocation of our resources allows. Employees are encouraged to volunteer their time and efforts off the job toward endeavors that make our communities a better place to live, and may do so on Company time within the limits set out in the Company's personnel policies.

Rose's Stores

Rose's will continue to support worthy charitable organizations, but no associate may personally solicit contributions from any supplier for any charity or similar organized endeavor. Associates are permitted and encouraged to accept positions of responsibility in fund raising activities of well organized and worthy charitable organizations, but they may not use supplier lists of Rose's as the basis for solicitation by themselves or others.

Panhandle Eastern

The Panhandle Eastern Companies contribute to charitable, educational, cultural and community activities to demonstrate responsible corporate citizenship in areas where the Companies have employees and business operations. Contributions will be made to certain types of educational institutions. As a general rule, giving to colleges and universities will be limited to those institutions which are a regular source of employees for the Company through its recruiting program and those which provide evening or other supplemental education in which employees may have an opportunity to participate. Educational contributions may be made to offset operating deficits, support for capital programs, or grants to specific departments where the Company has a particular interest, such as engineering, accounting, economics, etc.

The Companies support the concept of the United Fund-type of campaign; therefore, the main portion of the contributions for charity, social and community welfare activities should be contributed to the United Fund or similar agencies in the communities where the Company has facilities and employees.

Chapter 22

PROTECTING THE ENVIRONMENT

Businesses and their employees are affected in many ways by what happens to the earth's environment. In the 1990s, worldwide concerns have been voiced over issues such as air quality, water quality, wildlife and forest preservation, toxic waste disposal, pesticides in food, recycling, and land reclamation. These concerns sometimes have spilled over into political and physical conflicts that affect jobs, profitability, and the future of entire projects or industries. How a company approaches and deals with environmental issues not only can affect its public image but its bottom line and, among many employees and managers, the firm's desirability as a place to work.

The following examples show how a variety of leading firms have dealt with sensitive environmental concerns in their business codes. The statements range from Digital Equipment Corporation's direct, one-sentence declaration to Chevron's eloquent essay, which attempts to give the employee an understanding of why certain regulations and restrictions must be enforced. Each example presented in this section represents a somewhat different approach to the major environmental, health, and conservation concerns. In some cases, firms have combined several issues into one code statement, while other companies have chosen to develop separate statements for each major issue.

PROTECTING THE ENVIRONMENT AND HUMAN HEALTH AND PRESERVING NATURAL RESOURCES

Chevron

Few issues in modern times have stirred as much controversy as the protection of the environment and human health. The passions and positions that have arisen on this issue are framed by two extremes. At one extreme are those who seek to restrict any human activity that seems to mar the purity of nature. At the other extreme are those—a steadily decreasing number—who believe in their right to pursue their own objectives without regard for the environment. The company supports and encourages laws to provide adequate protection for the environment and public health while simultaneously allowing reasonable economic growth and improvement in living standards. To this end, the company cooperates with industrial, community and governmental groups to try to develop environmental, health and safety regulations that accommodate both economic needs and the need for a safe, healthy and attractive environment and work place.

In the U.S., federal, state and local governments have enacted legislation designed to protect the worker, the public and the environment. At the federal level, for example, the Clean Air Act was passed to protect and enhance the quality of the nation's air. The Clean Water Act is meant to restore and maintain integrity of United States' waters. The Resource Conservation and Recovery Act regulates the disposal of both conventional and hazardous wastes. The Toxic Substances Control Act seeks to prevent the manufacture and use of chemicals that present an unreasonable risk to health or to the environment. The Occupational Safety and Health Act is designed to assure that safe and healthful working conditions are made available to all employees. Federal and state legislation is concerned also with recreation and aesthetics. These include laws regulating the use and development of coastal and wilderness areas and protecting visibility near significant scenic attractions. The company is aware of the special character of coastal and wilderness areas and believes that they should be preserved for those activities for which they are particularly suited. At the same time, the company believes that the development of natural resources in those areas is often compatible with preserving their important public uses. Penalties for violating these laws are severe. Under the Clean Air Act, for example, each day of violation may be punished by a fine or penalty of up to $25,000. Individual violators may also be imprisoned for up to one year. These criminal punishments may be doubled for those who repeat a violation. There are also severe penalties for falsifying required records or monitoring data. The states, too, have severe penalties for violations of laws, even if those violations do not cause injury to human beings or the environment.

Chevron has established a comprehensive and rigorous environment, health and safety compliance program and has issued detailed guidelines which are contained in the company's Manual of Compliance Procedures and Guidelines. It is our policy to comply with the spirit and letter of all environmental, health and safety laws and regulations, regardless of the degree of enforcement. If we believe that a regulation or government policy is unsound or contrary to law, we work to change it through the regulatory, legislative or judicial process, but while it is the law, we obey it. The company's efforts extend beyond merely meeting its legal obligations. It voluntarily takes additional measures to assure that its activities do not jeopardize the environment or human well-being. For example, the company has undertaken a five-year tank integrity program to identify underground tanks with a potential for leaks and to replace or repair them before a leak occurs. In many areas of regulation in the United States, there is a complex interrelationship between the federal and state governments. For example, in the areas of air and water pollution control and hazardous waste management, the Federal Environmental Protection Agency has the principal responsibility for implementing and enforcing the federal statutes. Each state also has its own air and water pollution controls, as well as hazardous waste management. These federal and state controls interact in many ways. Generally, the Environmental Protection Agency sets goals which the states must meet by specified deadlines. The states may also have their own, more severe, standards. Increasingly, local governments are establishing their own requirements. This has been particularly apparent in ordinances setting forth requirements for the design and maintenance of underground storage tanks and requiring the publication of data on chemical substances stored and used in industrial operations.

PRESERVING NATURAL RESOURCES AND PROTECTING THE ENVIRONMENT

Boise Cascade

The company is dedicated to practicing sound stewardship of its natural resources and will take all necessary steps to maintain a safe, clean environment within national policies and those of the states or provinces in which the company operates. All employees are expected to comply with the spirit as well as the letter of this policy. Where laws and regulations do not exist or are judged inadequate, the company will adopt its own environmental performance standards.

Air Products

Air Products is firmly committed to protection of the environment and conservation of each nation's natural resources. Air Products will not only comply with applicable environmental laws and regulations, but it will also monitor the impact of its products and their manufacture upon the environment. It is recognized that the Company's environmental concerns will include the health and aesthetic needs of the community's citizens. The Company and its employees are expected to participate in the development of sound, equitable and realistic laws and other standards designed to preserve the quality of the environment, while recognizing the economic costs and benefits to the Company, other industrial concerns, their employees and the public at large.

Combustion Engineering

The Company is aware of its obligation to the public to preserve the environment. All Company employees are required to conduct the Company operations in compliance with government regulations that prohibit contamination or waste of air, water and other natural resources. Employees responsible for operating Company facilities are expected to be familiar with such regulations and to obtain the necessary permits. Where appropriate, relevant Company departments, such as Health & Safety, should be utilized to obtain permits.

Digital Equipment

As good citizens, we believe we have a responsibility to keep our environment free of pollution and to set an example.

Litton

Litton is committed to the protection of the environment and the conservation of natural resources in every way. Litton will fully comply with environmental laws and regulations and will closely monitor manufacturing processes to ensure that the method by which goods are produced does not unreasonably harm the environment. Each Division shall ensure that its employees are aware of applicable environmental laws and regulations and shall develop policies to ensure that Division operations are fully compliant with the requirements for treatment of hazardous waste.

COMPLYING WITH ENVIRONMENTAL LAWS

Universal Corporation

In the United States and many foreign countries, numerous laws have been passed regarding the discharge of waste into the environment. Accompanying the laws are stiff civil and criminal penalties for violations of the same. It is our policy to comply with the letter and spirit of these laws.

CONSERVING ENERGY AND PROTECTING THE ENVIRONMENT

Kraft

Every Company activity is to be conducted with due concern for the human and natural environment in which it occurs. A prime planning and operating priority is the conservation of energy. Proper attention to both environmental and energy matters will not help only the present, but the future well-being of the Company and the communities in which it operates.

COMPANY ENVIRONMENTAL PROGRAMS

General Electric

Corporate Environmental Programs will [1] develop and administer objectives for employee health and safety programs, as well as environmental protection programs; [2] provide leadership to Company professionals involved with employee safety, industrial hygiene, environmental protection, and hazardous materials transportation; [3] issue appropriate bulletins, procedures and guidelines on employee safety, industrial hygiene, environmental protection, and hazardous materials transportation; [4] have the authority to conduct appraisals of programs addressing safety, industrial hygiene, environmental protection and hazardous material transportation, and to make appropriate recommendations for actions to be taken by the responsible manager; [and, 5] provide functional advice and counsel on environmental protection matters concerning Company facilities and on environmental compatibility issues involved in Company products and services.

ENVIRONMENTAL AUDITS

Upjohn

[Re] Real Estate: All acquisitions of real estate, including those associated with business acquisitions, must be preceded by an environmental audit approved by the Engineering and Legal Divisions. Exceptions are only permitted in conjunction with contractual guarantees of indemnification by sellers. Such exceptions must be approved in advance by the Chief Executive Officer.

PROTECTING THE ENVIRONMENT FROM HAZARDOUS WASTE MATERIALS

PPG

PPG recognizes that the Earth's natural environment is the common heritage of all living things. Additionally, the linkage between human health and the quality of the surrounding air, water and soil has been convincingly documented. Accordingly, the Company recognizes its responsibility to protect the environment adjacent to its facilities against damage resulting from its industrial operations. Toward this end, the Company has adopted a number of measures to assure that its manufacturing, transportation and waste disposal activities are consistent with environmental protection. This includes assigning qualified personnel to manage PPG's environmental control programs, cooperating with government and industry groups to develop appropriate standards, engineering production facilities to reduce or eliminate the discharge of pollutants, informing employees and community residents about relevant environmental control matters, dealing only with reputable waste disposal contractors, and complying with all applicable laws and regulations. PPG's Environmental Control Policy describes the implementation of these steps. The Company's Air Toxic Control Policy and its Zero Discharge Policy outline strategies of compliance in relation to air and water.

Sundstrand

Sundstrand must fully comply with all state and federal laws relating to the protection of the environment in the conduct of its business. It is recognized that the use of hazardous materials is unavoidable. However, we have an obligation to use and store these materials properly to insure that contact with the environment is minimized and limited to established accepted circumstances. All wastes which are generated must be stored as required by applicable law and must be recycled or disposed of at state or federally approved facilities which have also been approved by the Company. Employees must report, in accordance with applicable Company policies, all circumstances under which hazardous materials or wastes come in contact with the environment, are improperly handled or disposed of, or where a potential violation of law may exist.

Chapter 23

ADMINISTERING THE CODE, ENSURING COMPLIANCE, REPORTING VIOLATIONS, AND ISSUING SANCTIONS

Key decisions when setting up a code of conduct are: (1) who will administer it; (2) who will ensure compliance; (3) how will violations be reported; (4) and what sanctions will be imposed. The model codes below illustrate several approaches used by successful firms.

ADMINISTERING THE CODE

Polaroid

The code will be administered by a Code Committee consisting of at least three of the Company's Officers or Directors appointed by the President subject to approval of the Board of Directors. The decisions of the Code Committee on all matters concerning the interpretation or operation of the Code and on all questions arising thereunder will be final and binding upon all officers and employees of the Company.

All questions arising under the code should, in the first instance, be referred to the Chairperson of the Code Committee. The Chairperson may or, if so requested by the individual concerned, must refer any questions to full Committee. In appropriate cases such questions will receive confidential treatment by the Committee.

Premier

1. This Code of Ethics will be administered by an Ethics Committee formed for that

purpose within Premier Bancorp and each of its subsidiaries. The mission of the various Ethics Committees is to review the need for ethical standards in the day-to-day operation of the subsidiary; to make recommendations to the Premier Bancorp Management Committee with respect to changes or additions to this Code of Ethics; and to resolve conflicts and/or uncertainties regarding these standards as they affect specific situations of individuals.

2. Responsibility for overall administration of the corporate ethics program will rest with the Premier Bancorp Management Committee. Specifically, the Committee will review the need for corporate ethical guidelines, publish such guidance as it deems necessary; and function as a "court of the last resort" in the resolution of complicated and/or technical corporate ethics problems arising through Premier Bancorp.

Norwest

The Reporting Officer is responsible for the distribution and administration of the Code of Ethics and each employee must be given a copy. New employees must be given a copy of the Code of Ethics as soon as possible after hire usually when payroll and benefits information is given to the employee.

On each request for approval, consent or exception, the Reporting Officer must note his or her approval or disapproval of the request, any comments or reasons therefore, and the date filed. A copy of each disclosure or request for approval, consent or exception as filed must be sent to the employee. Reporting Officers should report questions involving unique issues or areas of uncertainty to the Corporate Secretary. In appropriate cases, questions will be referred to the chief executive officer of the Corporation for decision.

Disclosures and requests for approval, consent or exception must be retained by the Reporting Officer in a confidential file separate from the personnel and employee files. If an employee transfers between Norwest subsidiaries, the employee's Code of Ethics file must be transferred to the successor Reporting Officer. An employee's file must be retained for ten years following his or her termination of employment.

Reporting Officers must annually certify to their Board of Directors, with a copy to the Corporate Secretary, that each employee has been given a copy of the Code, that all employees have been reminded annually of their duty to comply with the Code, that the Code is being administered in accordance with its terms, and that, to the best of his or her knowledge, all employees are in compliance with the terms of the Code.

Questions about the interpretation or administration of this Code are to be referred to the Corporate Secretary. Inquiries concerning the Code will be handled confidentially.

Employees who violate the provisions of the Code will be subject to disciplinary action including dismissal.

Burlington Northern

Questions of interpretation or application of this code may arise with respect to a particular situation. If so, the persons involved are encouraged to seek the advice of his/her superior, the appropriate Company law department or office of general counsel, or from the Vice President, Law, of Burlington Northern Inc. Such inquiries may be made in writing or orally and will be treated confidentially.

Responsibility for adherence of this Code rests with each individual. Any suspected violation must be reported promptly and directly to the senior legal officer of the appropriate Company or to the Vice President, Law, of Burlington Northern Inc. without regard to the usual lines of reporting.

Observing the law is a minimum. The code envisions a level of ethical business conduct well above the minimum required by law.

Violation of this Code of Conduct will be grounds for appropriate disciplinary action, including, where justified, dismissal.

ENSURING COMPLIANCE

Contel

Each member of the organization is responsible for complying with the Code. Each member shall be provided with a copy of the Code and instructed as to its application. Supervisors must be careful in words and conduct to avoid placing or appearing to place pressure on subordinates that would cause them to deviate from acceptable standards of conduct.

The Code should be viewed as more than mere words or abstract ideals. Adherence to the Code must become an individual's responsibility to the Company and to fellow members of the organization. Individuals should feel free to report suspected violations of the Code without fear of retribution.

Each member of the organization is expected to report actual and suspected violations of the Code. Violations must be reported to supervisors through normal management channels or through the toll-free "hotline" administered by the Internal Audit Department. Every effort will be made to safeguard employee confidentiality when reporting suspected violations through normal management channels or the hotline.

A program to familiarize all Company members with the Code and the hotline will be conducted by the Corporate Communications Department and the Human Resources Department. The program will be presented to all current members of the organization as well as to all new hires. The Code and the hotline should also be featured prominently on Company bulletin boards.

Each member of the organization shall be required to certify in writing that he has no knowledge of any violations of the Code other than those previously reported. Appropriate periodic certification shall be required and shall be conducted by the Human Resources Department.

A report on the Company's activities to enforce the Code shall be prepared and submitted to the Audit Committee annually. The report shall include verification by the Vice President-Internal Audit and Company's independent public accountants that the certification program is being properly administered.

Any violation of the Code will subject an individual to disciplinary action. This action may include reprimand, suspension, demotion, reduction in compensation or dismissal, depending upon the nature of the offense.

Giant

A. The statements of policy in this Code are to be liberally interpreted in favor of the highest standards of legal and ethical behavior, and any doubt as to the highest meaning or coverage of this Code shall be resolved by making inquiry of the General Counsel who shall consult with the Audit Committee.

B. All associates, officers, directors and other persons in the Company's employ shall immediately report any violation of this Code to the General Counsel who shall notify the Audit Committee.

C. Upon the direction of the Audit Committee, associates, officers, directors and other persons in the Company's employ shall annually be required to confirm in writing to the General Counsel that they have no knowledge of any violation of this Code or of any other law or regulation by anyone employed by or transacting business on behalf of the Company.

Harris

Harris intends to be fair in its interpretation of the provisions of these Standards of Business Conduct. However, failure to comply with the Standards contained here may result in discipline, including such actions as warnings, suspension, termination or criminal prosecution. As with all matters involving disciplinary action, principles of fairness will apply. Any employee charged with a violation of these Standards will be afforded a full opportunity to explain his or her actions before disciplinary action is taken, and upon request, shall have the right to appeal to the Corporate Ethics Committee.

Disciplinary action will be taken as appropriate, for the following circumstances: [1] Against any employee who is found to have authorized, participated in or concealed actions which are a violation of these Standards; [2] Against the supervisors of any violators, to the extent that the circumstances reflect approval or condoning of the violation or a lack of reasonable diligence in supervision to prevent violations and also against any supervisor who retaliates, directly or indirectly, or encourages others to do so, against an employee who reports a violation of these Standards. Any employee desiring more information, assistance or clarification concerning the Company Standards is encouraged to contact his or her immediate supervisor or his or her Division liaison officer. If the matter is not satisfactorily resolved, it should be brought to the attention of the Director of Business Conduct as soon as possible.

Mead

The Guidelines for Proper Business Practices confirm that as company representatives, Mead people are expected to act with the highest integrity. Individual judgment will always play a vital role. The following questions may be helpful in dealing with specific situations which arise in your application of the guidelines: [1] Am I obeying the law? [2] Is anyone's personal status/stature improperly comprised or endangered by this action? [3] Am I complying with company policy and approved practices? [4] Am I personally proud of this action? [5] Would I feel comfortable if it were known by my business associates, family, friends, or the public at large? [6] Is my personal code of behavior being compromised? Am I comfortable with this act?

Sears

From time to time, as the Company deems it appropriate, each officer of the Company and such other management personnel as may be designated will be requested to complete a questionnaire concerning personal compliance with this policy and return it to an independent auditing firm. The auditing firm will prepare a brief report for the Chairman covering the receipt of the completed questionnaires and citing any problem areas disclosed therein.

At other times, every Corporate employee should feel free and is urged to present to the Company for a determination any particular investment or relationship which he or she would like to have reviewed for compliance with the letter and spirit of this bulletin. Such inquiries should be addressed to the Vice President and Corporate General Counsel.

Gillette

The chief executive officer is responsible to the Board of Directors for compliance with this policy. Managers of staff and operating units are responsible for compliance within their respective units, and will submit annual statements of compliance to the Senior Vice President, Legal.

REPORTING VIOLATIONS

Perkin-Elmer

All employees are authorized and required to report instances of improper business conduct of which they have personal knowledge to the employee's immediate supervisor. However, in instances where the employee's relationship with his supervisor could be placed in jeopardy because of the circumstances involved in the particular case of misconduct in question, such report of misconduct may be made directly to any responsible representative of the Corporation, such as any

Corporate Director or Officer, a Division Manager, or a member of the Internal Auditing, Accounting, Industrial Relations, or Legal Departments or, as provided for in Policy No. 1-013, to the Corporation's independent public accountants.

US West

All employees are responsible not only for their individual compliance with these rules, standards and principles, but also for reporting violations and suspected violations by others. Thus, in the area of ethics, legality and propriety, each employee has an obligation to the company which transcends normal reporting relationships. This obligation requires that employees be alert to possible violations of this Code anywhere in the company and to report such possible violations promptly. Reports should be made to the employee's supervisor, the appropriate Security or Law Department or elsewhere as the circumstances dictate.

Employees will also be expected to cooperate in the conduct of investigating violations. In addition, any employee who is convicted of a felony, whether related to these rules or not, should also report that fact.

All cases of questionable activity involving the Code or other potentially improper actions will be reviewed for appropriate action, discipline, or corrective steps. The Company will keep confidential the identity of employees about or against whom allegations of violations are brought, unless or until it has been determined that a violation has occurred. Similarly, whenever possible, the Company will keep confidential the identity of anyone reporting a possible violation. Reprisal against any employee who has, in good faith, reported a violation or suspected violation is strictly prohibited.

In order to comply with the Drug-Free Workplace Act of 1988, all employees are required to notify the Company within five (5) days of any conviction of any criminal statute violation occurring on the job. In addition, any employee who is convicted of a felony, whether related to the rules or not, should report that fact to an appropriate representative of the Company.

Home Group

Information about known violations of any provision of this Corporate Code of Conduct on the part of any Home Group or Home Insurance Company employees, independent agents, adjusters, appraisers, suppliers or vendors must be reported immediately to the Corporate Security Department . . . In the case of a subsidiary with a compliance department, violations must be reported to that department or to the General Counsel. The Company shall neither impose penalties nor take any retaliatory actions against any employee who reports violations as long as the employee has not personally committed a violation.

No action (including the acceptance of restitution) should be taken against or on behalf of anyone suspected of committing fraud, a dishonest act, or unethical conduct without prior review by the Personnel Department. Employees are required to cooperate with all conflict of interest or business conduct investigations carried out by the Company. Requests for information by law enforcement officials should be immediately referred to the Corporate Security Department.

Litton

Litton conducts its relations with its employees in a manner intended to create an atmosphere of mutual respect and understanding. Accordingly, all Divisions shall establish in addition to normal and routine employee reporting procedures: 1) a Division Employee Appeals Procedure whereby an employee may, without fear of retaliation, appeal what that employee believes to be an adverse personnel decision, and 2) provide a mechanism for any employee to report, without fear of retaliation, any practices occurring within the company that the employee believes to be not in compliance with the company's Policy Directives.

IMPOSING SANCTIONS

Apple

Apple expects its employees to compel with all provisions of these guidelines, to rely on their own high standards and reasoned evaluation in ambiguous situations, and to seek the advice and counsel of management and the Law Department to clarify issues not covered by these guidelines or good judgment. These guidelines are based in part on various laws, and employees should be aware that violations of those laws can result in criminal fines and punishment of the company and its employees, or adverse judgments in civil lawsuits.

Because of this seriousness, the company may take disciplinary action against any employee whose actions have been found to violate these standards. Such disciplinary action may include termination from employment or other working relationships.

Sears

Failure to conform scrupulously to Sears Standards of Ethical Business Conduct can result in serious damage to the Company's reputation and business interest, in the possibility of civil or criminal prosecution, and in such individual discipline, including discharge, as may be appropriate.

US West

Violation of this Code can result in serious consequences to the company, its image, credibility and confidence of its customers and can include substantial fines and restrictions on future operations as well as the possibility of fines and prison sentences for individual employees. Therefore, it is necessary that the company ensure that there will be no violations. Employees should recognize that it is in their own best interest, as well as the company's, to follow this Code carefully.

The amount of any money involved in a violation may be immaterial in assessing the seriousness of a violation since, in some cases, heavy penalties may be asserted against the company for a violation involving a relatively small amount of money.

Disciplinary action should be coordinated with the appropriate Human Resources representatives. The overall seriousness of the matter will be considered in setting the disciplinary action to be taken against an individual employee. Such action, which may be reviewed with the appropriate Human Resources organization, may include: Reprimand; Probation; Suspension; Reduction in salary; Demotion; Combination of the above; [and/or] dismissal.

In addition, individual cases may involve: Reimbursement of losses or damages; Referral for criminal prosecution or civil action; [and] Combination of the above.

Disciplinary action may also be taken against supervisors or executives who condone, permit or have knowledge of illegal or unethical conduct by those reporting to them and do not take corrective action. Disciplinary action may also be taken against employees who make false statements in connection with investigations of violations of this Code.

The disciplinary action appropriate to a given matter will be determined by the company in its sole discretion. The listing of possible actions is information only and does not bind the company to follow any particular disciplinary steps, process or procedure.

The company's rules and regulations regarding proper employee conduct will not be waived in any respect. Willful violation is cause for disciplinary action including dismissal. All employees will be held to the standards of conduct described in this booklet.

The company never has and never will authorize any employee to commit an act which is inconsistent with this Code or to direct a subordinate to do so. With that understood, it is not possible to justify commission of such an act by saying it was directed by someone in higher management.

ACKNOWLEDGMENTS AND CERTIFICATES OF COMPLIANCE

Many firms require their employees to acknowledge in writing that they have received a copy of the code of business conduct and that they are familiar with its contents. The following are excellent examples of compliance documents that can be adapted by other firms.

Ameritech

I have read the booklet, "Code of Business Conduct," and fully realize the necessity of:

- Protecting the Company's reputation.
- Preserving the privacy of communications.
- Engaging only in fair competition.
- Adhering to the requirements imposed by the Modification of Final Judgment.
- Safeguarding proprietary and classified national security information and adhering to the FCC's requirements with respect to the disclosure of customer proprietary information.
- Complying with the Company's drug abuse policy.
- Refraining from discrimination and sexual harassment.
- Properly handling of Company funds, property, records, and accounts.
- Protecting computer systems, and
- Guarding against espionage and sabotage.

I realize that both the law and Company practices require factual reporting and accounting in all phases of the Company's operations.

I also agree that during or after my employment I will not, except as required in the conduct of Ameritech's business or when properly authorized in writing, publish, disclose, use or authorize anyone else to publish, disclose, or use, any private, confidential, or proprietary information that I may have in any way acquired, learned, developed, or created by reason of my employment.

I understand that my employment can be terminated by me or the Company at any time, with or without cause and with or without notice, and that nothing in this booklet or any other publication, practice, policy or manual is to be interpreted to the contrary.

Signature _____

Name (printed) _____

Title _____

Department _____ Date _____

ACKNOWLEDGMENT RECEIVED

Supervisor's or other authorized signature _____

Name (printed) _____

Title _____ Date _____

Home Group

HOME GROUP CORPORATE CODE OF CONDUCT

ETHICAL DISCLOSURE FORM

I have listed below any present or anticipated financial interest, outside employment or other activities and any additional information which may appear to influence the performance of my duties, my responsibilities or my judgment.

Listed below are all outside employment and activities, financial interests and other pertinent information which I am disclosing under The Home Group Corporate Code of Conduct.

I understand that if any changes should occur, I will immediately complete a new Ethical Disclosure Form.

Name (please print) _____

Signature _____ Date _____

Company _____

Department and Location _____

W.W. Grainger

CERTIFICATION

(ADMINISTRATIVE EMPLOYEES)

I have received and read the W.W. Grainger, Inc *Business Conduct Guidelines* dated January 1990. I certify that I am presently in full compliance with the policies stated in the *Business Conduct Guidelines*, and that I have no direct knowledge or factual evidence of any present violation of them by another employee, except as I have specifically disclosed to the Company:

Signature _____

Name (print) _____

Social Security No. _____

Department or Unit _____

Location _____ Date _____

Centel

I have carefully read the Centel Corporation Ethics Policy, November 1989, and understand its provisions.

Date _____

Signature _____

I obtained the above signed acknowledgment from _____

Employee's Name _____

City _____   State _____

Date _____

Supervisor's Signature _____

Title _____

Chapter 24

ETHICS TRAINING FOR EMPLOYEES

Firms sometimes offer formal training programs or orientation sessions covering a firm's ethical principles and code of business conduct. Often, however, a manager or supervisor is responsible for imparting the information to a new employee.

ETHICS PROGRAMS

McDonnell Douglas

The Ethics Program is designed to give the employees of McDonnell Douglas Corporation an introduction to the role of ethics in business decisions and to enable them to analyze the ethical dimensions of their own job responsibilities.

[The Program's objectives are to:] [1] Look at the concept of ethics and how it relates to our business environment. [2] Emphasize senior management's dedication to maintaining good ethical practice throughout MD. [3] Show the employee various ways to apply ethical values to business decisions. [4] Learn several specific techniques to apply ethical values to business decisions. [5] Encourage employees to enter into formal discussions of their own areas of concern. [6] Encourage employees to communicate with senior management about problems encountered as they pursue their own ethical goals.

[The Program's specifics include:] [1] Ethics training is 8 hours in length for salaried exempt/non-exempt and hourly employees. Employees covered by Union agreements receive 4 hours of training. [2] Attendance at ethics training is *mandatory* for all employees. [3] Training is facilitated either by a Human Resources representative or management from the work group attending the training. [4] A segment of the training includes a video tape of Sandy McDonnell introducing the Code of Ethics and Standards of Business Conduct booklets, a review of this material, and a discussion of how to report suspected violations of the Code of Ethics and Business

Conduct. [5] Each component conducts their own training, using a standardized program developed in conjunction with a consultant . . . .

Waste Management

It is imperative that all employees be informed and advised of the provisions contained in the Policy Statement. All supervisors and managers are responsible for ensuring that new employees receive initial policy indoctrination at the time they are hired. Annual policy overview and discussion sessions are also to be scheduled with all employees.

Chapter 25

USING CLOSING STATEMENTS IN CODES

Just as a code of business conduct needs a strong beginning, so should it have a well-worded closing statement, one that sums up and reinforces the firm's emphasis on ethical behavior. These examples can serve as handy starting points for drafting your own closing statements.

CLOSING STATEMENTS

Chevron

We close with the thought that the responsibility for meeting our legal and ethical obligations cannot be fully defined or assured by any set of written rules, however extensive. In the end, our confidence must rest, as it always has, upon the integrity of our people.

Control Data

You are responsible to act within the spirit of the guidelines in this handbook—and to seek help when you need it. Your best guide is often your common sense. Ask questions if you are unsure about a situation. Use any of the resources listed in this section under "Raising ethical issues."

Control Data encourages its employees to take worthwhile economic and technical risks. We need to do this to provide innovative products to our customers. However, you should never risk an illegal or unethical action. To do so would provide a disservice to our customers, our shareholders, and ultimately, yourself as an employee.

As you conduct Control Data's business, ethics must be considered along with other business factors. Sound ethics are fundamental to our business.

Becton Dickinson

A code of ethics and the rule of law are as valid to a business environment as they are to the political and social system as a whole.

Neither should conflict with the exercise of individual talents and freedoms or impose special hardships or challenges on any business or individual.

Your strict adherence to the principles discussed in this booklet is the surest way to guard your Company's most valuable asset—its reputation.

We suggest that you keep this booklet handy for use as a ready reference. It and the Code of Conduct should guide you in your activities as a member of the Becton Dickinson family.

Proctor & Gamble

This booklet is essentially a summary of key operating principles which have served for many years as guidelines for the actions and decisions of Proctor and Gamble employees. It reaffirms what all employees must keep constantly in mind: that P&G people, wherever they are located and whatever they do, are expected to conduct themselves as Company representatives in accordance with the highest possible integrity.

It is obviously impossible in a summary booklet of this type to cover every conceivable situation where an employee may have to deal with questions of law and ethics. Highly detailed policies and guidelines already existing within the Company cover most of the subjects covered in this booklet, and these should be the primary basis for actions/decisions. If neither this booklet nor the specific policies and guidelines seem to offer sufficient guidance to cover a particular situation, an employee should consult with his/her manager and other appropriate sources of guidance.

Early in the history of The Proctor & Gamble Company, its founders established a tradition of integrity in dealings within and without the organization. That characteristic—"try to do the right thing"—is the principal facet of the total character of Proctor & Gamble. And it is P&G's character which top management has often described as the underlying asset which holds the Company together in times of change or stress.

Because the character of the Company is always, in the final analysis, but a mirror of the conduct of its people, each employee has a continuing personal responsibility in all dealings with customers, suppliers, employees, shareholders and the public to see that the Company continues to "try to do the right thing."

AT&T

AT&T's Code of Conduct reaffirms the importance of following the highest standards of business conduct. Adherence to these standards by all employees is the only sure way the Company can maintain the confidence and support of the public and AT&T customers.

Each employee is responsible for his or her actions. For each, integrity is a personal responsibility. No one may justify an illegal act by claiming it was ordered by someone in higher management. No one, regardless of rank, is ever authorized to direct an employee to commit an illegal or unethical act.

As a summary of basic principles, this booklet does not include all the rules and regulations that apply to every situation. Its contents must be viewed within the framework of Company policies, practices, and instructions, and the requirements of the law. Moreover, the absence of a Company practice or instruction covering a particular situation does not relieve an employee from acting ethically. Employees with questions about a particular situation should consult their supervisor, the Law Department of the AT&T Corporate Security Organization.

Violations or suspected violations of any of the policies or principles in this booklet, or other Company rules and instructions, must be promptly reported to supervision or the AT&T Corporate Security Organization, as appropriate. Reprisals against an employee who, in good faith and with reasonable belief, reports such a violation or suspected violation is strictly forbidden. One important point bears repeating: **Violations can result in disciplinary action, including dismissal—even for a first offense in appropriate circumstances—and criminal prosecution.**

SECTION III

IMPLEMENTING AND ENFORCING A CODE OF BUSINESS CONDUCT

Chapter 26

IMPLEMENTING THE CODE

Once a code of business conduct has been drafted, reviewed and approved, the process of implementing the code can begin. The mere adoption of a comprehensive code will not ensure that employees will adhere to it. It must be communicated properly to its intended audience.

The manner in which a firm disseminates its code signals to all employees the significance and stature of the code. If the chairman, CEO, or president of the firm transmits the code to employees, the code gains a certain prominence. For example, in a 1987 study of codes of conduct, 73 percent of the respondents designated the company's chief executive officer as playing the largest role in setting ethical standards for the firm. Thus, a cover letter, signed by the CEO, chairman, or president and pointing out why adherence to the code is critically important, can have a significant impact on employees. Premark Vice President John Kelly agreed with that assessment. "The company's successfully communicating the importance and absolute necessity of the code serves a beneficial impact, as opposed to penalizing after the fact because employees violated the code through indifference," he said.

The objective of a code of conduct often determines the scope of its dissemination. Codes that are intended to guide employees in all areas of the firm naturally should be distributed to every employee. Codes structured to be public relations documents, on the other hand, may be distributed more widely to external groups than to employees. And codes that address only the conduct of managers and other high level personnel likely will not be handed out to the general audience of employees. For example, many banks are very concerned about conflicts of interest, and they may create specialized codes intended for officers and key employees who deal directly with customers, vendors, or other third parties.

Without proper dissemination to the right audience, a code of business conduct is destined to fail, through lack of familiarity and a corresponding lack of support. About seven out of ten firms surveyed by the Ethics Resource Center provide codes of conduct to new employees as part of their procedure manuals, orientation programs, or training sessions. But while a majority of firms (57%)

distribute their codes to all employees, the remaining 43% in the survey reported that the codes are distributed to specific subsegments of the employee population.

Sometimes, a code originally created for internal dissemination finds a useful life beyond the walls of the firm. Caterpillar, for example, distributed more than 25,000 copies of its code to association leaders, Caterpillar dealers, suppliers, and other opinion makers over a five-year period after the document was released.

CODE DISTRIBUTION

Several techniques are used to distribute codes to employees. FPL, Enron, and Geico are among the many firms that mail copies of the documents to all employees. Another frequently used technique is to place the code in each copy of the company's policy and procedures manual. According to Michael Brown, director of employee relations at Northeast Utilities, "placing the code in the employee handbook institutionalizes the code and ensures that it won't be lost as easily as a separate brochure alone—this integration is a key success factor to establish an effective code."

To be implemented successfully, codes of conduct require a basic accountability that can only be reasonably assured when the firm educates its employees about the code's contents and establishes an effective and fair enforcement mechanism. Codes that are neither explained to employees nor enforced suggest a mere window-dressing document.

EMPLOYEE EDUCATION

On the other hand, the employee education process, some observers contend, may help fill a void in ethical behavior that has been caused by a dearth of appropriate training outside the firm. According to Susan Koonsman, a United Banks of Colorado vice president, "education about codes is critically important because many people haven't developed values because of the breakdown in our schools, churches, and families in teaching values and ethics."

Another effective technique is to explain the code in the context of the firm's history and sense of values, as well. For example, at Disney University, a training department of Walt Disney, all new employees receive more than just a summation of ethics and good business conduct, according to the department's manager, Sharon Harwood. "Every new employee receives orientation which stresses the values and philosophy which have led to Disney's success—we correlate these values to the present through printed materials, videos, and group interaction."

Studies have shown that the most effective employee training sessions for codes of conduct are brief—two to four hours—and interactive. Group sizes should be kept small, so each employee can have an opportunity to discuss his or her experience with business conduct and ethical dilemmas.

Highly polished presentations also demonstrate the gravity of a code of business conduct and help employees pay attention to the information that is being imparted. For this reason, some firms hire outside trainers to make the presentations or hire consultants to train the firm's presenters. Lockheed, for example, used a "quite extensive" and well-developed presentation to introduce new and current employees to the firm's code of conduct. According to Donald Gore, Lockheed's director of business practices, the process included a brief orientation program with a videotape featuring Lockheed's chairman and "candid and unrehearsed commentary from a broad cross-section of Lockheed employees . . . stressing, in their own words, their own views on the importance of ethical business conduct." In addition, "comprehensive four-hour training sessions were attended by managers and supervisors at every level, from the chairman of the board to the factory floor . . . ." Moreover, "non-supervisory employees whose responsibilities present a high degree of ethical sensitivity (i.e., those involving considerable discretionary duties or complex regulatory requirements) also attended four-hour training sessions . . . [which] included segments that conveyed substantive information respecting particular duties and 'case study' workshops that provided employees with a framework for recognizing, analyzing and resolving ethical conflicts that might be encountered in the workplace," Gore reported.

RESISTANCE TO CHANGE

Sometimes, during the implementation process, employees or managers may resist change. "There is always resistance to change," Jack Reichert, Brunswick chairman and CEO, commented, "but I believe more than anything else, people really test you to find out whether it is simply today's value system or whether the business really believes in [the code standards] over a long period of time."

Resistance to change, according to other observers, is comprised of several elements: (1) the individuals' need for stability and for control or autonomy in their environment; (2) the individuals' need for maintaining their established power in the *status quo ante*; and (3) their need for protecting the present system, because they perceive it as better than the proposed changes.

A second hindrance to code implementation is that the new code may interfere with existing systems of management control by disrupting the normal functioning of the organization. For example, the code may require a change in standard reporting relationships. Or the code may make it more difficult for employees to exercise the same degree of control over their activities.

A third potential hindrance to code implementation is that the changes the code brings about may adversely affect the existing authority or power relationships among different groups or individuals.

DEFUSING RESISTANCE

Firms can take several steps, however, to defuse the resistance to a new code of business conduct.

The first action step is to identify and surface the dissatisfaction with the current state, thus "unfreezing" people from their present inertia so they will be more receptive to change.

Second, the firm can actively build employee involvement in the process of change. This can be done by having employees help create and implement the code. Questionnaires can be used to monitor employee values. And effective education programs can be offered to highlight the new code.

Third, top management can lessen the resistance by constructing rewards for the desired behavior in accepting the change. For example, resistance is often lowered when acceptance of a code and adherence to it is included in an employee's annual performance review to determine promotion, job assignment, and salary increases.

Finally, employees need a reasonable length of time and an opportunity to disengage from the present state. In short, a code should not be approved one day and put into action the next. It should be introduced and discussed, and a date for implementation should be announced, before the code actually goes into effect.

In the final chapter, the procedures for enforcing a code of conduct are examined.

Chapter 27

ENFORCING THE CODE

"A code which is created but not enforced" is, in the words of Independence Bancorp Vice President and Corporate Attorney Marcia Oeste, "an empty chalice."

Enforcement usually is not an issue for firms that create a code comprised only of general precepts. Instead, these firms rely on peer and hierarchical pressures, as well as the fundamental honesty of employees and managers, to generate compliance.

METHODS OF ENFORCEMENT

With codes of conduct containing directives that must be obeyed, however, firms typically rely upon two methods for assuring compliance: (1) surveillance and oversight; and (2) relying on individual integrity and senior-management role models.

In the surveillance and oversight method, employees are encouraged or required to report violations they witness through channels to a specific fact-finding agency or group that will investigate the allegations and take enforcement action. For example, at Olin, the code "invites any employee to report 'any activity which the employee in good faith believes is or may be a violation of this Code,'" according to McIntosh Cover, vice president and general counsel. "Reporting a violation is an expected, accepted and protected behavior, not the exception to the rule."

The second method relies on individual integrity and senior-management role models to produce the compliance. However, this method has not fared well, given the extent of top executives' involvement in the business scandals of the past two decades.

There are at least five reasons why many firms choose the surveillance and oversight method of code enforcement, instead.

First, managers can rely on the hierarchy of management to help them enforce the codes. In this chain-of-command system of authority, top managers can diffuse their values downward through the ranks. And they can require a signed certification that employees have read, understand, and will adhere to the code's provisions.

Second, historically, the Securities and Exchange Commission (SEC) has advocated that top management should exercise its authority regarding ethical concerns. For example, the Foreign Corrupt Practices Act, drafted by SEC auditors and attorneys, implies that top executives should use codes of conduct as vehicles to diffuse ethics throughout the various employment levels of their firms.

Third, many top executives subscribe to the position that firms must have "no-nonsense" mechanisms to effectively ensure compliance with codes. This attitude is based on the assumption that diligent detection and sure and timely punishment will deter wrongdoing.

Fourth, oversight procedures are easier to administer than general precepts, and the policy results are more tangible. Also, oversight procedures offer executives some protection from charges of not punishing, or even ratifying, wrongdoing among subordinates. Some firms have established surveillance-oriented oversight procedures to protect themselves against charges that executives have overlooked employees' violations of the law.

THE CONTENT AND FORM OF THE ENFORCEMENT AGENCY

When a firm chooses to enforce its code, it then must decide on the content and form of the enforcement agency. Will it be made up only of executives and managers and, possibly, some employees of the firm? Or will the enforcement agency include some outsiders as well, such as consultants, community leaders, or social scientists? Outside members can help enhance the uniformity and impartiality of enforcement. But company executives may be reluctant to have to expose and explain the inner workings of the firm to outsiders. And they may not want to set up any conflicts that would pit the "outsiders" against the "insiders."

A related issue poses some equally difficult choices. Should the enforcement process be incorporated as an ethical review into the procedures for periodically evaluating and rewarding employees? Or, should an employee suspected of a code violation be given a formal, quasi-judicial hearing similar to a trial? Many firms employ a combination of the two choices.

In firms where reporting code violations is encouraged, ways should be set up for top management to protect the employees who have revealed the wrongdoings. Such assurance often is included in a compliance form that many firms require employees and managers to sign, usually once a year. By signing the form, the employees and managers affirm that they have read the code and understand it. Often, they also are required to disclose any code violations that they have witnessed or of which they have knowledge or in which they have participated.

As an example, at Kaiser, according to General Counsel and Vice President David Perry, "Periodic inquiry is made into antitrust, conflicts of interest and accuracy of books and records issues with confidential surveys directed to a committee of the Board."

But not all firms favor the use of compliance forms or believe they provide a deterrence. Allan Goldstein, general auditor for Meritor, maintains that "detailed attempts to obtain acknowledgments . . . are not worth the administration effort."

Periodic audits are used by many firms to improve compliance with their codes. Auditors can bring impartiality, independence, and considerable knowledge of the firm's business to the process, and they may already have considerable experience investigating and monitoring various systems within the company. Chevron, for instance, relies on "periodic reviews by our full-time auditing staff . . . for compliance with our ethics guidelines," according to J.D. Hufford, manager of employment, policies, and administration.

Some firms take a multi-faceted approach to ensuring compliance. For example, at Bankers Trust, according to Senior Vice President James Byrne, Jr.: "Compliance with the policy is structured around three groups: the individual departments . . . [which are] responsible for assuring day-to-day compliance . . . [some of which have] compliance officers . . . [while] [t]he Central Compliance Department [the second compliance group] is responsible for enforcing certain active requirements under the policy specifically relating to employee security accounts . . . [and it] conducts a daily review . . . [and, last] [t]he Audit Department initiates standard periodic reviews of department to insure compliance with the policy, among other issues."

According to Ethics Resource Center reviews of codes of business conduct, in slightly more than half of the firms studied, one individual has the responsibility for evaluating violations. In just under 29 percent of the firms studied, ethics committees or management committees review the alleged violations. At many firms, employees may appeal a ruling to a management committee, the general counsel, the president, or sometimes even the chairman of the board.

Robert Souder, senior vice president for personnel at Rite Aid, describes the use of line management in that company's adjudicatory procedure: "Once an alleged violation has been reported or discovered, the Security Department, in conjunction with the head (usually vice president) of the department which employs the alleged perpetrator, investigates and presents its findings to that department head . . . [who] discusses the matter with the Senior Vice President of that department before making disposition." In instances when an offense is "very serious," Souder says that he is "consulted to discuss an appropriate sanction, and, if reporting the employee for prosecution is a possibility, the Legal Department will also advise . . . Sanctions include verbal and written warnings, suspension, termination and reporting for prosecution."

Many firms take reasonable steps to assure fairness, thoroughness, speed, and consistency in the adjudicatory process. Without an actual and visible system of due process and appeal, a code cannot maintain the confidence of those it addresses.

APPENDIX A

MEASURING VALUES AND ATTITUDES: A QUESTIONNAIRE FOR EMPLOYEES AND MANAGERS

Changing technologies, disappearing boundaries between industries, and fierce competition—these are just some of the facts of life for those who do business in the 1990s.

More than ever, two-way communication between management and employees is vital to the survival of the firm. One way to enhance the interactions and flow of information between these two levels is to measure the values and issues that employees and managers consider important and to address these values and issues in the business code of conduct. Such an approach shows that the firm cares about, and listens to, the opinions and concerns of those it employs. "There's a whole new kind of work force that has high expectations of being listened to . . . [there's] a new model of leadership built on shared responsibility and teams," asserts Allan Cohen, Babson College professor of management.

Scott McNealy, CEO of Sun Microsystems, points out that "codes [of conduct], their development and communication, are effective mechanisms for building the shared values necessary to permit empowerment to act." By "empowerment," McNealy refers to the new model of shared responsibility in the workplace and proactive, confident employee effort in behalf of the firm. Moreover, as Florida Progress CEO Andrew Hines, Jr., reminds, "[M]any [managers and employees] do not come to a business with the sense of values which that business attempts to foster."

Recent studies have turned up evidence of a growing shift away from the top-down decision making styles and toward participative work environments where employee input is encouraged. At some firms, such as United Technologies, which has instituted what it calls a PERL (positive employee relations leadership) program, the move to a work atmosphere where employees feel comfortable pointing out problems and making suggestions has proven very successful. The benefits include improved performance, better productivity, and higher employee morale and self-esteem.

One way to initiate the process of listening to employees and managers is to use a well-structured questionnaire that challenges them to respond and reveal their views, values, attitudes, and expectations concerning the business and its work environment. The values turned up by this questionnaire then can be addressed in various sections of the code of business conduct.

The following questionnaire is designed to measure attitudes, values, and expectations of employees and managers. It can be adapted as needed to best fit the exact needs of a small, medium-sized, or large firm.

MEASURING VALUES AND ATTITUDES: A QUESTIONNAIRE FOR EMPLOYEES AND MANAGERS

1. The first questions in this survey ask for your opinion about the firm overall, how the company relates to customers, employees, shareholders, and how it manages several important business issues. Please pick from this list those statements that best describe the firm as a whole.
   The firm...

	Check
a. is likely to grow in the future.	☐
b. has a good overall reputation.	☐
c. is concerned about providing high-quality service to its customers.	☐
d. is a modern, up-to-date company.	☐
e. is good at planning for the future.	☐
f. is a leader/pacesetter.	☐
g. is a well-run company.	☐
h. provides good job security.	☐
i. lives up to its social responsibilities.	☐
j. practices high ethical standards.	☐
k. is interested in employees' ideas and opinions.	☐
l. pays competitive salaries.	☐
m. is able to attract high-quality employees.	☐
n. manages its employees well.	☐
o. shows concern for employees.	☐
p. is able to retain high-quality employees.	☐
q. rewards good job performance.	☐

2. Considering your experience here, as well as what you may know of other organizations, how would you rate the firm on each of the following? Circle one number for each statement.

		Very Good	Good	Average	Poor	Very Poor	Not Applicable
a.	Treating you with respect and consideration.	1	2	3	4	5	6
b.	Communicating information about job opportunities.	1	2	3	4	5	6
c.	Providing training so that you can handle your present job.	1	2	3	4	5	6
d.	Providing training to help you qualify for a better job.	1	2	3	4	5	6
e.	Responding promptly to your safety concerns.	1	2	3	4	5	6
f.	Ability of the firm's top management.	1	2	3	4	5	6
g.	Job security.	1	2	3	4	5	6
h.	Concern for employees' safety.	1	2	3	4	5	6
i.	Letting you know what's going on in the corporation generally.	1	2	3	4	5	6
j.	Willingness to do something about employee problems and concerns.	1	2	3	4	5	6
k.	Opportunity for advancement.	1	2	3	4	5	6
l.	Sensitivity to cultural differences.	1	2	3	4	5	6

m. Sensitivity to international differences. 1   2   3   4   5   6

n. Applying company policies and work rules the same way in all divisions or departments. 1   2   3   4   5   6

3. Please read each of the following statements about the firm, and decide how much you agree or disagree with it. Then circle the number on the AGREE:DISAGREE scale that is closest to your opinion in general.

	Strongly Agree	Tend to Agree	Neutral	Tend to Disagree	Strongly Disagree	Not Appli-cable
a. The firms understands employee needs.	1	2	3	4	5	6
b. The procedures for considering employees for job openings are fair.	1	2	3	4	5	6
c. The firm recognizes employees for service in their communities.	1	2	3	4	5	6
d. The firm avoids excess management levels.	1	2	3	4	5	6
e. The firm provides equal opportunity for training and development for those qualified.	1	2	3	4	5	6
f. The firm provides equal opportunity for promotion for those qualified.	1	2	3	4	5	6

g. The firm exhibits
    sufficient concern
    for employees
    whose jobs have
    been changed or
    eliminated.   1   2   3   4   5   6

h. The firm rewards
    managers and
    supervisors for
    developing
    subordinates.   1   2   3   4   5   6

i. It is easy to obtain
    accurate
    information about
    company policies at
    the firm.   1   2   3   4   5   6

j. The firm
    encourages
    teamwork.   1   2   3   4   5   6

k. The firm rewards
    teamwork.   1   2   3   4   5   6

4. How strongly do you agree or disagree with the following statements about
   management in your division or department? (Circle one number for each
   statement.)

		Strongly Agree	Tend to Agree	Neutral	Tend to Disagree	Strongly Disagree	Not Applicable
a.	provides a clear sense of direction.	1	2	3	4	5	6
b.	creates an environment which fosters innovation.	1	2	3	4	5	6
c.	acts on employee problems and concerns.	1	2	3	4	5	6
d.	acts on employee suggestions for improvement.	1	2	3	4	5	6

e. creates an atmosphere of openness and trust.	1	2	3	4	5	6
f. actively seeks the opinions of employees.	1	2	3	4	5	6
g. keeps employees informed about what's going on in division or department.	1	2	3	4	5	6
h. promotes the most competent people to key management positions.	1	2	3	4	5	6
i. encourages teamwork.	1	2	3	4	5	6
j. rewards teamwork.	1	2	3	4	5	6
k. works out unit disagreements.	1	2	3	4	5	6

5. Please read each statement that follows and decide how much you AGREE or DISAGREE with it. Circle the number of the AGREE: DISAGREE scale that is closest to your opinion in general.

	Strongly Disagree	Neutral	Strongly Agree	Does Not Apply
Overall, the firm:				
1. understands customer needs.	1 2 3	4	5 6 7	0
2. emphasizes customer service.	1 2 3	4	5 6 7	0
3. services customer orders *promptly.*	1 2 3	4	5 6 7	0
4. understands its employees' needs.	1 2 3	4	5 6 7	0
5. recognizes employee potential.	1 2 3	4	5 6 7	0

6.	evaluates employee performance fairly.	1	2	3	4	5	6	7	0
7.	practices open communication with employees.	1	2	3	4	5	6	7	0
8.	works out disagreements among units.	1	2	3	4	5	6	7	0
9.	supports its employees.	1	2	3	4	5	6	7	0
10.	experiments with new ideas.	1	2	3	4	5	6	7	0
11.	considers new ideas and suggestions in an organized way.	1	2	3	4	5	6	7	0
12.	develops innovative programs.	1	2	3	4	5	6	7	0
13.	pays competitively compared to similar jobs in other companies.	1	2	3	4	5	6	7	0
14.	produces products with "the priceless ingredient" (Quality).	1	2	3	4	5	6	7	0
15.	pays adequate attention to productivity measurement.	1	2	3	4	5	6	7	0
16.	seeks to improve productivity.	1	2	3	4	5	6	7	0
17.	strives to reduce costs.	1	2	3	4	5	6	7	0
18.	develops its employees.	1	2	3	4	5	6	7	0
19.	provides an orderly process for career development.	1	2	3	4	5	6	7	0
20.	moves decision-making to the appropriate level.	1	2	3	4	5	6	7	0
21.	avoids excess management levels.	1	2	3	4	5	6	7	0
22.	excels in management.	1	2	3	4	5	6	7	0
23.	shows concern for people.	1	2	3	4	5	6	7	0
24.	provides equal opportunity for *development* for those qualified.	1	2	3	4	5	6	7	0
25.	recognizes employees for services in their communities.	1	2	3	4	5	6	7	0

26. shows social responsibility/
supports charities and other
good works.   1 2 3   4   5 6 7   0

6. How do employees get ahead at the firm? (Circle the number of the AGREE :
   DISAGREE scale that is closest to your opinion.)

		Strongly Disagree	Neutral	Strongly Agree	Does Not Apply
a.	By knowing the "right people."	1 2 3	4	5 6 7	0
b.	By making sure their immediate supervisor likes them.	1 2 3	4	5 6 7	0
c.	By performing their job well.	1 2 3	4	5 6 7	0
d.	By being willing to accept responsibilities.	1 2 3	4	5 6 7	0
e.	By getting along well with other employees.	1 2 3	4	5 6 7	0
f.	By making sure they don't "rock the boat."	1 2 3	4	5 6 7	0
g.	By attending training and development programs.	1 2 3	4	5 6 7	0
h.	By having a college degree.	1 2 3	4	5 6 7	0
i.	By being willing to transfer elsewhere within the Company.	1 2 3	4	5 6 7	0
j.	By demonstrating technical competence.	1 2 3	4	5 6 7	0
k.	By having highly visible work assignments.	1 2 3	4	5 6 7	0
l.	By having long Company service.	1 2 3	4	5 6 7	0
m.	By being lucky.	1 2 3	4	5 6 7	0
n.	By making significant contributions to the Company.	1 2 3	4	5 6 7	0

o. By working a lot of extra
   hours.   1 2 3   4   5 6 7   0
p. By using leisure time to
   improve themselves.   1 2 3   4   5 6 7   0

7. From which of the sources listed below would you say you *currently* receive
   information and from which sources would you *prefer to* receive information
   about the firm?

	Currently Receive	**Would Prefer**
EYES AND EARS		
a. Grapevine, fellow employees.	☐	☐
b. Bulletin board.	☐	☐
c. My own supervisor.	☐	☐
d. Departmental memos.	☐	☐
e. Departmental meetings.	☐	☐
f. Meetings with management.	☐	☐
g. Personnel Office.	☐	☐

8. Which of the following services do you feel is the duty of any firm to provide
   for its employees? (Circle your responses.)
   a. Child-care programs.
   b. Parental and pregnancy leave.
   c. Personal days of leave for sick child care.
   d. Safe parking facilities including business guards if the firms are located in
      urban areas or high crime risk areas.
   e. Work-environment that will not be hazardous to an employee during her
      pregnancy.
   f. Flex-time to allow an employee to spread his contracted hours of work
      (usually 8) over the entire hour-span of a day.
   g. Work-at-home arrangements.
   h. Same rights for both fathers and mothers regarding child care.
   i. Other: _____

Comments, if you wish:

9. Which of the following do you strongly consider as being obligations of the
   firm? (Circle as many as you wish.)
   a. Avoiding direct harm to employees.
   b. Respecting employee rights.

   c. Communicating honestly.

   d. Honoring promises and labor contracts.

   e. Obeying laws and complying with government regulations.

   f. Helping employees in need.

   g. Treating employees fairly.

   h. Adhering to an equal-opportunity employment policy.

   i. Other: _____

Comments, if you wish.

10. Which of the following would result in termination of the employment of an employee in your firm? (Circle as many as you wish.)

   a. Any conduct that causes the firm to lose confidence in the manager's ability to perform in accord with company standards.

   b. Unsatisfactory work performance.

   c. Dishonesty, theft, fraud, or embezzlement.

   d. Serious misconduct.

   e. Obtaining employment on the basis of false or misleading information.

   f. Outside employment which constitutes a conflict of interest.

   g. Falsifying company documents.

   h. Excessive absences or tardiness.

   i. Unauthorized use of computer-related resources.

   j. Soliciting or accepting gifts in connection with a company transaction of any kind.

   k. Bringing firearms or illegal weapons on company premises.

   l. Accepting temporary employment elsewhere while on a leave-of-absence.

   m. Other:

Comments, if you wish:

11. With which of the following statements do you mostly agree or mostly disagree?

	Mostly Agree	Mostly Disagree	Neither Agree nor Disagree (Neutral)
a. Corporations do not have a conscience; they are legal entities, not persons.	☐	☐	☐
b. The only corporate social responsibility is to increase profits.	☐	☐	☐

c. Unequal incomes are the cause of injustice in society.   □   □   □

d. Corporations should not undertake any action at all which does not have a positive cost/benefit relationship.   □   □   □

e. Personal values should be subordinated to corporate values.   □   □   □

f. Companies should be managed solely for the benefit of the shareholders.   □   □   □

g. Capital punishment is a necessary deterrent to some types of murder (i.e., murder after rape or kidnapping).   □   □   □

h. Workers should be given at least sixty days notice of an impending plant closing.   □   □   □

i. Business ethics do not exist.   □   □   □

j. Information is power; therefore, your own information should not be shared with fellow workers.   □   □   □

k. Corporations should not discriminate in the hiring or promotion of persons with AIDS.   □   □   □

l. Corporations should not be allowed to make monetary or monetary-equivalent contributions to political candidates or groups.
Comments, if you wish: □   □   □

12. If you discovered that certain policies of your firm were socially injurious to workers or to the public what would you do? (Circle your response.)

   a. Do nothing.

   b. Discuss the policies with a superior.

   c. Try to change the company's policies.

   d. Resign, if the company refused to change the policies.

   e. Avoid conforming to such policies.

   f. Other: _____

Comments, if you wish:

13. Who is morally responsible for the corporation's conduct? (Circle your response(s))

a. Directors.   b. CEO.

c. Shareholders.   d. Public.

e. Government.

f. Other: _____

Comments, if you wish:

14. If your firm were considering moving one of its offices or plants to another location, which of the following actions would it more likely take? (Circle actions more likely taken.)

a. Arrange for employees' representatives to confer with management to discuss possible locations of the office or plant.

b. Move without asking the employees their opinions.

c. Tell the employees the future plans, and indicate that, if they object to such a decision, they will be terminated.

d. Terminate the employees that cannot be relocated.

e. Hire new employees for the new plant.

f. Other: _____

Comments, if you wish:

15. Which, of the following statements about transferring moral responsibility to firms from individuals, do you believe to be true? (Check true or false beside each response.)

	True	False
a. Social-control mechanisms are ineffective in firms.	☐	☐
b. Societal values may only be agreed upon in a general way, rendering them inadequate for rule-making in a firm.	☐	☐
c. Some traditional personal methods of responsibility are inapplicable to firms.	☐	☐
d. Firms are often more progressive than society which makes rule-making in society as a whole considerably less advanced.	☐	☐

e. Other: _____

Comments, if you wish:

16. With which of the following statements regarding environmental concerns do you *mostly* agree?

	Mostly Agree	Mostly Disagree	Neither Agree nor Disagree (Neutral)
a. Environmental concern is an excessive economic burden to the firm.	☐	☐	☐
b. The demand for a cleaner environment creates expanded markets for almost every industry.	☐	☐	☐
c. The values of ethical growth more than offset overhead costs in following a strict environmental policy.	☐	☐	☐
d. Environmental improvement opens new markets for the firm.	☐	☐	☐
e. Environmental concern results in the organization of new, more effective political units.	☐	☐	☐
f. Environmental concern results in better management of public programs.	☐	☐	☐
g. Environmental concern forces business to establish needed standards to protect the environment.	☐	☐	☐
h. Environmental improvements result in overall economic benefits for the firm.	☐	☐	☐

i. Other: _____
Comments, if you wish:

17. How do you define "ethics" in the context of business competition: (Circle only one)

a. Personal standards.   b. Social rules.

c. Statutes.   d. Business rules and standards.

e. Honesty without exception.   f. Concerns for fellow humans.

g. Other:_____

Comments, if you wish:

18. To whom or what would you most look to for advice in ethical or business conduct dilemmas? (Circle only one.)

    a. Large firms in my business sector.

    b. My lawyer.

    c. Business associates or friends.

    d. Someone in my firm appointed to answer such questions.

    e. The business press.

    f. Newspapers and television.

    g. Family.

    h. Myself (using my own rules of conduct).

    i. My religion.

    j. Teachers in academia.

    k. My supervisor or superior.

19. What do you think is the most important strategy, in general, in dealing with business conduct or ethical problems? (Circle only one.)

    a. Don't take a leadership role in responding to such problems and, hence, play it safe.

    b. Share the risk by involving others.

    c. Confer with your competitor(s) to establish the guidelines that you'll both follow.

    d. Look to precedent in the firm for guidance.

    e. Consult with lawyers and other experts.

    f. Allow your conscience to dictate your response.

    g. Place the question before the public for opinion and feedback.

    h. Simply ignore the ethical portion of the dilemma.

    i. Allow someone else to decide the issue and absolve yourself of any responsibility.

    j. Refrain from taking action until all other alternatives are removed.

    k. Other:_____

Comments, if you wish:

20. (Circle your responses) In the last twelve months have you:

    a. Taken a stand on a serious matter of principle?

    b. Taken any step to improve the ethical environment of your firm?

    c. Been involved in any voluntary activities?

    d. Provided donations, money or time, to an organization?

    e. Given money to a religious organization?

    f. Donated time to helping the poor or disadvantaged?

    g. Donated time to religious work?

    h. Written a letter to a political official or signed a political petition?

    i. Other: _____

Comments, if you wish:

21. Which of the following is most important in the implementation of a firm's code of ethics, conduct or values? (Circle your response(s).)

    a. Employee awareness through firm publications and meetings.

    b. A committee assigned to evaluate policy ramifications of code statements.

    c. Orientation programs for employees, providing information concerning an understanding and acceptance of the code.

    d. Utilization of and reference to the firm's code when recruiting employees, conducting management training, or chairing any other programs.

    e. Appointing a committee of firm elders to monitor and critique the application and effectiveness of the code.

    f. Creation of an incentive system that rewards behavior commensurate with the firm's code of values.

    g. Other: _____

Comments, if you wish:

22. If a fellow employee violates a provision of your firm's code of ethics or conduct, which step(s) should you take knowing that the code imposes a duty on every employee to report violations? (Circle your response(s).)

    a. Do nothing since everyone violates a rule occasionally.

    b. Tell the employee not to violate the rule again, and take no other step.

    c. Follow (b); however, if the fellow employee violated the rule again, report the violation.

    d. Report the violation only if it is a breach of a very important code section, even if the sanction for the offender is termination of employment.

    e. Report all violations, since the firm's code requires it.

    f. Other: _____

Comments, if you wish:

23. Answer the following questions by checking the appropriate box.

a. Have you ever known of a case of alcoholism or drug abuse in your firm?
    Yes ☐   No ☐   Don't know ☐

b. Does your firm have an effective policy dealing with such issues as alcoholism and drug abuse?
   Yes ☐   No ☐   Don't know ☐

c. Have you ever known of a case of alcoholism among the general managers?
   Yes ☐   No ☐   Don't know ☐

d. Do you feel that firms should have a special rehabilitation program to deal with alcohol and drug abuse?
   Yes ☐   No ☐   Don't know ☐

e. Do you believe that alcoholism is a serious disease?
   Yes ☐   No ☐   Don't know ☐

f. Do you consider alcoholism as resulting from lack of "will" power?
   Yes ☐   No ☐   Don't know ☐

g. If you discovered that one of the best and highest ranking executives in your firm was an alcoholic or drug abuser would you report it to your mutual supervisor or superior?
   Yes ☐   No ☐   Don't know ☐

h. If an employer has a reasonable basis to suspect an employee's on-the-job substance or alcohol abuse, should the employer have a right to order a mandatory physical examination of the suspected employee?
   Yes ☐   No ☐   Don't know ☐

i. Do you believe that a firm's employee who is an alcoholic or drug abuser should be terminated?
   Yes ☐   No ☐   Don't know ☐

j. Can a person with drug or alcohol addiction be successfully treated and returned to productive work?
   Yes ☐   No ☐   Don't know ☐

k. Other:_____

Comments, if you wish:

24. Which of the following are, in your opinion, cases of sexual harassment?

	Sexual Harassment	Possibly Sexual Harassment	Not Sexual Harassment
a. A secretary's boss occasionally flirts with the secretary by casually touching the latter's arm.	☐	☐	☐

b. A manager tells that person's secretary that it would be good for her career if she dated the manager. □   □   □

c. A manager asks an employee to have sex with the manager. The employee refuses, and later discovers that the manager has assigned the employee a poor performance evaluation. □   □   □

d. An employee is having an affair with the manager of the employee's department. The employee relates to the manager a desire to terminate the affair. The manager replies, if the affair is ended, the employee's career will be harmed. □   □   □

e. An employee, upon entering the office, often suffers the supervisor's "up" and "down" look. □   □   □

f. A supervisor starts the day with his secretary with a sexual remark. □   □   □

g. Every time a female employee and her manager meet, the manager kisses her on her cheek. □   □   □

h. The manager puts a hand around a secretary's arm when making a point. □   □   □

i. Other: _____

Comments, if you wish:

25. Indicate whether you agree or disagree generally with the following statements.

	Agree	Disagree	No Opinion
a. Perceived seriousness of sexual harassment depends on who is making the advance, degree of interpreted intent and the victim's perception of the consequences.	☐	☐	☐
b. A man and a woman have a different perception of harassment.	☐	☐	☐
c. There are different perceptions of harassment at different management levels of the firm.	☐	☐	☐
d. Men and women have different opinions on treatment by superiors when sexual harassment is reported.	☐	☐	☐
e. Women must take "what comes" in order to survive in the business world.	☐	☐	☐
f. Sexual harassment prohibitions are good in theory but unworkable in practice.	☐	☐	☐
g. Smaller companies rely on peer pressure rather than formal rules to deal with harassment problems.	☐	☐	☐
h. Usually, companies fail to communicate rules, policies or expectations in sexual harassment matters.	☐	☐	☐
i. Men do not know where "the line is."	☐	☐	☐
j. Cursing on the job is a natural way to relieve stress and should not be sanctioned.	☐	☐	☐
k. Employees should be allowed outside employment if it doesn't compete directly with the firm.	☐	☐	☐
l. Inventions and discoveries on the job should belong to the employee making them since it is his creative genius which allowed the invention or discovery.	☐	☐	☐

m. Handicapped people should be hired and
    given special privileges by the firm.   ☐   ☐   ☐

Comments, if you wish:

26. An estimated 1.5 million Americans are infected with the AIDS virus today,
     and 450,000 of them are expected to suffer full-blown AIDS symptoms by
     1993. Do you agree or disagree with the following statements?

	Mostly Agree	Mostly Disagree	Neither Agree nor Disagree (Neutral)
a. Firms should be able to require testing for diagnostic purposes of any employee suspected of being infected with the AIDS virus.	☐	☐	☐
b. Firms should be able to terminate employees who have tested positive for the AIDS virus, but who show no symptoms of the disease.	☐	☐	☐
c. Firms should be able to terminate employees who have tested positive for the AIDS virus, and who show symptoms of the disease.	☐	☐	☐
d. Firms should terminate AIDS-infected employees if the work of fellow employees is adversely affected because of the latters' fears of disease.	☐	☐	☐
e. Landlords and insurance companies should be allowed to refuse to enter contracts to provide housing and insurance, respectively, to persons who have the AIDS virus and who show AIDS symptoms.	☐	☐	☐
f. Firms should have the right to remove AIDS-infected employees from certain tasks that could expose others to AIDS-tainted blood (for instance, those AIDS-infected persons working with heavy machinery or sharp instruments).	☐	☐	☐

g. Doctors should be allowed to contact the sexual partners of people diagnosed as having the AIDS virus if those AIDS-infected persons fail to contact their sexual partners. ☐ ☐ ☐

h. No discrimination in any way should be allowed against AIDS-infected persons, without regard to the public welfare. ☐ ☐ ☐

i. Other:_____

Comments, if you wish:

27. If you determine that your firm shortly will announce a new product which will enhance the value of the firm's stock price, which step would you take? (Circle one.)

   a. Tell no one but buy all the firm's stock you can afford, wait for the price to increase, sell and take a profit.

   b. Only buy a small amount of stock—after all you're just doing what everyone else does.

   c. Tip your best friends and relatives of the imminent stock price rise while buying all the stock you can afford.

   d. Do not buy any stock or tell anyone of the product announcement.

   e. Other:_____

Comments, if you wish:

28. How would you react to a firm and very attractive job offer from your present firm's competitor? (Circle only one).

   a. Reject it immediately.

   b. Inform your firm, resign, and then accept the offer.

   c. Resign without informing your firm of the offer, then accept the offer.

   d. Inform your firm, and negotiate with your firm for increased benefits.

   e. Accept the offer, then inform your firm.

   f. Other:_____

Comments, if you wish:

29. Would you feel that your present employer is entitled to some of the key competitive information which you possess and which was gained by you during prior employment with a competitor of your present firm? (Circle your response.)

   a. Yes, definitely.   b. Perhaps, or probably.

   c. Neutral (depends on other circumstances).   d. Probably not.

e. No.

f. Other:_____

Comments, if you wish:

30. Here are some questions concerning how satisfied or disatisfied you are with various things about your life. Check the appropriate blanks.

	Very Satis- fied	Satis- fied	Dissat- isfied	Very Dissat- isfied	Un- desig- nated
a. Your standard of living.	☐	☐	☐	☐	☐
b. Your education in preparing you for the work you do.	☐	☐	☐	☐	☐
c. They way things are going in your own personal life at this time.	☐	☐	☐	☐	☐
d. Your family life.	☐	☐	☐	☐	☐
e. Your job and the work you do.	☐	☐	☐	☐	☐
f. The business ethics of your firm.	☐	☐	☐	☐	☐
g. Your education in preparing you for life.	☐	☐	☐	☐	☐
h. Your relationship with your children.	☐	☐	☐	☐	☐
i. Your relationship with your spouse.	☐	☐	☐	☐	☐
j. Your free time.	☐	☐	☐	☐	☐
k. The way things are going in this country at this time.	☐	☐	☐	☐	☐

l. Other:_____

Comments, if you wish:

31. If my supervisor or boss asked me to tell a lie to disguise one of his or her mistakes, I would:

a. Resign my employment.

b. Lie.

c. Indicate to the supervisor that I felt such a request was wrong.

d. Lie on this occasion, but not lie again.

32. If I believed a fellow employee, a supervisor, or an employee under my supervision had a drug problem, I would:

    a. Discuss it with that person.

    b. Do nothing until that person's performance declined.

    c. Seek guidance from the personnel department or other department dealing with such matters.

    d. Write an anonymous note to someone in authority in the firm.

33. If I believed a fellow employee, a supervisor, or an employee under my supervision had an alcohol problem, I would:

    a. Discuss it with that person.

    b. Do nothing until that person's performance declined.

    c. Seek guidance from the personnel department or other department dealing with such matters.

    d. Write an anonymous note to someone in authority in the firm.

34. Please circle as appropriate:

    a. Sex: Male   Female

    b. Highest level of Education: 1. some high school
                                 2. high school graduate
                                 3. college attendance
                                 4. college degree
                                 5. Master's degree
                                 6. Ph.D.

    c. Length with company: 1. less than 1 year
                               2. 1 to 4 years
                               3. 5 to 9 years
                               4. 10 to 19 years
                               5. 20 years or more

    d. Your age: 1. under 20 years
                   2. 20 years to 29 years
                   3. 30 years to 39 years
                   4. 40 years to 49 years
                   5. 50 years to 59 years
                   6. 60 years or over.

    e. How many hours of work do you normally spend for the firm each week? 1. 40 hours or fewer
                   2. 41-50 hours
                   3. 51-55 hours
                   4. 56-60 hours
                   5. More than 60 hours.

f. Do you supervise or manage employees?   Yes ☐   No ☐

The following questions should be added to Questions 1-34, above, and administered only to managers:

35. An American steel company was the largest and most profitable of all steel firms on a global basis. Earning after 1977 deteriorated rapidly, forcing the management to a diversification decision. Should the company have diversified from its normal business into the oil industry, given the foreseeable adverse consequences on employment and economic development in the original communities in which its plants and employees were located? What action would you have recommended to the company? (Circle your answer.)
   a. Diversification regardless of the adverse effects on employees.
   b. Expansion, though acquisition of companies in the same industry.
   c. Termination of employees who cannot or are not willing to be relocated.
   d. Establishment of an employees' training program in order to establish a "bridge" between company employment and other firms.
   e. Do nothing.
   f. Other:_____
Comments, if you wish:

36. A manufacturer of cigarettes utilizes a large-scale advertising campaign designed to promote the idea that using the company's product will make men more masculine. What do you consider such advertising to be? (Circle your response.)
   a. Completely ethical
   b. Mostly ethical
   c. Barely ethical
   d. Slightly unethical
   e. Mostly unethical
   f. Completely unethical
   g. Other:_____
Comments, if you wish:

37. Assume that an automobile manufacturer has developed a safety device that could reduce traffic injuries in its automobiles by 50%. The company's consideration is that the device could increase the cost of each car by at least $600, which could cause the company to lose sales to competitors. The

company decides not to use the safety device at this time, but to wait until all car manufacturers are legally required to use such a device. What would you consider such a decision to be? (Circle your response.)

a. Highly unethical
b. Unethical
c. Ethical
d. Highly ethical
e. Other:_____

Comments, if you wish:

38. Do you agree or disagree with the following statements?

	Agree	Disagree	Neither Agree nor Disagree (Neutral)
a. A manufacturer should be liable for hazards posed by its product that may result in injuries many years after product use, even if scientific knowledge cannot detect hazards it may cause at the time the product is marketed.	☐	☐	☐
b. A manufacturer should be liable for hazards posed by its product that may result in injuries many years later, after product use, if scientific knowledge could have detected hazards at the time the product was marketed.	☐	☐	☐
c. The individual user, not the manufacturer, should be held entirely responsible for injury in case of that user's intentional misuse of a product.	☐	☐	☐
d. The manufacturer should be held responsible for injury to a user, even in the case of intentional misuse of a product by that user.	☐	☐	☐
e. A manufacturer should be liable for injuries if a product does not perform safely when used as intended.	☐	☐	☐

f. A manufacturer cannot design products
   that will prevent injuries from all
   possible accidents resulting from product
   use.   ☐   ☐   ☐

g. In creating a product, managers should
   choose a design that affords the most
   practicable protection from injuries in the
   most frequent types of accidents.   ☐   ☐   ☐

h. Other:_____

Comments, if you wish:

39. Which of the following statements *mostly* represents your personal opinion?
    (Circle the statement(s) with which you *mostly* agree.)

    a. Business bluffing or deception is ethical.

    b. Business bluffing or deception is unethical.

    c. Bluffing or deception in business is a game-strategy.

    d. In order to succeed, one must master the principles of the bluffing or
       deception game.

    e. Bluffing or deception is a violation of the ethical ideals of society, not of
       ethical business principles.

    f. Bluffing or deception in work is guided by different ethical standards
       than the ones practiced at home.

    g. Other:_____

Comments, if you wish:

40. If you were to decide between promoting a black or a caucasian with
    comparable experience and background, which of the following would
    influence your decision? (Please circle those factors which influence your
    decision and rank them in importance.)

	Rank in importance
a. Color	_____
b. Personality	_____
c. Seniority	_____
d. Past Performance	_____
e. Extent of Formal Education	_____
f. Moral Standards of the Candidate	_____

g. Other:_____
   Comments, if you wish:

Thank you.

BIBLIOGRAPHY

Ackerman. "How Companies Respond to Social Demands." *Harvard Business Review* (July-August 1973).

Aetna Compliance Manual.

American Banker's Association. *Developing or Revising a Bank Code of Ethics*. July 1986.

Andrews. "Can the Best Corporations Be Made Moral?" *Harvard Business Review* (May-June 1973).

Andrews. "Ethics in Policy and Practice at General Mills." *Business Roundtable* (February 1988).

Andrews. "Ethics in Policy and Practice at GTE Corporation." *Business Roundtable* (February 1988).

Arrow. "Social Responsibility and Economic Efficiency." *The Public Interest* (Summer 1973).

Beauchamp. *Case Studies in Business, Society and Ethics*, 2nd ed. Englewood, Cliffs, NJ: Prentice-Hall, 1989.

Beauchamp. *Philosophical Ethics*. New York: McGraw-Hill, 1982.

Behrman. *Discourses on Ethics and Business*. Oelgeschlager, Gunn, & Hain, 1981.

Bell. *The Cultural Contradictions of Capitalism*. New York: Basic Books, 1976.

Bennett. "Ethics Codes Spread Despite Skepticism." *Wall Street Journal* (July 15, 1988).

Berenbeim. *The Conference Board: Corporate Ethics*, 1988.

Berney. "Finding the Ethical Edge." *Nation's Business* (August 1987).

Bok, D. *Beyond the Ivory Tower*. Cambridge, MA: Harvard University Press, 1982.

Bok, S. *Lying, Moral Choice in Public and Private Life*. New York: Pantheon Books, 1978.

Bowie. *Business Ethics*. Englewood Cliffs, NJ: Prentice- Hall, 1987.

Bowman. "The Management of Ethics: Codes of Conduct in Organizations." *Public Personnel Management Journal* (1981).

Bradshaw and Vogel (editors). *Corporations and Their Critics*. New York: McGraw-Hill, 1981.

Braham. "Tips from the Top." *Industry Week*.

Brandt. *A Theory of the Good and the Right*. London, England: Oxford University Press, 1979.

Buchholz. *Fundamental Concepts and Problems in Business Ethics*. Englewood Cliffs, NJ: Prentice-Hall, 1989.

Center for Business Ethics at Bentley College. "Are Corporations Institutionalizing Ethics?" *Journal of Business Ethics* (April 1986) cited in Buchholz.

Chamberlain. *The Place of Business in America's Future*. New York: Basic Books, 1973.

Collins and Blodgett. "Sexual Harassment. . .Some See It. . .Some Won't." *Harvard Business Review* (March-April 1981).

The Conference Board's Management Briefing: Human Resources (October 1987).

"The Corporate Elite." *Business Week* (October 21, 1988).

Cressey and Moore. "Managerial Values and Corporate Codes of Ethics." *California Management Review* (Summer 1983).

Donaldson. *Key Issues in Business Ethics*. Boston: Academic Press, 1989.

Donaldson and Werhane. *Ethical Issues in Business*. Englewood Cliffs, NJ: Prentice-Hall, 1988.

Drucker. "Management's New Role." *Harvard Business Review* (November-December 1969).

Dworkin. *Taking Rights Seriously*. Cambridge, MA: Harvard University Press, 1978.

Estes. *Corporate Social Accounting*. New York: John Wiley and Sons, 1976.

Ethics Resource Center. *Implementation and Enforcement of Codes of Ethics in Corporations and Associations*, 1980.

Ewing. "Civil Liberties in the Corporation." *New York State Bar Journal* (April 1978).

Ewing. *Do It My Way or You're Fired*. New York: John Wiley and Sons, 1983.

Ferrell and Fraedrich. *Business Ethics*. Boston: Houghton Mifflin, 1991.

Fletcher. *Situation Ethics*. Philadelphia: The Westminster Press, 1966.

Frankena. *Ethics*, 2nd ed. Englewood Cliffs, NJ: Prentice-Hall, 1973. Paperback.

Fried. *Right and Wrong*. Cambridge, MA: Harvard University Press, 1978.

Friedman. "The Social Responsibility of Business Is to Increase Its Profits." *The New York Times Magazine* (September 13, 1970).

Glickman (editor). *Moral Philosophy, An Introduction*. New York: St. Martin's Press, 1976.

Goodpaster. "The Concept of Corporate Responsibility." *Journal of Business Ethics* 2, 1983.

Goodpaster and Mathews. "Can a Corporation Have a Conscience?" *Harvard Business Review* (January-February 1982).

Greiner. "Patterns of Organizational Change." *Harvard Business Review* (May-June 1967).

Haney. *Communication and Organizational Behavior*. Irwin, 1973.

Harris. "Structuring a Workable Code of Ethics." *University of Florida Law Review* (1978).

Hare. *Moral Thinking*. London, England: Oxford University Press, 1981.

Harvard Business Review — On Human Relations. New York: Harper & Row, 1979.

Hoffman and Moore. *Business Ethics*. New York: McGraw- Hill, 1984.

Jackall. "Moral Mazes: Bureaucracy and Managerial Work." *Harvard Business Review* (September-October 1983).

Kline. *International Codes and Multinational Business*. Westport, CT: Quorum, 1985.

Kouzes and Posner. *The Leadership Challenge*. San Francisco: Jossey-Bass, 1987.

Kristol. *Two Cheers for Capitalism*. New York: Basic Books, 1978.

Ladd. "Morality and the Ideal of Rationality in Formal Organizations." *The Monist* 54 (1970).

Litzinger and Schaefer. "Business Ethics Bogeyman: The Perpetual Paradox." *Business Horizons* (March-April 1987).

Lodge. "The Connection between Ethics and Ideology." *Journal of Business Ethics* 1 (1982).

Lodge. *The New American Ideology*. New York: Alfred A. Knopf, 1975.

Lorsch. *Managing Change*. Harvard Business School Publication, 1974.

Lorsch and Kotter. *Managing Change. Part I: The Problem of Resistance*. Harvard Business School Publication #476-102, 1976.

Maccoby. *The Leader*. New York: Simon and Schuster, 1981.

McCoy and Twining. "The Corporate Values Program at Champion International Corporation." *Business Roundtable* (February 1988).

Merz and Groebner. *Toward a Code of Ethics for Management*. National Association for Accountants, 1981.

Minnesota Power Corporation Code.

Molander. "A Paradigm for Design, Promulgation and Enforcement of Ethical Codes." *Journal of Business Ethics* 6, 1987.

"The Most Admired Companies in America." *Fortune* (January 30, 1989).

Nadler. "Concepts for the Management of Organizational Change." Reading 54 in *Perspectives on Behavior in Organizations*. New York: McGraw Hill, 1983.

Nash. "Ethics without the Sermon." *Harvard Business Review* (November-December 1981).

Nash. "Johnson & Johnson's Credo." *Business Roundtable* (February 1988).

Nash. "The Norton Company's Ethics Program." *Business Roundtable* (February 1988).

Novak. *The Spirit of Democratic Capitalism.* New York: American Enterprise Institute/Simon and Schuster, 1982.

Nozick. *Anarchy, State and Utopia.* New York: Basic Books, 1974.

Nozick. *Philosophical Explanations.* Cambridge, MA: Belknap Press (Harvard University), 1981.

O'Neill. "Creating and Promoting a Code of Ethics." *Association Management* (November 1972).

Opinion Research Center. *Implementation and Enforcement of Codes of Ethics in Corporations and Associations*, 1980.

Pastin. *A Code of Ethics for Your Organization.* New York: Lincoln Center for Ethics, 1987.

Pastin. "Ethics and Excellence." *New Management* (Spring 1987).

Pastin. *The Hard Problems of Management.* San Francisco: Jossey-Bass, 1986.

Peters and Austin. *A Passion for Excellence.* New York: Random House, 1985.

Posner and Schmidt. "Values and the American Manager: An Update." *California Management Review.* (Spring 1984).

Purcell. "Management and the 'Ethical' Investors." *Harvard Business Review* (September-October 1979).

Rawls. *A Theory of Justice.* Cambridge, MA: Belknap Press (Harvard University Press), 1971.

Russell. *A History of Western Philosophy.* New York: Simon and Schuster, 1945.

Sanderson and Varner. "What's Wrong with Corporate Codes of Conduct." *Management Accounting* (July 1984).

Sherwin. "The Ethical Roots of the Business System." *Harvard Business Review* (November-December 1983).

Smith. "Make Your Code of Ethics Work through a Program of Education." *Association Management* (April 1976).

Sneath. *Vital Speeches* 64 (1979), 302.

"Statement on Corporate Responsibility." *Business Roundtable* (October 1981).

Stone. *Where the Law Ends.* New York: Harper & Row, 1975.

Texas Instruments. *Ethics Cornerstone.*

Toffler. *Future Shock*. New York: Random House, 1970.

Touche Ross. *Ethics in American Business: A National Opinion Survey*, 1987.

U.S. Department of Commerce (December 1980). *Business and Society: Strategies for the 1980s*. Cited in *Business Roundtable* (October 1981).

Wall Street Journal (July 21, 1988).

Weiss. "Minerva's Owl: Building a Corporate Value System." *Journal of Business Ethics* (1986).

Westin. *Whistle Blowing!* New York: McGraw-Hill, 1981.

"What Bosses Think About Corporate Ethics." *Wall Street Journal* (April 6, 1988).

White and Montgomery. "Corporate Codes of Conduct." *California Management Review* (Winter 1980).

Index